SYMBOLIC EXPERIENCE:

A STUDY OF POEMS BY PEDRO SALINAS

SYMBOLIC EXPERIENCE: A STUDY OF POEMS BY PEDRO SALINAS

RUPERT C. ALLEN

THE UNIVERSITY OF ALABAMA PRESS
University, Alabama

cl/

Library of Congress Cataloging in Publication Data

Allen, Rupert C.
  Symbolic experience, a study of poems by Pedro
Salinas.

  Bibliography: p.
  Includes index.
  1. Salinas, Pedro, 1891–1951—Criticism and
interpretation.   2. Symbolism in literature.
I. Title.
PQ6635.A32Z54   861'.62   81-10307
ISBN O-8173-0081-3   AACR2

to my teachers

Nancy

and

Gus

Contents

Preface

While the present work is a contribution to Salinas studies, that is not its main purpose. I have addressed myself to the general reader, who may not profess even a casual interest in Spanish letters. My title, *Symbolic Experience: A Study of Poems by Pedro Salinas*, indicates where the center of gravity lies. I am concerned with the meaning and significance of reality experienced symbolically, just as the contemplative and the poet may experience it. My study is therefore wide-ranging, since the symbolic experience possible to each individual mind is as wide as the world itself.

Pedro Salinas (1891–1951) was born and educated in Madrid. He completed his doctoral program while he was lecturer in Spanish literature at the Sorbonne (1914–1917). In the eight years following he taught at the University of Seville and (in 1922–1923) at Cambridge University. His literary activity and growing reputation as poet and scholar eventually drew him back to Madrid, the cultural center of Spain, where he occupied a post as researcher for the Center for Historical Studies. It was there that he founded the critical review *Indice Literario* and promoted the establishment of the International Summer University of Santander.

With the outbreak of the Spanish Civil War Salinas emigrated to the United States as visiting professor at Wellesley College, where he taught for three years, after which he moved to Johns Hopkins University, which was to remain his home base throughout the forties. As guest lecturer he traveled considerably in this country, and spent the years 1942–1945 as visiting professor at the University of Puerto Rico. In 1951 he died of cancer in the Massachusetts General Hospital in Boston.

Salinas belonged to the so-called Generation of 1927, a remarkable group of young Spanish poets of whom the best known is Federico García Lorca, the totally dedicated poet-dramatist. By contrast Salinas was the poet-intellectual, a man of wide culture and spiritual equilibrium, a citizen of the world, and it is this about him that makes his poetry particularly appropriate for the present study. Salinas was no shaman of mystery; he was, so to speak, one of us, not an isolated comet of alien splendor. The material he brought into the poetic light of day was assimilated into a cosmopolitan awareness of reality; his work presents no idiosyncratic, ethnic obstacles, and there is no need to penetrate the "mystery of Spain" before getting down to cases.

The Salinas bibliography grows. Several books on his work have appeared (principally doctoral dissertations), as have dozens of articles in journals and periodicals. None of this published material is basically symbological, probably because the main tone has been set by the critical approach of that school known in Spain as *la estilística*, or Stylistics.

La estilística has at bottom a philological orientation, which means that it (unlike the symbological approach) is concerned with the poem as a linguistic phenomenon. At the risk of simplifying we may say that the symbologist sees the diction of the poem as a feat of ego-intellect, whereas the symbols are the raw *données* of consciousness, and attention is concentrated on these. The immediate spiritual function of such symbols is to encourage an integration into consciousness of nonego realities: the significance of world reality as perceived before each society begins to make up its own collective mind about the matter. Poets, like seers and prophets, seem to maintain an ability to transcend the metaphysical assumptions of their own time and place in the world, in order to return to the sources of human consciousness. But the poets, unlike the prophets, do not usually seem to be very interested in proselytizing; they are concerned mainly with bearing witness to the nonego sources of their own lives.

In the work of Pedro Salinas the question of symbolic reality vs. the reality of ego-intellect is treated time and again in poems concerning the symbolic process itself: how he finds himself passing from the routine, everyday consciousness that keeps him going as a successful inhabitant of his society into the exalted consciousness of nonego, where he is something more than a timebound, social entity.

Since the symbological approach to Salinas's poetry has hardly been used to date, I believe that specialists in twentieth-century Spanish literature will find some fresh conclusions as to the specific meaning and scope of this man's work. I emphasize *specific*, because I have tried to avoid being vague in a subject that invites vagueness. But the poetry of Salinas acts as a curb here, since Salinas himself, being a trained thinker and an excellent literary critic, wrote poems that were rooted in the three-dimensional ground of his immediate world.

Part One

Ego and the Self

Chapter One

THE MEANING OF SELF-INTEGRATION

Esta cadena de hierro	This chain of iron
que tanto pesa, me es leve	that weighs so heavily is light for me
de llevar y no la siento.	to carry and I do not feel it.
Hay otra cadena hecha	There is another chain made
de olas, de tierras y vientos,	of waves, of lands and winds,
de sonrisas y suspiros,	of smiles and sighs,
que me ata yo no sé adónde,	that binds me to I know not where,
que me esclaviza a ese dueño	that enslaves me to that unknown
desconocido, a ese dueño . . .	master, to that master . . .
No. 27, *Presagios* (1924)	

The published poetry of our century has largely been written by cosmopo-lites speaking to their very own kind. As poets they have characteristically addressed themselves to what may be formally called the problem of reality. We say they have done this as poets, not as philosophers; for to the poet the problem of reality is posed by a living experience that cannot be much illuminated by abstract speculation. It is really a problem created by the living ambiguity of each person's day-to-day ego-consciousness.

The city-dweller has difficulty in striking a balance between what the reality of the city demands and what the reality of the Self needs. One requires an aggressive ego in order to compete, but then again, one wants a spirit large enough to make its way without any competitive nonsense. And the dilemma often enough promotes neurotic behavior. We are taught, or somewhere we learn, that the meaning of reality is given us by life in the city; but we may suspect that reality is nothing if it does not have much to do with the movements of the spirit—that spirit that was early eclipsed by the establishment of the metropolitan ego-intellect.

The cosmopolitan society is commonly criticized as being "plastic," and this seems to imply that each one of us is similarly "plastic": we are science-fiction people. But this notion stems from the fact that we are supposed to identify the reality of the individual's own selfhood with the reality of society. If a society is science fiction, then so are its inhabitants. The idea, however, is a variant of the old missionary belief that a savage society is inhabited by savages, and it begs the question of what people may be, beyond mere members of a society. Certainly the human being is not primarily an ego, nor even principally so; rather, the ego is the shell of the egg, while the Self lies within, awaiting incubation. At the deepest level the Self is ahistorical. It exists out of time and is immune to the vicissitudes of history. It is not twentieth-century, not medieval; it is neither occidental nor oriental, male nor female, child nor adult.

All of us modern city-people, as ego-personalities, are increasingly aware that the quality of our consciousness, its secular content, is determined by the technology, the economics, and the ideologies of the century. Perhaps we at last accept the determinism of the naturalist writers, even if without the large dose of pessimism they prescribed. If we are not entirely the victims of our milieu, at least we are its typical products, and if so, it is well that we be aware of the kind of mentality with which we have been programmed. At the present time "consciousness-raising" is an activity that may be taken seriously by the city-dweller, for now it is recognized that one may become aware of one's self-image in order to do something about it.

The Meaning of Self-Integration

John McHale, a collaborator on the World Resources Inventory, has pointed out in his essay, "The Plastic Parthenon," that the human being of today's civilization belongs to a global community; we cosmopolites are more likely to feel at home in any of the large cities of the world than in the rural areas of our own country, for we are sustained by an "international cultural milieu"—mass culture.[1] McHale's essay appears in the Dorfles anthology, *Kitsch*, which naturally concerns the questionable quality of the contemporary mass culture. Kitsch is (among other things) the expression of a mentality, almost entirely obedient to the canons of modern ego-consciousness, that has a very limited notion of how one "ought" to be conscious at all. And from the beginning of the century the Freudian image of the negative "subconscious" mind made an important contribution to the idea that ego-consciousness could be stabilized by coming to terms with a kind of enemy within.

Carl Jung's reassessment of this subconscious mind helped some of us to accept the proposition that there is a creative unconscious, contact with which can lead toward individuation, or self-integration, whereby ego-consciousness no longer needs to feel that it ought to be engaged in a battle to dominate the house of the psyche. Jung characterized modern secular mentality as a kind of cult: "We lack knowledge of the unconscious psyche and pursue the cult of consciousness to the exclusion of all else. Our true religion is a monotheism of consciousness, a possession by it, coupled with a fanatical denial that there are any parts of the psyche which are autonomous. . . . We even deny that such autonomous parts are experienceable."[2] Such was the picture in the first half of this century. In recent years, however, we have seen a surge of sympathetic interest in the world of the unconscious, though this interest too often appears to be informed by the "scientific" approach to "psi" phenomena and by what we might call the kitsch of psychic pursuits, occultism.

Pedro Salinas was generously endowed both as a lyric poet and as an academic intellectual. He lived successfully in both worlds without compromising his effectiveness in either. He was a man of spiritual equilibrium, and did not succumb to any feeling that he was futilely attempting to serve both God and Caesar. The reader who becomes aware of this and who seeks some answer to Salinas's style of living, eventually finds the solution in the man's poetry, for it is there that we see how aware he himself was of the big issue in his life: the integration of ego-consciousness with the Self, and the expression of this in creative activity. Integration means that neither the intellectual nor the poet tyrannizes over the other. Had he committed his total energies to the cultivation of ego-intellect, obviously he would have become something else than the exemplary humanist-scholar that he was; he would have become a formidable academician engrossed in a higher criticism beyond the general reach (or interest) of the students to whom he was dedicated. He would have treated his field more "scientifically," in that manner described by R. G. Smith in the introduction to his English translation of Buber's *I and Thou*: "The world of objects or things . . . presupposes a single center of consciousness, one subject, an *I* which experiences, arranges, and appropriates. This is the characteristic world of modern activity; in it the scientist and the statesman and the economist carry on their particular work."[3] This result of the "I-It" relationship comes about through strengthening the barrier of repression whereby ego-intellect, as king of the psyche, is formed as an entity attempting to operate without interference from unconscious tendencies; hence the "hard line" that ego-intellect insensibly learns to follow in the desire to deal "realistically" with what it conceives to be the stony truths of contemporary life in the city—the world reality seen as an alien "it."

If, on the other hand, Salinas had given most of his energies to the poetic vocation, he would probably have left a body of work so dazzling that few of us would suspect its human cost. The totally committed poets whose image of self-worth must stand or fall on a body of lyric poetry become sacrificial victims whose very lives—and the lives of those around them—suffer accordingly. Two convincing examples of this deserve to be cited here.

The first is that of the unfortunate Italian poet, Dino Campana (1885–1932), who ended his days in a madhouse, and of whom his American translator says, "The marks of his insanity are like stigmata on the corpus of his work."[4] Campana devoted himself to his vocation, was indeed a *poète maudit*, and in a covering letter accompanying a manuscript he told a publisher, "In order to prove to myself I exist and to keep on writing I need to be published."[5] Here we see the toll in human cost of what it means to be possessed by a drive: "in order to prove to myself I exist." Of course Campana recognized the all-too-real existence of his own vocation, but unless he could join the human community through public recognition of his status, how could he place much faith in the reality of his own ego-consciousness? Other people seem to assume readily enough that ego enjoys an autonomous existence. This view too is lopsided, but if the assumption leads to a deranged notion of reality, it is at least a collective derangement and so breeds few doubts.

Our second example is furnished by the American poet, David Ignatow (b. 1914), who for many years attempted to live both as poet and as a working-class breadwinner. In his self-abasing *Notebooks* he describes himself as a man "who used to come home and sulk at dinner, eat and go into his room, shutting the door behind him leaving his wife and son outside seated at the table in silence, depressed. That was me for many years." He was consumed by the poetic vocation, lived the agony of nonrecognition, and took full blame for the psychotic episodes of his adolescent son: "I was alone and committing murder[;] in my mad violence at disappointments and loneliness I was terrifying a child to escape into a dream world. . . . I screamed my rage at the walls. . . . No one came to help, my wife smoking cigarette after cigarette in mounting hysteria for me, for herself, for the child. I was fit to be driven out into the streets where I could do no harm to anyone except myself, but I was tolerated in my own house, I was lived with through hell and drowning."[6]

Pedro Salinas escaped anything like this. He was always a success in the eyes of the world, was always recognized at large, and lived at ease with his reputation. Hence he was in a position to ponder tranquilly, without panicking, the task of spiritual integration. It was essential to his own well-being, and so why should it not become a subject important in his poetry? He lived in no ivory tower, happily "integrating" while civilization was coming down around his ears; he was an exile from the Spain of Franco, and the years of World War II were inauspicious for spiritual isolationism. His reaction to nuclear warfare is recorded in a long poem, "Cero," and his novel, *La bomba increíble*, is a bitter satire on the technocratic mentality of the mid-century.[7]

But he was a humanist-scholar, and considered himself to be a continuer of the liberal tradition on the side of spiritual equilibrium. In a preface published (in English) for an early translation of his poems, he expressed himself on the function of poetry for the modern city-dweller, who, he thought, is much too anxious to escape from the self, and so is hardly aware that poetry exists—and certainly has little idea of why anybody should pay it much mind: "Because instead of dis-tracting us it re-tracts, withdraws, us into ourselves. And what most persons wish to-day is to go out of themselves, not to enter into themselves." Salinas, who wrote this in his late forties, had spent his adult years aware of the process of self-integration, and so was quite conscious of the resistance to be encountered. For him the "great infirmity" of us moderns is our inability to establish contact with the "deepest and most mysterious self." As much as any Jungian, Salinas recognized our unconscious anxiety to avoid any such contact.[8]

In the present study I am concerned with poems by Salinas that express both his conviction and experience of compatibility with the "deepest and most mysterious self," the *persona honda* ("deep person") within, which Salinas, in his book on the poet Rubén Darío, contrasted with the *persona superficial*, the social image.[9] The poems I have chosen for study are about his meetings with that Self, and they document his belief that poetry is one of the ways the reader meets encouragement to honor the *persona honda*; this is what Salinas means when he writes (in English) that "poetry demands intense collaboration, not simple reading"; "only a certain class of frigid professor or students can be spectators of poetry, for, like love, it either conquers or does not exist."[10]

An "intense collaboration" with the poet is, of course, the purpose of the close reading. Since Salinas was concerned with the "deepest and most mysterious self," this means that the close reading of his poetry will be based not merely on a knowledge of his poetry; on the contrary, not much knowledge of his poetry can come about unless the reader cares to know what it is that requires collaboration: the world of the Self, and not the world of a specific man called Pedro Salinas. It is the Self with which we are really collaborating in the long run, and that is why our collaboration is grounded in symbology; for symbology is the study of the symbol, the language of the Self.

This leads me to a further consideration. The world of the Self is revealed to us, not invented by us; hence my preparation for this study has to be grounded not only in an adequate acquaintance with symbology, but also sufficiently documented by the experience of others who, like Salinas, have told us about that world. Otherwise the reader who is not already convinced by the realities of which I speak can have no reason not to believe that I am simply making up the rules as I go along. In his poetry Salinas has shown that he belongs to a society of human beings that goes back several thousand years. In the substance of what he says Salinas is not a modern poet at all, nor is he the product of any school immediately preceding him. Substantially he belongs to no time; he is a contemporary of Lao Tzu, of Basho, and of Thoreau, which is to say that his spiritual development eventually led him to experience the reality of the nonhistorical unified consciousness, the truth of his own deepest and most mysterious Self. He, one of the most successful examples of a twentieth-century ego-consciousness one could name, was successful both in the common, secular meaning of the term and in the deeper sense that he was able to function in his metropolitan world without depriving himself of his basic strength: self-integration.

Salinas did not pursue spiritual integration as a goal. He simply lived it, and in his poetry we may understand its meaning in four principal ways: (1) he early experienced the simple penetration of consciousness by the creative unconscious, and understood that a strength was being offered him; (2) he raised into awareness the spiritual meaning of woman for man, and intuited that his own conscious behavior toward woman was the outward expression of an attitude toward the feminine components of his own spirit; (3) he experienced and accepted the positive significance of the superstitious, and turned it into a creative force; and (4) he eventually experienced for himself what we call unified consciousness, the illumination that comes with the temporary transcending of our secular, dualistic thinking, the *satori* of unity, the brief perception of the Eternal Now in the world of nonego.

These are the ways in which Salinas lived with himself, with the consequence that he was able to give that much more to the many people who shared in his strength and who were the beneficiaries of his selflessness.

The Ego and the Self

We readily recognize that if our metropolitan civilization, as the product of ego-reality, is to exist at all, the mystic spirit of nonego must be held in check. That we live convinced of this is evidenced by the powers of resistance that ego characteristically mobilizes against intrusions from the world of nonego. The story about Oliver Wendell Holmes the elder under the influence of a psychedelic substance (nitrous oxide) illustrates the persistence with which our everyday ego rejects the significance of the other world. A dentist administered to him a dose of laughing gas, Holmes succumbed to its influence, and his experience "was so powerful that . . . he was convinced that he had discovered the golden key to eternal truth. Wanting to recapture his holy vision, he persuaded his dentist to put him under the gas once again. As he was going under . . . he hastily scribbled a few precious words. When he awoke, he anxiously asked to see what he had written. The words were: 'Lord, what a stench!' "[11]

Ralph Fine cites this story as an amusing analogy to what happened when "a University of California researcher" conducted an experiment with students "who claimed that marijuana gave them great insight and heightened their creative processes." The experimenter tape-recorded their conversation while they were intoxicated and later played them the tape. "He reports that they were so appalled at the verbal drivel being played back to them that they wept."[12]

The Holmes anecdote reappears in a popularly written handbook on marijuana, *A Child's Garden of Grass*. There the authors describe it as "the definitive story of false profundity," and attribute the episode to "a well-known writer" who, while under the influence of a mind-bending substance, "was struck by a revelation of universal truth." He was "overwhelmed by its significance and managed to bring himself back to reality long enough to scramble to his writing desk and frantically scribble his new-found wisdom on a scratch pad. The next morning . . . he found that he had written,

'There's a funny smell in the room.' "[13] A similar story is sometimes told of the oneiric insight: the subject half-awakens during the night and scrawls on a pad a few words that turn out to be gibberish.

That these stories circulate as examples of false profundity points up the ingrained skepticism of our ego-intellect, which through years of development and constant attention to practical problems and goals has so alienated itself from symbolic reality that it no longer sees that these anecdotes beg the question, and that they illustrate nothing except a commitment to the everyday ontological assumptions.

The stories refer to the experience of transcending routine ego-consciousness. When this state is achieved the habitual mode of perceiving reality collapses and one enters into a less restricted state of awareness. As the effects of the drug wear off, one returns to the old mode of reality, and so sees the visionary experience as absurd. But this lapse back into ordinary ego-awareness proves nothing beyond the obvious fact that one has simply returned to the repression of symbolic reality; the doors of perception have closed again on that state of consciousness which creative people commonly know as inspiration.

But that momentary amazement was not raised by the revelation of any new data. The sense of finding out an astounding secret was conveyed by transcending commitment to the dualism of ego-reality ("I" vs. the world "out there"); one has suddenly awakened in unity. William James took nitrous oxide on occasion and saw no difficulty in granting validity to the vision, while at the same time recognizing the after-sense of false profundity: "Depth beyond depth of truth seems revealed to the inhaler. This truth fades out . . . at the moment of coming to; and if any words remain over in which it seemed to clothe itself, they prove to be . . . nonsense. Nevertheless, the sense of a profound meaning having been there persists; and I know more than one person who is persuaded that in the nitrous oxide trance we have a genuine metaphysical revelation." Of his own experience with nitrous oxide he says: "One conclusion was forced upon my mind at that time, and my impression of its truth has ever since remained unshaken. It is that our normal waking consciousness, rational consciousness as we call it [i.e., ego-intellect], is but one special type of consciousness."[14]

Similarly Sir William Ramsay reports that his experiments with ether caused him to pass from an "outer" (profane) to an "inner" (sacred) reality: "An overwhelming impression forced itself upon me that the state in which I was then, was reality; that now I had reached the true solution of the secret of the universe, in understanding the secret of my own mind; that all outside objects were merely passing reflections on the eternal mirror of my mind."[15] Here the symbolic aspect of numinous reality is touched upon: the significance with which external reality is charged seems clearly to be an intimate part of inner reality; or, to put it differently, the reality "out there" and the mind of the observer are both parts of a single phenomenon. Reality is no longer something that one is conscious *of* ("I-It"); rather, one's consciousness *is* reality ("I-Thou"). Reality is no longer discontinuous; the breach of continuity between subjective experience and objective experience is no longer discernible. The universal mind is that which is, and one's "own" awareness is the universal mind. Then the threefold *sat-chit-ananda* of Hinduism becomes exceedingly clear: "Being (is) Consciousness (is) Bliss." Every object that is, sits there in its "suchness," as a holy object.[16] Reality is seen to be overflowing with the Buddha-nature; therefore one reverences it. One suddenly perceives that reality has always been like this, but that one has just now awakened to the sly realness of objects, the open secret of the universe:

> Like the empty sky it has no boundaries,
> Yet it is right in this place, ever profound and clear.
> ·
> When you are silent, it speaks;
> When you speak, it is silent.
> The great gate is wide open to bestow alms,
> And no crowd is blocking the way.[17]

Thus Hsüan-chüeh, in his *Song of Realizing the Tao*. The illumination suddenly hits home with the force of a mystery revealed. "No crowd blocks the way"—only the dualistic thinking of our everyday ego-intellect. When one enters through the great gate of unity one has just been initiated into the most exciting truth that it is possible to know: reality *is* consciousness, and to experience this *is* bliss.

After Thoreau had taken ether he wrote: "You are told that it will make you unconscious, but no one can imagine what it is to be unconscious—how far removed from the state of consciousness and all that we call 'this world'—until he has experienced it. The value of the experiment is that it does give you experience of an interval as between one life and another—a greater space than you have ever travelled."[18] For Thoreau this is neither temporary insanity nor "false profundity." It is a passing from a limited state of consciousness into a new and larger life, and we note here how Thoreau, writing in 1851, immediately falls into the language of psychedelic experience to become popular more than a hundred years later—"tripping."

Transcending the Opposites

We have observed that the hallmark of these nonego experiences is the liberation from dualism. Without losing one's spiritual differentiation as an individual human being in the world one nevertheless suddenly sees through the veil of separateness—"I" vs. "the world"—created by ego. Reality is one, even as it was before any ego-intellect came along to split it in two. There is no line of division anywhere. This experience, the *coincidentia oppositorum*, the transcending of the opposites, or categories by which we normally perceive reality, is a phenomenon well attested to in mystic literature, where "union with God" means awakening in unity—the oneness, the at-one-ment—of the universe. It is nirvana, which in the West is popularly equated with a state of nothingness, since in the West ego dominates our sense of reality. For us, reality *has* to be two ("I" vs. "It"), not one ("I" and "Thou"). But when the opposites have been transcended experientially one does not easily grant them the ontological validity that used to seem their natural right. William James's enjoyment of nitrous oxide was centered in the bliss of the *coincidentia oppositorum*, and he tells us that "the keynote of it is invariably a reconciliation. It is as if the opposites of the world . . . were melted into unity. Not only do they, as contrasted species, belong to one and the same genus, but one of the species, the nobler and better one, is itself the genus, and so soaks up and absorbs its opposite into itself. This is a dark saying, I know, when thus expressed in terms of common logic, but I cannot wholly escape from its authority. . . . Those who have ears to hear, let them hear; to me the living sense of its reality only comes in the artificial mystic state of mind."[19] James knows that he is trying to express that which has to be experienced in order to be believed or grasped—or, as the Zen master put it, "If any man cannot grasp this matter, let him be idle and the matter will grasp him."[20]

When we overcome the opposites then there can be no distinction between mind and matter, since mind/matter is a dualistic postulate; rather, we experience that so-called mind and so-called matter are different aspects of the same thing.[21] Reality is the universe being aware of itself. Maurice Nicoll, in his analysis of Ramsay's ether experiments, observes that the universe is seen "as a *mental process* and not as a *sensible object*." Ramsay, after his fourth dose of ether, writes ("hastily scribbles"?) "I may be the central person in the Universe—I don't mind, I can't help it"; and after the sixth he comes to the obvious conclusion: "The Universe is in our brain."[22] If we say that this is obvious it is because the *coincidentia oppositorum* lays bare to perception the consummate continuity of the universe. Naturally Ramsay's statement that he feels himself to be "the central person in the Universe" is not to be taken as the credo of a megalomaniac; it is the expression of the experience of unity in which *any thing at all* is central to the self-conscious universe. In the state of enlightenment "I" am everything else and everything "else" is the experiencing consciousness. To grasp this is to sense intimately the "suchness" of things—the principal theme of classical haiku in the East, and an important element of much twentieth-century Western lyric poetry.

Since language expresses the dualistic prejudices of ego-intellect, the poet's development involves learning how to give linguistic expression to the alogical content of symbolic reality.

Ego and the Self in Symbolic Reality

By now it is no doubt clear that whenever we speak of symbols and of symbolic experience we are referring to the perceptions of nonego reality. The symbolic reality of nonego is not alien, but on the contrary is universally experienced as significant images in that world of the Self we call the dream. To the extent that we dream we are all intimately familiar with the fluid becoming of oneiric images that "magically" overcome all logical resistance to transcending the opposites. To transcend the opposites is to be transcendental, and whenever we are vouchsafed a numinous dream we are struck by the higher significance of it, no matter how far removed it may be from dualistic thinking. We intuit that logical distinctions are simply irrelevant to the truth that it bears.

Because symbolic reality has its roots in the Self, it points toward God. Thoreau observed of his dream-life: "I am conscious of having, in my sleep, transcended the limits of the individual. . . . As if in sleep our individual fell into the infinite mind." "On awakening," he says, "we resume our enterprise, take up our bodies and become limited mind again. We meet and converse with those bodies which we have previously animated. There is a moment in the dawn . . . when we see things more truly than at any other time."[23]

The confrontation between ego and the Self is a very deep part of the meaning of symbolic reality. Consider the poem "The Dream," by David Ignatow, which shows the dream functioning at its best—as a prophetic diagnosis of spiritual lopsidedness:

Someone approaches to say his life is ruined
and to fall down at your feet
and pound his head upon the sidewalk.
Blood spreads in a puddle.
And you, in a weak voice, plead
with those nearby for help;
your life takes on his desperation.
He keeps pounding his head.
It is you who are fated;
and you fall down beside him.
It is then you are awakened,
the body gone, the blood washed from the ground,
the stores lit up with their goods.[24]

Here we see dramatized the activity of the Self attempting to deflate the ego in the interests of spiritual wholeness, and it is with the greatest relief that the recalcitrant ego awakens to escape from the suffering caused by the guilty realization that it, with its "goods," is indeed ruining the life of the spirit (cf. Mark 8:36). Ignatow characterizes our everyday, secular reality as the market place, a negotiable reality; but the goods of which he speaks suggest ironically the abstraction and its opposite—evils. Charles Bennett, in his study of mysticism, notes that the mystics turn away from "the whole elaborate system of goods which men have discovered and laboured to establish," and it is no doubt these illusory goods—or rather love of them— that is ruining the life of that shadowy Someone within.[25]

Pedro Salinas, besides being an excellent poet, was a worldly success by any measure, and the problem of the relationship between the ego and the Self appears early in his poetry. He freely recognized that the extraordinary talent and vitality that he brought to the task of living his life were, as a matter of fact, a willing bondage to secular reality; and in the poem at the beginning of these pages, "Esta cadena de hierro," he acknowledges the claims of the Someone. He, the promising young cosmopolite, is fully conscious that his rewarding commitment to profane reality is a bondage in any case. For most of us dualistic ego-reality is our *querencia*, our favorite haunt, our most comfortable perch in the cage of the world. We have grown up with our chain, and we think we would be lost without it.[26] H. G. Baynes has observed that "the extraverted habit of life can . . . assume a compulsive character, . . . especially . . . when extraversion is seized upon as a means for avoiding the needs and claims of the inner [self]." As long as we are "chained to extraversion" we have little chance to grow inwardly.[27]

The creative artist, less removed than others from the world of the Self, seems to have no difficulty in recognizing its higher claims. The successful inhabitant of the metropolitan reality will not hide the fact that secular bondage is no hard thing to endure, but at the same time, by virtue of the vocation as artist or poet, one may carry within a powerful sense of being "bound" to follow the dictates of another, "unknown master" of cosmic proportions, a master (or mistress) as great as the world reality. The *dueño desconocido* cannot be defined, but only intuited. It appears to David Ignatow in a dream, in the vague form of a faceless Someone; for Pedro Salinas, this someone is not to be known:

> There is another chain . . .
> that enslaves me to that unknown
> master, to that master . . .

The final ellipses perform the same function as the vagueness of Ignatow's reference to Someone.

We are now in a position to see fairly clearly that when Holmes "tripped out" and in a flash of illumination wrote, "Lord, what a stench!" he was giving verbal expression to the truth of symbolic reality. From this new vantage point he was struck by the limitations of conventional consciousness, found it to be thrashing about in a self-imposed bondage ("the sound of one hand clapping") and experienced the dark realization that something was rotten in Denmark. He intuited an inner reproach: "This is ruining my life! Lord, what a stench in here!" So his exclamation easily represents an insight into the cramped and frequently stinking living quarters of routine ego-consciousness. There was no false profundity here, but rather an immediate insight into the question of bondage to ego and the significance of liberation from it. That he exclaimed, "*Lord,* what a stench!" has its symbolic meaning—since in symbolic reality everything has a meaning; for after all, who is to say that at that moment of illumination the cry "Lord!" was a mere expletive? Chances are much greater that he was addressing that "unknown master" whose human rights Salinas unhesitatingly acknowledged.

Chapter Two

THE PASSAGE FROM EGO TO NONEGO

The rich poets, as Homer, Chaucer, Shakespeare, and Raphael, have obviously no limits to their works, except the limits of their lifetime, and resemble a mirror carried through the street, ready to render an image of every created thing.—Ralph Waldo Emerson, "The Poet"

El Negocio del Ocio: The Business of Idleness

In discussing the drive toward activation of the *persona honda* we have used, as examples of this kind of awakening, episodes from the drug experience and from the dream-world—examples which, for many of us, are no recommendation at all. Evidently most of us civilized people believe that unless the ego is captain of the ship irrational forces will take over and disintegrate us. We have all learned the need for "self-control," and so have come to think of growth and development as an either/or situation: either ego-intellect takes charge of our life, or chaos results, and this is the credo we pass on to our children.

But of course this is no choice fatally given. All religious traditions present us with examples of selfless persons who were effectively organized; self-integrated persons who learned that their own sense of selfhood was not inevitably chained to the ego, but was rather rooted in the existence of the unknown master or mistress.

This Someone does not stand in an "I-It" relationship with the world "out there," as ego does. Ego is the principle of differentiation between our own individuality and the world around us—the environment. When the Self mediates these two spheres, however, the world ceases to be an environment. There is a sense of at-one-ment which, when experienced sharply (as an illumination), changes the experience of who "I" am, of self-identity. An instance of this change can be seen in the experience of a certain person who is reported to have suddenly awakened into unity; when he looked upon the world, he says (and we note here a tendency to avoid the personal pronoun *I*), "I was in it, through it, participating in it—not an observer. This awareness was sudden, yet timeless. This other realm was very *real*—not a glimpse, but the whole of it was there. Did not want to possess it, or reject or love—no feeling *toward* it, but *in* all being. Too close to respond or react to it, but *in* it."[1]

The experience of at-one-ment seems paradoxical, since we have all become individual selves by cultivating duality, "I" vs. "the environment." When the illumination occurs, "I" plus the world equals a new, all-encompassing It—which is reality-as-consciousness. Thus Plotinus comments: "But one must not ask, Whence comes it? For there is no question of whence. For it neither comes nor goes, but it appears and it does not appear. . . . And when it has passed one says: After all it was within; and yet it was not within."[2] Unified consciousness is the culmination of the selfless condition, and so will be discussed in greater detail when we consider poems by Salinas written at the time of his own experience of unity. For the present it is needful to bear in mind that unified consciousness has both an ontology and an epistemology. Ontologically it demonstrates that reality is One, not two; epistemologically it comes about through cultivation of egolessness.

This kind of consciousness is what made Salinas both a humanist-scholar and the poet he was. R. H. Blyth, who in his monumental work on haiku quotes George Moore's definition of pure poetry, might almost have been describing Salinas's achievement: "something that the poet creates outside of his own personality." By this, says Blyth, we understand "that the world is reflected in the mind of the poet as in an undistorted mirror, the growth and life of the poet's mind being identical with that movement of things outside."[3]

Of course when we speak of the movement of things outside the poet, we mean things that are normally only thought to be outside the mind. The poetic awakening comes in the moment of nonego, when the mind experiences itself as reality. This manner of nonego experience, its epistemology, is recorded in a striking poem from Salinas's second book of poetry, *Seguro azar* ("Dependable Chance"), where it is indeed a chance incident that shows him in an extraordinary way how the nonego consciousness begins to operate.

MADRID. CALLE DE...

¡Qué vacación de espejo por la calle!
Tendido boca arriba, cara al cielo,
todo de azogue estremecido y quieto,
bien atado le llevan.
Roncas bocinas vanamente urgentes
apresurar querrían
su lenta marcha de garzón cautivo.

¡Pero qué libre aquella tarde, fuera,
prisionero, escapado! Nadie
vino a mirarse en él. Él sí que mira
hoy, por vez primera es ojos.
Cimeras ramas, cielos, nubes, vuelos
de extraviadas nubes, lo que nunca
entró en su vida, ve.
Si descansan sus guardas a los lados

acero, prisa, ruido,
corren. Él, inmóvil
en el asfalto, liso estanque
momentáneo, hondísimo,
abre. Y le surcan
—de alas, de plumas, peces—
crepusculares golondrinas secas.

No. 25, *Seguro azar*
(1924–1928)

MADRID: ON ANY STREET

What a mirror's vacation along the streets!
They carry it turned face up to the sky,
all quiet, trembling quicksilver,
securely tied down.
Raucous auto horns, vainly urgent,
would like to hasten
the leisurely gait of the captive blue heron.

But how free that afternoon, out-of-doors,
a prisoner, escaped! No one
came to look in it. *It* looks
today: for the first time it is eyes.
The topmost branches, the sky, clouds, flights
of errant clouds, what never
came into its life, it sees.
If its guards rest at either side:
steel, haste, noise
rush past. It, immobile
on the asphalt, opens up
for a moment a deep, deep
pool of still water. And darting through it
—winged and feathered fishes—
dry twilight swallows.

The transition from ego to Self is traditionally exemplified most clearly in the meditative state, for the idea behind meditation in both East and West is to cultivate detachment from one's customary ego-oriented point of view. Sitting in meditation, one quiets the mind, makes it a blank—without dozing off. One remains wide awake, completely attentive, with minimal interference from ego-business. This is to become aware of a reality from which one has withdrawn ego-projections. Mystics think of this as seeing things "as they really are," in a poverty of consciousness—for such is what it means to learn to be poor in spirit.

This ego-transcendence is conducive to seeing things without attempting to negotiate a relationship between them and ego-aims. Ego is constantly negotiating with its environment, in what is known as karmic involvement, or motivated actions.[4] My daily life is a series of "deals" wherein I negotiate for my place in the sun. I use the word *negotiate* here because the history of that word points up the difference between the two modes of perceiving reality: with ego-attachment and without it.

There is a curious cultural contrast in the psychology underlying the English word *business* and the Spanish *negocio* (cognate to our *negotiate*). Our words *business* and *busy* are derived from the Anglo-Saxon *bysig*, meaning "diligent," and they connote an active, conscious, and deliberate striving. But the Spanish word *negocio* does not lend itself to this connotation; "I'm busy" must be rendered in Spanish as "I'm occupied" (*estoy ocupado*). The Spanish *negocio* is ultimately a negative formation from the Latin *nec + otium* (cf. Eng. "otiose") and meant originally "not-ease," "not-leisure." Etymologically, the *negocio* in life is that part of life that is not concerned with leisure—that interferes with it, as it were. Because the term is negative it suggests strongly that our *negocio* is not our principal concern—a notion which in turn suggests the attitude of the leisure class, or of the contemplative life.

Seeing secular business affairs negatively, as "not-leisure," then, implies a greater commitment to *otium*, since it is *otium* that produces our greatest spiritual treasures. Pushed to its farthest extreme, the "otiose" attitude to life has the most significant consequences for one's manner of being a human being, for ultimately it means quiet detachment and selfless attention to reality. It means cultivating (like the ascetics who take the vow of poverty) an egoless ontology, seeking a new sense of reality by ceasing to negotiate with it in terms of ego-intentions.

The Epistemology of Enlightenment: "¡Qué vacación de espejo!"

Speaking allegorically we may say that the mirror normally functions in the world of *negocio*: it has a job to do, which is to serve as a cosmetic glass, and so it is usually "busy" reflecting our own self-attachment, our own face, and our own concern with the karmic appearance of our face in the world of negotiations. When Salinas, in a mood of quiet detachment, was lucky enough one day to see a couple of street porters carrying a large mirror through the streets of Madrid, he suddenly saw it as being something other than a cosmetic glass. He saw it as a symbolic projection of his own mood of tranquil observer, his own state of *ocio*. The mirror showed him his own mind doing what it was doing at that moment, which was to perceive things in a nonnegotiable reality. And his poem begins with the exclamation, "What a mirror's vacation . . . !"

In current Spanish the word for *vacation* is conventionally plural: one takes one's *vacaciones*. Salinas may or may not have been familiar with a local usage of this word in the singular; but in any case he uses that form here: *vacación*, just as he says of a character in a story, "He was empty of all will; the vacating [*vacación*] of his will put him at the mercy of the first thing that might come his way."[5]

The title, "Madrid. Calle de. . ."[6] is important since we are concerned with crossing the threshold from "negotiations" to "otioseness"; from *necotium* to *ocio*, and the metropolis is, of course, the negotiating place par excellence. But now the mirror is on vacation from its cosmopolitan job. Literally *vacación*, like *vacation*, means the act of making vacant; and "to be on vacation" means not only to be free from business or other activity in the popular sense, but also "to be in a state of mental emptiness" in the contemplative sense, which the Zen Buddhist thinks of as the natural, i.e., the nonego, mind: "Natural mind means more flexible mind, without sticking to [anything]. When our mind is perfectly free and open to everything— like a mirror—it is natural mind."[7] Among Spanish mystics the verb *vacar*, "to vacate," means "to meditate," to practice mental prayer. In secular usage it still carries the meaning of complete devotion to anything: cf. the Royal Academy's definition, "To devote oneself . . . entirely to a specific activity."[8]

The Dominican friar Luis de Granada (1504–1588) uses the verb this way in the biographical introduction to his translation of the anonymous, mystical *Ladder to Paradise*. Of its author Fr. Luis says, "Antes que tomase el sueño, tenía por costumbre vacar a oración," that is, "Before going to sleep it was his custom to meditate"—literally, to "vacate to prayer." Similarly Fr. Juan de los Angeles (1536–1609) says, "San Isidoro dice que la vida contemplativa es vida libre de todo negocio y que en sólo el amor se fija, y los santos dijeron que era vida ociosa, y el Filósofo (IV *Ethicorum*), la llama vacación." Which is to say, "Saint Isidore says that the contemplative life is a life free of all business and that it attends only to love; and the saints said that it was an otiose life; and Aristotle (*Ethics*, IV) calls it vacation." Finally, Miguel de Molinos (ca. 1640–1697), the central figure of the Quietist movement, writes in his *Spiritual Guide* that the contemplatives normally engage in simple quietism: " . . . vacan a sencilla, y desnuda contemplación de Dios." "They vacate to simple and naked contemplation of God."[9]

Spanish mysticism was one of the academic specialties of Pedro Salinas, and he, like all readers of mystic literature, soon became aware that the emptying of the mind is a commonplace idea. It is essential to the mystic task in the East as well as the West; a Chinese Zen master has written, "Only when you have no thing in your mind and no mind in things, are you vacant and spiritual, empty and marvellous."[10]

The secular notion of going on vacation is connected with all this through the idea of idling or playing, which is to indulge in free activity unencumbered by serious ego-goals. Johan Huizinga, in *Homo Ludens*, has much to say about the significance of play as mental recreation, and he notes that Aristotle himself stressed the importance of knowing how to "idle well," since, says Huizinga, for Aristotle "this idleness or leisure is the principle of the universe." This principle of the universe is the Dance of Life, the free play of reality. Only when the mind is emptied of all constraint can it be filled with the play of reality: "Clay is moulded into a vessel, but the empty space is the useful part."[11] The *spiritus*, the breath of life, can penetrate consciousness only if we leave it room to do so. Thus Charles Reznikoff says of the beginning of springtime:

> Sit still
> beside the open window
> and let the wind,
> the gentle wind,
> blow in your face;
>
> sit still
> and fold your hands—
> empty your heart of thoughts,
> your mind of dreams.[12]

These nine short lines constitute a treatise on meditation, on Quietism, on *zazen*. The rest is technique, about which volumes continue to be written.

All this is what we have called the epistemology of enlightenment, the manner in which one attains to knowledge of the Self. The cheval glass observed by Salinas revealed to him his own mind. The porters had tied it securely to keep it from swiveling in transit, and they were carrying it face up. It had been vacated from its usual environment (a domestic or business interior) and was now in the meditative posture recommended: "todo de azogue estremecido y quieto," literally, "completely of trembling quicksilver and quiet." This means that the reflecting surface (of the mind) is all of a piece, no longer discontinuous; for the preparation for meditation requires one to establish a *continuous* awareness, an awareness that suffers no breach of continuity from the intrusion of vagrant thoughts, free associations, idle personal images, or the like.

The mirror observed by Salinas is seen to have entered into a quietistic, reflective state. Since it is being carried face up it is reflecting the sky, and so becomes that which it reflects. Salinas compares it to the quiet passage of a blue heron, blue, of course, because the reflecting surface is all sky. But the symbolism is specifically that of an aquatic fowl, an earth-water-sky bird in whose living being the realms have ceased to exist as separate. Similarly the cheval glass is likened to sky and water simultaneously in the last three lines.

Context establishes that the symbolism of the heron is positive, not negative; further, the aquatic fowls in general (swan, duck, goose, heron, crane, pelican, etc.) carry the symbolism that arises in connection with transcending the opposites, e.g., the separateness of sky and water. Equally at home in the "below" and in the "above," they symbolize the union of the realms and matrimonial bliss plus domestic felicity, the peace of union as opposed to strife and discord, longevity and wisdom. This suggests why the crane is connected with poetry (the "Word of wisdom") "all the way from Ireland to China," since poetry, in the deepest sense, is a manifestation of union: consciousness conjoined to the unconscious.[13]

The general image of the poem involves the apparent paradox of liberation through bondage: the mirror, lashed down securely and escorted by "guards," is seen as being on the path of freedom; today it is truly seeing for the first time. Liberation from the bondage to ego's negotiable, dualistic reality is traditionally associated with the self-imposed slavery of ascetic discipline. The ascetic seeks to vacate the mind and so awaken in unity as an escaped prisoner, morally free at last. It is as Jung has noted: in meditation there is the sense "of having been 'replaced,' but without the connotation of having been 'deposed.' It is as if the direction of the affairs of life had gone over to an invisible centre. Nietzsche's metaphor, *'in most loving bondage, free'*, would be appropriate here."[14] By entering into the poverty of vacancy, by escaping from the richness of cosmopolitan consciousness, the seeker approaches the point of seeing truly, as if for the first time.

Salinas, as a poet, was regularly familiar with the informal vacating of the mind whereby fresh material could be raised into consciousness. This harmonious and constructive interaction of ego with Self is basically a part of what it means even to have a poetic spirit at all—a point not easily conceded by people who believe that poetry is primarily a linguistic art. Robert Graves, speaking of T. E. Lawrence (they were acquaintances), says that Lawrence "frankly envied poets. He felt that they had some sort of secret. . . . Lawrence envisaged the poets' secret as a technical mastery of words rather than as a particular mode of living and thinking."[15] It is a particular mode of living and thinking that Salinas illustrates so frequently, and which actually becomes the theme of many poems describing the "epistemology" of the poetic process, as it is in "Madrid. Calle de . . ."

The poem progresses to a point where the speaker sees that the mirror has been transformed into a pool of quietism out of time. The surface noise and bustle of metropolitan confusion is blanked out, to be replaced by profundity, the profundity of unity with the natural macrocosm. The birds flitting across the sky *are* the reflecting surface; hybrid creatures (bird/fish) moving in the crepuscular depths of the "deep, deep pool" within.

The motif of the mirroring pool is used universally in contemplative literature. In the *Cántico espiritual* of Saint John of the Cross, for example, the pool within becomes a "crystalline fount" (*cristalina fuente*, punning on the name of Christ, or *Cristo*) wherein the mystic seeks to discern the reflected image of the divine glance. And Heinrich Zimmer, speaking of yoga, describes the Eastern idea of the mind as a reflective pool. Yoga stills consciousness, he says, and when this happens the life-monad stands revealed "like a jewel at the bottom of a quieted pond."[16] Zimmer here notes that yoga stills the mind, since it is one of the techniques perfected to this end. But of course the techniques are countless, whereas the poetic spirit seems to be in native possession of the secret.

Salinas's poem contains an implicit pun that tells us something important about the mirror as a symbolic projection of the poet's own mind. We have noted that a cheval glass is involved, that is, a full-length mirror that swivels in a frame and must be tied down securely before it can be safely carried about. Salinas makes a point of including this detail. Now it is a fact that in the nineteenth century a popular name for the cheval glass was "psyche." In English one said "psyche-glass," or simply "psyche"; in Spanish, *psique*. The old 1912 edition of the Pequeño Larousse Spanish Dictionary gives this domestic meaning of *psique*, and even includes an illustration of the cheval glass.

Salinas, born in 1891, came from a middle-class Madrid household.[17] He grew into maturity during the beginning of the age of depth-psychology (Freud, born in 1856, began publishing at the turn of the century), and so we must note that by the time Salinas was a young man with his college degrees the word *psique* had undergone a semantic change. By the 1920s, when this poem was written, it certainly would have seemed unusual—particularly among university people—to speak of acquiring a "psyche" for one's living quarters. The *OED* gives a nineteenth-century example from Lytton: " 'How low the room is . . . !' said Caroline; . . . 'And I see no Psyche.' " By the 1920s a sentence like this must have seemed like the evocation of a bygone age.

Salinas excludes the word *psique* from his poem, and evidently does so as a semantic strategy, since the poetic effect would have been quite different had he used an explicit allusion: "Today I saw a psyche being carried down the street." This wording will not do, since the semantic confusion of a deliberate pun intrudes upon our reading. Nevertheless to a middle-class person born before the turn of the century we may suppose that both the object and its name still enjoyed an existence, if only as a latent memory; so that the unity of the symbolic projection may be expressed in the closest possible fashion: "That 'psyche' is indeed a psyche! My nonmaterial psyche is experiencing itself as a material psyche."[18]

Chapter Three

THE MESSAGE OF THE CREATIVE

UNCONSCIOUS

Agua en la noche, serpiente indecisa,
silbo menor y rumbo ignorado;
¿qué día nieve, qué día mar? Dime.
¿Qué día nube, eco
de ti y cauce seco?
Dime.
—No lo diré: entre tus labios me tienes,
beso te doy pero no claridades.
Que compasiones nocturnas te basten
y lo demás a las sombras
déjaselo, porque yo he sido hecha
para la sed de los labios que nunca preguntan.

No. 2, *Presagios* (1924)

Water in the night, indecisive serpent,
faint hiss and unknown path;
what day snow, what day sea? Tell me.
What day cloud, echo
of yourself and dry river bed?
Tell me.
"I will not say: you have me between your
 lips,
I will give you a kiss but not clarities.
Be satisfied with nocturnal compassion
and leave all the rest
to the shadows, because I was made
for the thirst of lips that never ask questions."

Of the secular reality of ego Okakura Kakuzo observed, in *The Book of Tea*, that "nothing is real to us but hunger, nothing sacred except our own desires."[1] In the world of the Self one awakens to what reality signifies when experienced without ego-desires. One is alive here and now, in the Eternal Present, where each thing is perceived as a culmination, as the full ripeness of itself. The past fades into insignificance and the future does not yet exist. The present moment is not experienced as an exciting event that happens and fades away (like the sexual or esthetic event) but rather is always in the process of playing, like a fountain or like the fire on the hearth. It cannot die and it cannot go beyond what it is busy being, since what it is busy being is already an overflowing abundance. "To arrive at reality . . . is to go beyond *karma*, beyond consequential action, and to enter a life which is completely aimless. Yet to Zen and Taoism alike this is the very life of the universe, which is complete at every moment and does not need to justify itself by aiming at something beyond."[2] Everything is already ripe, fully mature. A child is not a little incomplete adult; a child is the magic of childhood, suddenly alive and vibrant in any individual boy or girl. All is archetypally alive, and so nothing is to be "done" with it.

This mode of participating in the life of the universe is intuited by Salinas in his poem "Agua en la noche," which presents ego-intellect as the time-bound inquirer, and the Self as alive in unity. Here the Eternal Present appears both as a ceaselessly flowing river and as a serpent that underlies all vital movement and that precedes all attempts on the part of human consciousness to separate itself as a subject distinct from reality as an object.

The Symbology of the Serpent

The inner becoming of the nonego reality raises into consciousness a realization of symbolic meanings that are not necessarily in agreement with the symbols of one's culture—symbols that have long been divested of their archetypal significance, and that now function as mere moralistic allegories. Most of us have learned, for example, that the serpent symbolizes evil; we have not learned this experientially, but rather have been educated to the idea.

In "Agua en la noche" the speaker experiences a river at nighttime (whether empirical or oneiric makes no difference) and it becomes the carrier of part of his own instinct. By projecting upon it an element of his own psyche he enters into dialogue with it, and we see that this symbolic serpent escapes entirely the moralistic characteristics with which occidental tradition has endowed it. The serpent, being one of the telluric, earthbound creatures (like spiders and toads) becomes the carrier of whatever attitudes one has toward the earth-body (instinctual realm) itself.

Christianity has traditionally stressed the spirit/body dualism as a conflict of interests (cf. "the world, the flesh, and the Devil") in which sensuality (the outward show of instinct) is the work of the Devil, which must be overcome or sublimated in the interests of the upward-striving, uranic soul. The very first appearance of the Ancient Enemy is the serpent's tempting of Eve, and among Christians this is popularly taken to be a reference to sexuality; the Freudian interpretation of the serpent as a phallic symbol encounters little resistance among us.

But this concern for associating the serpent with sexuality may be largely a conditioning by the occidental Christian tradition; for comparative mythology shows the snake to be an archetypal symbol of such immense importance that to restrict one's discussion of it to sexuality is hardly more than a severe, self-imposed limitation. To equate the snake with sexuality is to do the same thing to the Earth Mother herself. This is well known to mythologists, and no one would want to argue that the veneration of the serpent in the Orient has ultimately a sexual significance. For when we speak of veneration we mean reverence on the part of consciousness for an unconscious force that ego recognizes as being more powerful than itself. Refusal to recognize any such force within is the spiritual flaw that the Greeks called hubris.

Serpent symbolism in the Orient (and in our own dream-world) entails a recognition of the transcendent powers of instinct as a divinity that must be treated with reverence; acknowledged, not repressed; a divinity that in itself is neither benevolent nor malevolent, but accessible.

Reverent recognition of transcendent forces implies the belief that we are part and parcel of the surrounding world, and not really a subject facing an object. Conscious life itself has been evolved out of the world reality, and this is a creative feat on the part of nature. The natural world's reality underlies all that we can hope to be spiritually, and so it merits veneration. The psychological projection affords the mechanism whereby such veneration is implemented, since our instinctual life is projected onto and experienced as a telluric creature. This is the "I-Thou" experience of the contemplative act; or, as Wallace Stevens puts it, contemplating fruit on a table:

> It is something on a table that he sees.
> . . . .
> Himself, may be, the irreducible X
> At the bottom of imagined artifice,
> Its inhabitant and elect expositor.[3]

The serpent has commonly been the creature chosen as the object of chthonic worship. Jacob Grimm has noted the ancient mythological theory that springs and wells are guarded by snakes (or dragons)—guarded, because they contain something of value.[4] Ego can become a separate subject in an objectively seen world only by climbing out of those depths, only by leaving our original home in nature. But our origin must be the *source* (the French word means "wellspring") of valuable material, since it has produced consciousness, and so the Hindu naga (serpent) kings and queens are everywhere the guardians of the earth-treasures.[5]

Alfred Métraux, in his study of voodoo in Haiti, points out the archetypal significance of the serpent apropos of Haitian ophiolatry (which he rightly denies as being mere snake-worship). The serpent "is a being with a dual nature, both male and female. Coiled in a spiral form round the earth [it] sustains the world and prevents its disintegration. . . . Because [its] nature is motion, [it] is also water."[6]

The serpent is androgynous because it carries a projection of the preconscious instinctual realm that contains all latent potential. The slithering movement of the snake appears to be purposeless locomotion (cf. Salinas's *serpiente indecisa*), since it encompasses all directions at once. The sinuous snake is a magic river, an intelligent river, as it were, that is no longer the complete prisoner of gravity. It is the river that has learned how to seek higher ground.

Primitive mythology transcends Darwinian evolution: the river, having discovered the secret of overcoming inertia, magically sprouts wings and flies heavenward in the form of a dragon, or it simply hurls itself into the sky as a rainbow, the symbol of the earth-rooted spirit. The rainbow is a river-serpent magically transmuted into the uranic spirit of the human being.

The archetypal symbol of the Rainbow Serpent of North Central Australia is considered by those aborigines to be at the beginning of their creation in the Dream Time, and through it they periodically renew themselves ritually by making contact with Mother Earth. The significant episode occurs in the ritual when "a whistle summons the Rainbow Snake. The Serpent moves, arches [its] body, and ascends to the sky. '[It] is the harbinger of rain, rejuvenator of the earth: [it] is the instrument through which the rebirth of nature is achieved.' "[7]

Edgar Thurston, discussing primitive beliefs of Southern India, even cites the opinion that the comet is a celestial snake, a flying dragon or serpent-principle united to the principle of human consciousness. Within the earth, serpents are continually making gold nuggets. "The moment their work is finished, the serpents are transformed into winged serpents, and fly up into the air with the stones in their mouths."[8]

In Malabar it is the hissing of the snakes that performs the magic trans-formation of the treasure that they guard: "In time . . . the reptile is said to get wings, and the treasure, by the continual hissing, to assume the form of a precious stone. When this is done, the snake is said to fly with its precious stone. So strong is this belief that, when a comet appeared some ten years ago, people firmly believed that it was the flight of the winged serpent with the precious stone."[9]

Edgar Herzog, in his study of the mythology of death, connects the snake both with the water principle and the feminine principle (i.e., the chthonic realm): "Snakes themselves are supposed to possess the equivalent of hidden wisdom and of knowledge of the hidden, whether it is that they are thought of as the souls of the dead guarding hidden treasures, or that they them-selves are thought to be enchanted girls, or whether it is believed that since they dwell in secret depths they are in contact with the water of life, hidden wisdom and healing counsel."[10]

Thus in studying the mythology surrounding the figure of the serpent, one constantly gets back to its uroboric aspect: the original serpent is the tail-biter, the circular world-snake of the original pleroma—the primordial plen-itude out of which the world reality has been formed, analogous to the foetal world out of whose waters the human being comes forth. Nothing that is was not originally in the primordial waters, and so it is that the snake represents both the power to prophesy and the power to heal. Human ego-consciousness, cut off from its instinctual sources, easily falls sick, and the healing process can come about only by a return to the source of the healing water. Whatever is to be lies already present, as a potential, below the threshold of conscious life.

So the artist and the seer do not invent anything out of whole cloth. By means of opening the inner doors of perception they raise into consciousness elements that were awaiting discovery. Consciousness sets it into order, imposes patterns upon this material, structures it, which is to say that consciousness plays the role of demiurge, the subordinate divinity who creates a world out of the original supreme fiat.

A modern version of the magic transformation of river into serpent occurs in the entry in Thoreau's journal for August 17, 1851: "The rill I stopped to drink at I drink in more than I expected. I satisfy and still provoke the thirst of thirsts. . . . I do not drink in vain. I mark that brook as if I had swallowed a water-snake that would live in my stomach. I have swallowed something worth the while. . . . I have drunk an arrowhead. It flows from where all fountains rise."[11] Here Thoreau feels his assimilation of a stream of water as the conversion into a snake within himself; then, curiously enough, there occurs to him the notion of an arrowhead, which is to say the initiation of the flight of an arrow (cf. the Rainbow Serpent and the comet snake). Natural forces have been raised into conscious participation in the life of the spirit that flies heavenward, and the drinker is again at one with the realm "where all fountains rise," the source of all life.

Ego-consciousness can only surmise its own sources, of course, but the materials at its disposal are such as these: the symbolic contents from religion and art which antedate the civilized differentiation of ego-intellect, and which transcend the latter-day postulates of Freudian empiricism. The universality of this archaic, archetypal material requires one to object to the limitations which Freudian symbology lays upon archetypal meaning, as when Ernest Jones points out that "the serpent symbolizes not simply the male member in general, but particularly the male member of the father."[12] This limitation in itself represents a kind of spiritual provincialism on the part of a male-oriented, profane rationalism that seeks to impose upon ancient material the prejudices of late-nineteenth-century Europe. Universally considered, the primordial insights of human beings concerning the serpent (or the moon or ocean or sun or any other archetypal phenomenon) cannot be realistically reduced to the scope of the family problems besetting the cosmopolitan neurotic of 1900.

Thus the serpent as an archaic symbol must be related not to the phallus, which is specifically male but rather to the spinal column, whether male or female, as is the case in kundalini yoga. The snake, as the guardian of the treasures of the unconscious, is the sign par excellence of all human beings' capacity to live "vertically," i.e., to rise toward heaven—whether in the shape of the heavenly dragon of the Chinese or that of the Rainbow Serpent of Australia. And indeed, this is the primary insight of Salinas's poem, "Agua en la noche," where the river/serpent is a minimal symbol for differentiated Earth-flowing; a flowing bound to inertia which spirit overcomes in the process of differentiating a human consciousness.

The Salinas poem shows us here how the modern lyric poet is our mythologizer, and what it means to mythologize. The myth is a dramatization of human becoming, not an allegory nor yet a pathetic, primitive attempt to explain the world scientifically, as nineteenth-century anthropologists were fond of saying. The myth shows us the nature of spiritual metamorphoses, just as the dream, where the magic *coincidentia opposi-*

torum is typically accepted as quite normal by the dreamer. Symbols may thus be seen as involved in an endless becoming, which is to say, a becoming sometimes highly differentiated, sometimes barely so. An oneiric river gradually turns into a snake; or it may gradually become a horse, seen as the surging force of libido in a magnificent and highly differentiated form, a steed that the dreamer may leap upon and ride heroically. Delmore Schwartz, in his poem about the child's dreaming, "O Child, Do Not Fear the Dark and Sleep's Dark Possession", gives expression to this ambiguity of symbolic differentiation in a manner parallel to that of "Agua en la noche":

> And in sleep's river you sleep
> Like the river's self and the marine
> Beings who mouth as they glide,
>   nosing
>   And sliding lithely and smoothly
>   Gleaming serenely and sleekly.[13]

Here sleep itself is a snake/river that flows, "gleaming serenely and sleekly."

The River/Serpent and "Agua en la noche"

For Salinas the primary characteristic of the double symbol of river and serpent is its indecisiveness: "River in the night, indecisive serpent." The sinuous flowing of preintellectual spirit is, by definition, as yet undifferentiated, as yet consciously undirected. Indeed, the spiritual direction that consciousness will take (what Salinas likes to call its *rumbo*, "route") is something to be supplied unconsciously.

The movement of the river/serpent is accompanied by a faint hiss. The *silbo* ("whistle," "hissing"), when heard from out of the unconscious, is the "still small voice" of the Self, as the author of I Kings 19:12 has it: "Y tras el terremoto un fuego: mas Jehová no estaba en el fuego. Y tras el fuego un silbo apacible y delicado." "And after the earthquake a fire; but the Lord was not in the fire; and after the fire a still small voice." Similarly Saint Teresa hears God speak to her with an internal *silbo* ("Oí que me hablaba una voz muy suave, como metida en un silbo," "I heard a voice speaking softly to me, as if within a *silbo*"), and likewise Saint John of the Cross: "así como el silbo del aire causado se entra agudamente en el vasillo del oído," "just as the *silbo* made by the wind penetrates into the eardrum." According to the quietist Miguel de Molinos, the contemplative hears at times "una voz interior de su amada que . . . llama, y un silbo muy delicado, que sale de lo íntimo del alma," which is to say, "an inner voice calling, and a very soft *silbo* that issues from the deepest part of the soul."[14] So we gather that the *silbo* is literally a sibilant sound, symbolizing the manifestation of the *pneuma*, the *spiritus* ("breath," "wind") within; the primordial spirit that underlies ego-consciousness. Ultimately the sibilant sound of the magic serpent is a more differentiated form of the sibilant sound of the *spiritus*, just as the sinuous flowing of the serpent is a more differentiated form of the flowing of the river.

This "inspired" *silbo*, the still small voice heard when we are silent, is not only a sibilant wind heard in the stillness of consciousness; it is also a *rumbo ignorado*, an "unknown path." This voice from the other side of consciousness speaks of transformation, of new paths that cannot be known before they come into being:

> what day snow, what day sea? Tell me.
> What day cloud, echo
> of you and dry river bed?

But the future of the *pneuma*, the *spiritus*, cannot be known, even as Christ informed Nicodemus: "El viento de donde quiere sopla, y oyes su sonido; mas ni sabes de dónde viene, ni a dónde vaya: así es todo aquel que es nacido del Espíritu." "The wind bloweth where it listeth, and thou hearest the sound thereof, but canst not tell whence it cometh, and whither it goeth: so is every one that is born of the Spirit." (John 3:8)

The creative artist, just like the prophet, is one who is born of the spirit, one who is silent in the presence of the still small voice. As long as ego-consciousness chatters away, as long as it is noisily busy with being its routine, secular self, it can never enter into union with the spirit on the other side. In "Agua en la noche" the speaker wants to know straight out: When? What? Where?

Nicodemus asked Christ the literal-minded question: "How can a man be born when he is old?" Christ told him, "Except a man be born of water and of the Spirit, he cannot enter into the kingdom of God" (John 3:4–5). Christ, using the truisms of symbolic reality, says, "That which is born of the flesh is flesh; and that which is born of the Spirit is spirit" (John 3:6). The kingdom of God is, for the poet, the kingdom of the spirit, the kingdom of the Self, the sacred ground of our own being. Poetry is the spirit that is born of the Spirit.

Salinas perceives the nocturnal river as a symbol, which is to say that he perceives it in the realm of meaning beyond the contrarities, the realm of the preintellectual world, where our conscious categories have not as yet been critically differentiated. Thus the presence that he intuits is a creative force, a movement; at once a river, a serpent, a still small voice and a surging along an uncharted course. As river it carries the waters of life, and these cover the entire world in the form of river, ocean, cloud, and rain. To perceive the presence of the inner fountain—and the symbol is the magic sign of its presence—is to recognize its existence, and this is tantamount to knowing that it will one day be raised into consciousness. It is not tantamount to knowing ahead of time what the spiritual evolution will be, because this comes in its own due time and cannot be forced. The *spiritus* bloweth where it listeth. Thus the secular question must remain unanswered; the answer always comes in the form of a vitalizing presence, not in the form of a preconceived plan of action.

That ego-question put by the speaker ("what day snow, what day sea? What day cloud . . . ?") is couched in the form of an image which Yeats had already used in speaking of the poetry of Shelley: "Alastor calls the river that he follows an image of his mind, and thinks that it will be as hard to say where his thought will be when he is dead as where its waters will be in ocean or cloud in a little while."[15] Ego-consciousness is only a fragment brought into awareness; a fragment of the mind that is always here whether ego knows it or not. When ego sleeps, it speaks; when ego dies, it continues to speak. When we hear it speak, it prophesies, which is to say that it awakens ego-consciousness to latent possibilities for future growth. It does not say exactly where or when or how one is to proceed, but rather that one will indeed proceed beyond the present limits of one's course already charted by ego-consciousness. These are the instinctual secrets of the Earth Mother through which the spirit speaks. Thus Aelian singles out this important attribute of the serpent: "It seems that one peculiarity of snakes is their faculty of divination."[16] And Herodotus, speaking of the sacred value which the Athenians placed upon the serpent: "The Athenians say that they have in their Acropolis a huge serpent, which lives in the temple, and is the guardian of the whole place."[17] Which is to say that the hissing snake, the serpent of the still small voice, is guardian of the sacred *temenos*, the precinct of the Self. Hence the Hindu naga symbolizes the superior consciousness: "The naga is a being of superhuman potency, immediately above the rank of [human beings], endowed with superior skill and wisdom. [It] can assume human form at will, but when [it] sleeps becomes again a serpent."[18] To assume human form means to be assimilated into ego-consciousness, so that a creative expansion occurs. In "Agua en la noche" the still small voice tells the speaker that fertile union is the goal of the transformation:

> "I will give you a kiss but not clarities.
> Be satisfied with nocturnal compassion
> and leave all the rest
> to the shadows, because I was made
> for the thirst of lips that never ask questions."

Here the union is called compassion. The clarities are, of course, the clear ideas of ego-intellect that cannot be supplied by this water. When clarity comes upon one from within we speak of it as illumination. The route to enlightenment involves the fusion of what is above with what is below, and as one of its fruits it yields compassion, which the Buddha, after his awakening, considered to be an all-important consequence; for to be compassionate means to be at one with life in its other forms and in its transformations.

Years later, in the forties, Salinas would reach the culmination of this process; in this poem he is concerned with the realization that the means are indeed available: available both for satisfying a certain thirst, and (as Thoreau puts it) for provoking "the thirst of thirsts." The ego-questions cannot be formulated at all unless one has some notion as to what the answers "ought" to be. The questioner anticipates the answerer—leads the witness, as it were—and so makes no progress toward transcending the limitations of ego-intellect. But falling silent, vacating the mind of conscious ego-intentions as to the course of one's spirit, allows the Spirit to blow where it will.

Chapter Four

THE ETERNAL PRESENCE OF THE
CREATIVE UNCONSCIOUS

MONEDA	COIN
Será quizá porque hay niebla	Perhaps because it is foggy
por lo que yo te acaricio.	do I rub you.
Porque hay niebla,	Because it is foggy,
masas disueltas, precisos	with masses dissolved, exact
resultados abolidos,	results abolished,
y todo se va a otro vago	and everything becomes another vague
no sé qué sin dimensión.	something without dimension.
Te acaricio a ti, moneda.	I rub you, coin.
Anochecer de diciembre	December nightfall
y tú aquí en mi mano, tú	and you here in my hand, you,
contorno estricto, tú, dura	definite outline, you, hard
existencia resistente,	resistant existence,
tu cuerpo de fina plata.	your body of fine silver.
Moneda	Coin
con un número invencible	with a numeral invincible
por la duda o por la niebla	by doubt or by fog
y un rostro	and a visage
que no dudará jamás,	that will never doubt,
de reina antigua, mirándome.	ancient queen looking at me.

No. 16, *Fábula y Signo* (1931)

My discussion of "Agua en la noche" incorporated a certain amount of archetypal material associated with the water-serpent. I have reviewed some of the reasons underlying the primitive (and unconscious) connections between the serpent principle and the earth-instinct, and have noted the dual nature, or androgyny, of the chthonic principle that sustains the world—the world of human consciousness, that is.

The Taoists recognize that life itself, the living world, comes about through the creative mingling of the feminine and masculine principles. The feminine principle, yin, relates to Mother Earth, and includes those qualities we associate with night, darkness, and the unconscious—the mysteries hidden to conscious understanding. It is the becoming that occurs below the surface of the earth and below the surface of the mind. The masculine principle, yang, is the fertilizing action bespeaking sunlight and daytime. It is clear and steadfast. While we hesitate to speak in riddles, it is nevertheless true that the whole point of the yin-yang "distinction" is the doctrine that the two are actually different aspects of the vital principle, and this applies equally at the level of human consciousness.

In all societies the feminine principle—woman herself, who conceives and carries the foetus—is the incarnation of the mysterious ways of nature, whereas the man functions as the carrier and principle sustainer of the tribal traditions. It has become common to speak of ego-consciousness as the "masculine principle," and of the instinctual realm of unconscious tendencies as the "feminine principle." The poets themselves have characteristically associated inspiration with the feminine figure of the muse. Of course it is not necessary to insist upon the association of nature with the feminine principle, since we are all familiar enough with the notion of Mother Nature, just as we traditionally associate the sun (that is, consciousness) with God the Father. What we do need to keep in mind, however, is the idea that spiritually each man and woman is a culturally conditioned product. Each culture develops a psychological ideal of the man and the woman, and this ideal is not a simple result of natural development. The culturally conditioned male and female consciousness represents a fragment of the original potential, and it is a specialization, as is suggested by particularly specialized forms like the Mexican image of the *macho* and the antebellum southern belle. And of course the repressive measures needed to produce a society where "men are men and women are women" may even yield the remarkable pathological phenomenon of the transsexualist.

The spiritual drive toward self-integration may mean, then, something much more specific than the assimilation by consciousness of creative, unconscious tendencies; it may mean specifically the assimilation of the feminine unconscious. "Agua en la noche" exhibits the former; and the poem we are now to examine shows how the confrontation crystallizes the "ancient queen" of the unconscious.

The confrontation, in any form, can come about only when the normally dominant operation of the civilized ego-consciousness is by some means curtailed, in some way clouded. In the poem "Moneda" this happens when the poet finds himself in the midst of a December fog that has descended at night upon the city. This fog surrounds the city-dweller physically with all those qualities associated with the yin principle—"cold, wet, soft, dark, mysterious, secret, changeable, cloudy, dim, and quiescent"—and it encourages a passivity of spirit in the masculine consciousness, which is (like Salinas, the active intellectual) "bright, clear, and steadfast," as is the yang principle.[1] Since the conscious mind is in a solvent state, the speaker—who is, after all, a poet—finds himself walking in the realm of the *creative unconscious*. Because of a minor incident, the bemused touching of a silver coin in his pocket, he enters into relation with the world of nonego.

Fog over the city is a variant of the motif of the timeless moment, the falling out of the duality that is the measured clarity of separateness. An excellent example of this is furnished by Charles Reznikoff, who notes how the magic of mist evokes the reality of consciousness blurred:

I like this secret walking
in the fog;
unseen, unheard
among the bushes
thick with drops;
the solid path invisible
a rod away—

and only the narrow present is alive.[2]

We are dealing with a phenomenon best known as a symbolic expression in the misty and foggy landscapes of Japanese and Chinese painting. This foggy blankness pervading the scene creates intervals that may be filled in imaginatively with any kind of material rising up from below the threshold of secular consciousness. The latter functions by connecting events causally, whereas what Edmund Carpenter calls the "art of the interval" seeks some new significance: "An alternate to the art of connecting events is the art of the interval. Oriental art doesn't use connections, but intervals, whether in flower arrangement or Zen poetry or dress. Free time [and] space are perceived as the meaningful pause. . . . Practically every aspect of Japanese life asserts the integrity of the interval. The *ma* ('spaces between' objects in the scene or simply 'spacing' of objects) . . . are integers, realities." The civilized Western mind seems to seek a fullness of ego-consciousness: "According to the Western 'Principle of Plenitude,' the universe is full: there are no gaps, no intervals: 'Nature abhors a vacuum'—at least, Western *human* nature does."[3]

The *ma*, then, provide the meaningful emptiness, the potential site of a new spiritual content. It is the emptiness that calls for participation and new forms. The Western mind seeks to fill in the void by means of connecting links already known; it seeks to reestablish a pattern. But the interval may be sensed as an opening, as a breathing space, rather than as a faulty gap.

Perhaps the most effective way to experience deliberately this meaningful blankness is to make the experiment suggested by Carpenter, who notes that "to the blind, all things are sudden." "Test this yourself: move about the room with your eyes closed. All encounters become abrupt. Emptiness combines with sudden interface. Connections are lacking; the gradations, shadings [and] continuities of the visual world are gone."[4] With eyes closed, connections gone, we sense an attentive expectancy in the void; we know not what to expect, but we know that something will be there, and we are ready to be surprised.

Expectancy in the fog is a common theme in classical haiku:

The morning mist
Painted into a picture:
A dream of people passing.

> In the dense mist,
> What is being shouted
> Between hill and boat?[5]

An extraordinary haiku on the theme of the creative interval of the fog concerns the Japanese tale of Momotaro, the peach-boy. "One day, an old woman was washing clothes by a stream, when a huge peach came floating down. She took it home, and when she and her husband cut it open, they found a little boy . . . inside."[6] The poet Issa, contemplating the river bank during the spring haze, senses the potential of the vacated, hazy mind out of which may be born a new spiritual content, readily symbolized, of course, by the newborn child; and so, alluding to the story of Momotaro Issa writes:

> Will that peach
> Come floating down?
> The spring haze.[7]

The blurring of the two allows the One to surge into the mind:

> Sing, sing, you symbols! All simple creatures,
> All small shapes, willow-shy,
> In the obscure haze, sing![8]

Thus Theodore Roethke, with his customary enthusiasm.

The possibility of contact with unconscious contents appears in "Moneda" as the evocation of a majestic figure. It is the motif of the *numen*, the creative unconscious in the form of an indwelling divinity or royal personage—the "ancient queen" borne on the face of the coin.

Since the poem is concerned specifically with a coin we must not lose sight of the motif of the lucky coin, related to a number of superstitions connected with money. The relevance of this theme to the poetry of Salinas will become clearer when we discuss the general subject of the dynamics of superstition and the important role played by superstition in his work.

The symbology of money has two general aspects, the secular and the sacred, the collective and the private. In the larger sense, money is well known to symbolize "one's own energy, one's psychic capital,"[9] though this symbolism is probably most often quite conscious, particularly in a capitalistic society. Now the poem "Moneda" is clearly not concerned with money as a social medium of exchange, since the coin is not experienced there as potential purchasing power. William Desmonde, in his *Magic, Myth, and Money*, writes at length on money's symbolizing not only one's "psychic capital," but more specifically one's deepest spiritual capital. For money, like gold and silver, began to be used in a context of spiritual meaning which was only gradually secularized. This is the usual evolution of the most ancient artifacts of culture that wind up as simple secular objects. H. G.

Baynes, in speaking of gold, echoes Desmonde's assertion when he points out that gold, like any other precious substance, is valuable for symbolic reasons which are subsequently degraded.[10] If there is a pot of gold at the end of rainbow, it is not for material reasons, but rather because it represents the reason why the rainbow itself is valuable: it is the bridge between the two worlds that leads to the "treasure hard to find": self-integration. Similarly, the gold sought by the alchemists was recognized to be a spiritual gold long before the secular alchemists treated their discipline as a get-rich-quick scheme. The vast amount of alchemical material reaching back to pre-Christian times leaves no doubt about this.

The use of coins as amulets is well known: "Coins . . . originally served as charms possessing magical powers. The use of coins as amulets is very well known [as a charm] against sickness, poverty, and danger. In the Middle Ages this belief was highly prevalent. . . . Coins to protect the holder from plagues were . . . given out by the church, and similar practices existed in ancient Rome."[11] Here the use of the coin as a magic medallion renders the symbolic meaning of money sacred once more, and the owner of such a coin has no intention of using it as a medium of exchange.

Desmonde traces the relationship between the coin and the signet ring, and notes that signet rings "exerted a formative influence upon the origin of coins, the signet eventually becoming the image on the coin."[12] Here, of course, the coin becomes particularly significant (cf. *signet*) as a medallion: the object is ultimately a sacred image: "The king would give his portrait to loyal subjects as an expression of a close personal relationship. Like other ancient works of art, coins functioned as memorials, serving to immortalize an important, highly regarded person or occurrence." Thus the royal image upon the coin "was . . . not originally a sign guaranteeing the value of the metal, but was . . . a symbol of the emotional bond between giver and receiver." Here (with respect to the Salinas poem) we get to the crux of the matter: "Part of the religious significance of the early coins stemmed from the fact that the stamped metal carried the *mana* of the king."[13] As Salinas crosses over into the magic world of the fog he senses that his own being is actually partaking in the *mana* of the Self. That "ancient queen" is always there, always looking at us, whether we are aware of this or not. To wake up in that other world typically has the quality of a homecoming, the return to a place that is forever there, awaiting us.

In our brief survey of coin symbolism I have noted the principal motifs of the lucky coin that represents a bond between the stable, time-bound ego-personality (cf. the date on the coin, the "invincible" numeral) and the transpersonal forces of the world of the spirit. To recognize this bond at all expresses faith in the existence of such spiritual capital, and of course it is this faith that matters, not the superstition of letting a lucky coin symbolize that faith. In this sense the lucky coin is analogous to a religious artifact.

Carrying the coin on one's person, however, is a token of recognition, a sign of one's willing adherence to faith in transpersonal forces. The coin is an amulet in the sense that it proclaims one's submission, and it is actually this submission itself that functions ipso facto as an amulet, since it preserves one from the spiritual dangers of hubris, or belief in the self-sufficiency of secular ego-intellect. The image of the coin becomes, then, a symbolic image of the royal signet ring, the symbolic extension into the visible world of the *mana* inhering in the invisible presence of that ancient queen who is always looking at us.

Part Two

The Male and

the Feminine Unconscious

Chapter Five

THE SOCIAL PARTNERSHIP

OF MAN AND WOMAN

FONT-ROMEU, NOCHE DE BAILE

Cada montaña tiene
su nombre, su estatura
(consúltense las guías)
y una señal de "libre," de "se alquila."
Pero no para estarse allí, no.
Llamo a aquella escurrida, silbo.
Es un taxi, tarifa de infinitos.
Viene ya. Me equivoco, lo que viene
es una nube rubia
con un álbum de discos bajo el brazo
a tocar foxtrots cándidos,
en sordina con títulos de estrellas.
Y los bailan
sílfides de aluminio y celuloide,
duras, resbaladizas, con anuncios
de automóviles nuevos en la frente.
Y tan solas, las pobres,
tan sin pareja,
que se enamora sucesivamente
de una, de dos, de tres, de todas,
la voluntad vacante aquí en lo blanco.

No. 15, *Fábula y Signo* (1931)

FONT-ROMEU: DANCE TONIGHT

Each mountain has
its name, its height
(consult the guidebooks)
and a sign: "Unoccupied," "For Hire."
But not in order to be standing around, no.
I call to that one in the tight skirt: "Psst!"
She is a taxi, good for any number of fares.
Here she comes. I'm mistaken: what's coming
is a blonde cloud
with an album of records under her arm
to put on naive fox-trots
played with muted horn by star performers.
And they dance them,
these sylphs of aluminum and celluloid,
hard-boiled women of easy virtue, with
new-car ads on the brain.
And so alone, the poor things,
so partnerless,
that my vacant will falls in love successively
with one, with two, with three, with all of
them—
my will: vacant here, and blank.

Gwyneth, always prepared for troublesome customers, clasps a small knife open inside her fist during intercourse.—C. H. Rolph, *Women of the Streets*

Within the economy of the masculine psyche, the personification of the feminine unconscious (as muse or as the Sleeping Beauty) was first formally described by Carl Jung, who called it the anima.[1] This inner soul mate mediates between the conscious and the unconscious, and can be experienced as inspiring, as breathing life into the products of masculine, rational activity. This latter, the so-called *logos* function, is concerned with abstracting and distinguishing; as Baynes puts it, it is "the ability to name one's goal and to find or create the means to achieve it," whereas the anima function is the "inner attitude . . . of psychic relatedness."[2] The *logos* function is traditionally associated with the male principle, since the male, for whatever reason, has cultivated with greater assiduity the intellectual capacity to work with abstract constructs—to think of reality as discontinuous. The contrary

tendency, that of relatedness, is usually thought of as the natural habitat of
the female, since traditionally her imposed role as mother and psychic
center of the family has demanded not abstract mental constructs, but rather
a spontaneous, intuitive feeling for the spiritual continuity of the lives
around her.

In a society where these sexual roles are traditionally accepted, boys and
girls are taught to cultivate the social personalities appropriate to them, and
to repress the inappropriate tendencies. This monosexual development cre-
ates the so-called feminine unconscious in the male; and when it happens
that he meets a flesh-and blood woman who appears to embody his own
repressed side, she will exert a great power of attraction. She is a sign
incarnate, a walking symbol of whatever it is she has awakened in the man:
"If some special quality which a man needs to complete himself as an
individual is buried so deep in his own unconsciousness that he cannot get at
it, or if he represses it, then some woman possessing this quality may seem
to him almost to possess his soul, and he feels . . . she *has* his soul. . . . The
power of the projection is so great that the woman . . . will exert a compul-
sive fascination."[3] That is to say, the beloved has awakened the man's own
"latent femininity,"[4] not in the sense that he suddenly becomes effeminate,
but in that he suddenly raises into consciousness a powerful capacity for
instinctual relatedness that manifests itself both physiologically and spiritu-
ally. The beloved has awakened his own capacity to relate to his instinctual
side. When G. K. Chesterton opined that "men are men, but man is a
woman,"[5] he may well have meant that no man can ever complete himself
until Sleeping Beauty awakens him by flooding his consciousness with her
proximity to nature. Baynes has observed that the beneficent character of
the anima appears as "the spirit of a man's vocation," showing him what he
has a calling for; hence it is that the anima is regarded as the "personification
of fate in the individual psyche."[6] A man can never know what he is fated to
be unless his other, repressed half is awakened within him. When this
happens it becomes possible for him to transcend his own personal place in
time and history. As the artist, he may create works out of time, nonmortal,
not subject to the idiosyncratic limitations of his society. Readers of the great
Spanish poet of the Renaissance, Garcilaso de la Vega, are familiar with his
depiction of the anima function in the form of nymphs dwelling at the bottom
of a pool or river—a universally known motif, since peoples the world over
have always intuited that the relationship between consciousness and the
unconscious is (among other things) one of time vs. timelessness. The surface
of the water embodies the moving surface of the mind that dwells in sidereal
time; the still depths of the water, the region of the feminine unconscious, is
inhabited by beautiful nymphs who cannot be experienced except by the
timeless eye. A typical tradition is that one reported of the Mermaid's Pool at
Hayfield, Derbyshire: "There is a local tradition that a beautiful nymph . . .

comes to bathe daily in the Mermaid's Pool, and that the man who has the good fortune to see her whilst bathing will become immortal."[7] The motif of the anima's origin in the depths of the spiritual waters is certainly best known in the form of Aphrodite, born of the foam.

Equally important is the symbolic motif of the mirror, since, as we have noted previously, the divinatory mirror so readily activates the projection of unconscious contents. I have discussed elsewhere the symbol of the androgyne, the image of male and female components simultaneously manifested in one body,[8] and the mirror, with its duplicating function, easily enables this to take place symbolically. When the young man experiences the illumination of his own indwelling feminine component, this may be projected onto a beloved, or it may come directly into consciousness as an indwelling numen, as it does in the Perrault fairy tale, "The Little Green Frog," where the magic is accomplished by means of a divinatory glass. In this story the hero, Prince Saphir, had lost his mother when he was but three years old. When he reached adolescence, "the fairies suddenly took fright lest his love for his father should interfere with the plans they had made for the young prince. So, to prevent this, they placed in a pretty room of which Saphir was very fond a little mirror . . . such as were often brought from Venice. . . . What was his surprise to see reflected in the mirror not his own face, but that of a young girl . . . ! As might have been expected, the young prince lost his heart completely to the beautiful image."[9]

Here the growth into wholeness is expressed by use of the anima figure as counteracting the masculine lopsidedness of the motherless boy, who might attain to manhood without ever meeting his feminine, instinctual other half. That it is the fairies who fear this (that is, the magic forces of nature herself) points to what in analytical psychology is postulated as the holistic movement of the psyche, which seeks its own wholeness apart from whatever limited, self-seeking goals that ego may establish for itself.[10] In folklore and in the world view of the primitives the incorporation into the spirit of instinctual goals, of spiritual equilibrium, is intuited as instinctual wisdom. By itself ego can never stumble onto the meaning of wisdom, because by itself ego can only become shrewd, masterful, and "smart."

So the fairies see to it that the young prince (who no doubt already had been given plenty of cosmetic mirrors) is given a magic, divinatory glass "such as were often brought from Venice," the city whose inhabitants live in daily contact with the deep waters. And in it he sees the unconscious prefiguration of himself, a lovely young girl. She herself has a similar speculum in the story. Here we have the typical magic image of the fairy tale, as beautiful as it is cogent: the androgyne, the symbol of the male and female components together in one psyche. The fifteen-year old boy is fascinated with the specular image of a lovely maiden who is herself fascinated with the specular image of the young man.

A modern, civilized, sophisticated version of this motif appears in the striking symbolic story, "The Water Pavilion," by Théophile Gautier (1811–1872). Set in China, the story concerns two wealthy gentlemen who were such fast friends that they built their estates side by side. Over the years, as their dispositions changed, they grew to despise each other to such a degree that each of them forbade members of his household to have any intercourse with those of the other. Separating their property was a large pond that the landowners owned jointly. With the growth of their enmity they arranged for the erection on pilings of a great spite-wall running across the center of the pond. A boy is born to one family, and a girl to the other. As they grow into adolescence they become more curious about what might lie on the other side of the ugly wall, especially because they can look into the water between the arches supporting the wall and see a small part of the neighboring estate reflected there. It is this mirror-world that entrances them both, each unknown to the other; it becomes a divinatory speculum quite like the one we saw in "Madrid. Calle de . . .": "The trees on the bank were so accurately reflected . . . that it was hard to tell the image from the reality; they looked like a forest planted upside down and uniting its roots with those of an identical wood; like a grove that had drowned itself for love. . . . The fish seemed to swim in the foliage, and the birds to be flying in the water." Though many suitors are available to the girl, and many eligible maidens to the young man, neither shows interest in the prospect of marriage. And then it happens that one day they are standing at the same time gazing into the mirror-world. Each sees the silent reflection of the other, true love surfaces, and the young man thinks: "Though I have never seen her, I recognise her: she is indeed the woman whose image is engraved on my heart, the fair unknown to whom I address my distichs and my quatrains."[11] And so here, as in the Perrault tale, the young people fall in love with the inner aspect of themselves which the speculum raises into consciousness.

In the poetry of Salinas the anima figure appears both in the form of the deep waters and as the divinatory mirror. Since water is commonly used as a speculum, the two motifs easily combine. The authors who write about the feminine unconscious seem generally to recognize two ways of going about it, the general and the specific. That is to say, they may apprehend the feminine unconscious as a vast realm of instinctual possibilities somehow connected with the feminine principle, or they may come to it with the help of a specific woman—either a fantasy muse that guides a man safely through that world (ocean or forest), or a flesh-and-blood beloved who awakens him to a whole secret world of spiritual potential. These modes of assimilating the feminine unconscious are all represented in the poetry of Salinas, and it is now our task to examine a number of his poems concerned with this kind of individuation.

One of Salinas's earliest efforts to express the general connection between

the ocean and the feminine is quite literal, and will serve as evidence of the
clarity with which he intuited this archetypal material. It is a poem about a
sea-going vessel, the *Manuela Pla* (No. 33 of *Presagios*), which he supposes
to have been named after the builder's wife. The ship has been in service for
quite a few years, and so he imagines that the builder has died, and that his
widow, Manuela Pla, is now a well-to-do old lady who lives placidly and
conventionally, surrounded by material comfort. Every night she tells her
beads and dozes off:

> And while the builder's wife is
> navigating through the tame sea
> of prayer, where she falls asleep,
> the *Manuela Pla* is underway
> upon the real sea,
> young, strong, and proud.

Salinas, true to his poetic style, grasps in an artifact the means of symboliz-
ing the creative spirit of *homo faber*. Because the ship bears a woman's name
it becomes possible for the poet to present us with the two forms that the
feminine may take vis-à-vis the man: the flesh-and-blood beloved, and the
inner guide awakened by her. Manuela Pla is here imagined as the woman
whom the builder married long ago; she presumably represented to him a
desirable embodiment of the feminine, for she inspired the name of a ship.

But the carrier of the anima projection is only an accidental carrier. The
man conceives of her as the one woman in the world capable of inspiring him
to his best efforts, capable of transforming his spiritual life and enriching it.
But why her rather than another? It is because in some significant way she
reminds him of his own forgotten feminine half. She, like the man himself, is
subject to time and change, and may eventually become a placid old mate-
rialist incapable of exerting any attraction upon anyone. But the thing that
she once awakened in the man, the thing that she inspired, that she made
come alive: *that* is not subject to time. Symbolically, it is out of time and is
always underway, "young, strong, and proud," upon the oceanic conscious-
ness.

The poem "Manuela Pla" presents the anima phenomenon in nonpersonal
terms, since it concerns some unknown shipbuilder and his imagined widow;
later, when I come to discuss the anima figure as it appears in personal,
specific form, my commentary on the poem "35 bujías" will show how
Salinas interprets the "Manuela Pla" material personally, in terms of his own
spirit. For the present, I want to examine in detail several poems dealing
with the poet's own general attitude toward the feminine—an attitude that
implies his faith in it, his belief in its inner, creative presence, without which
we must live restricted to the lopsidedness of ego-intellect.

In the first of these poems, "Font-Romeu," Salinas intuits the difference between the lower masculinity and the higher masculinity: that is, the social man's notion of woman as an alien being to be used by him, and, conversely, the idea of woman as constituting one half of the human spirit. Without the spiritual joining of these two halves, either half lives in solitude and poverty. In the second poem, "Atalanta," the male, as woman's lover, intuits her psychosexuality as being an instinctual guide to him; such is the meaning of the old Greek fable about the fair maiden whom no man can outdistance.

This material, arising from encounters with flesh-and-blood women, leads us naturally to a transition in which the feminine component of the male psyche is raised into consciousness. The poems "Otra tú" and "Marco" illustrate this in the most general way, while "Underwood Girls" allows us to see how the old idea of the muse begins to take shape in the creative imagination. This vague awareness comes into sharp focus in "35 bujías" where the poet fantasizes his own personal muse in a remarkable fairy tale spontaneously generated—and this turns out to embody the motif impersonally alluded to in "Manuela Pla": the anima within becomes the figure that will rise into consciousness in order to navigate the ocean that lies before the voyager-poet.

A detailed analysis of "Font-Romeu" makes an appropriate introduction to the anima in the work of Salinas, because we see here his understanding that the feminine unconscious is the necessary partner to the culturally conditioned male ego-consciousness. The latter, when it attempts to function without such partnership, becomes isolated spiritually, and easily produces the *macho* attitude that strives to degrade the woman. It is a competitive attitude, whereby the isolated male ego-consciousness attempts to assert itself as spiritually independent from the Eternal Feminine. In "Font-Romeu" the speaker becomes aware of the difference between the male-female relationship as a rivalry on the one hand, and as a partnership on the other. As we read through the poem it becomes clear that Salinas is not talking mainly about a cabaret with taxi dancers, but rather about the insurmountable difficulty he senses to be inherent in the prostitute-customer relationship, whether this occurs in a cabaret, a call-house, a "resort palace," or a massage parlor.

The remark with which the poem begins alludes to the *guías*, the "guide-books":

> Each mountain has
> its name, its height
> (consult the guidebooks).

Why he calls these women mountains is a subject for later consideration; for the present we are interested in what may be a now-historical reference to

the guidebooks. Research materials available to us concern the old guide-
books of the United States and England only, but it is reasonable to suppose
that research on the Continent would turn up similar material on methods of
advertising in the world of prostitution. In this country the most famous of
such guides are those of New Orleans—the *Green, Red,* and *Blue Books*
published during the latter half of the nineteenth century and at least up to
the time of the First World War. Since Salinas uses the word *guías,* it is
pertinent to note that the classic report by the anonymous Semper Idem
(privately printed in New Orleans in 1936) uses the equivalent term in its
title: *The "Blue Book": A Bibliographical Attempt to Describe the Guide
Books to the Houses of ill fame in New Orleans as They Were Published
There.* The author notes that by 1907 the guidebook was a well-established
feature in the public life of New Orleans.[12] Curt Gentry says that Denver,
Colorado had its *Red Book,* subtitled *A Reliable Directory of the Pleasure
Resorts of Denver* (1892), and that in extraverted San Francisco the guides
were actually "hawked, loudly, on most downtown street corners."[13]

John Gosling and Douglas Warner report the existence of similar guides in
London, called "Registers of Ladies," as late as 1959.[14]

In "Font-Romeu" we read that the *guías* carry the name and height of the
ladies listed, and Gentry tells us that the format of the New Orleans *Blue
Book,* "common to all, contained a list of the prostitutes . . . with pertinent
physical data on each."[15] In turn-of-the-century New York City, according to
George J. Kneeland, the call-house madams could "usually" show customers
photographs of the girls, plus "a description of them, with measurements to
show their physical development."[16]

Kneeland gives special attention to the dance halls "that encourage inde-
cent dances and supply long intermissions for the consumption of liquor,"
since these were considered to be mere fronts for the business of
prostitution.[17] Salinas's poem carries as its title the announcement "Font-
Romeu, noche de baile," and this special announcement may be of the type
described by Kneeland as the "open date" in the New York dance hall: "The
proprietors of the dance halls in question have 'open dates,' on which their
halls may be rented by social clubs. . . . The usual method of advertising
dances is by distributing 'throw aways.' . . . These . . . intimate the charac-
ter of the proposed frolic."[18]

The setting for the proposed frolic in the poem by Salinas is identified
simply as "Font-Romeu," which may be either a dance hall in a metropolis
(Paris or Barcelona, for example), or else a dance hall actually in the town of
Font-Romeu. Taken literally the title will be understood to be an allusion to
the little French town in the Pyrenees, just north of the Spanish border,
about eighty miles due north of Barcelona and some fifteen miles east of
Andorra. The Larousse Encyclopedia calls Font-Romeu an important tourist
center for winter sports. Over a mile high (1800 meters), it is situated on a

slope of the mountain of the same name. If Salinas is referring to the Pyrenean town, the opening reference in the poem to "each mountain" makes sense: every eminence in that mountain chain has its name and height.

The main point of the poem springs from an intuition of the basically lonely character of the prostitute's life, and it is this that seems to lie behind the negative association of prostitute with mountain: each peak of the multitude of peaks in the Pyrenees stands in lonely isolation.

But if the speaker sees an analogy between these women and the lonely peaks like Mt. Font-Romeu, he also sees a humorous difference, because the mountains simply stand there, whereas taxi dancers and common prostitutes, whose careers involve a good deal of standing, are not there, however, for that purpose. This being the case, we had better say that they are more like taxicabs.

Robert Wilson's explanatory remarks on the "cab" (or cab joint) are appropriate here: "Underworld argot for a whorehouse, evidently based on the facts that taxicabs are sometimes used as mobile brothels and that many cabdrivers in large cities receive a cut of the take for steering customers to whorehouses. Compare 'taxi dancer,' a female employee of a dance hall where dancing is a good deal more intimate than is usually acceptable elsewhere."[19] The term *taxi dancer* itself as originally coined expresses a scornful attitude toward women who hire themselves out; they are entitled to no more concern than is a taxicab.[20] A man with wife or mistress has his own private automobile, while the taxis ply the red-light district.

These women at the dance hall are waiting around, each displaying a "sign" ("Unoccupied," "For Hire"). The sign of the unoccupied prostitute is her mien; she is ready for the next solicitation, and this seems to be primarily a matter of eye-contact. The "taxi" who is occupied does not like to establish eye-contact with a new, interested customer, since at that moment he represents an intrusion into a going transaction. The speaker summons one of the women who has her sign out. If we would see what he is seeing here, we have only to look at Toulouse-Lautrec's *Salon in the Rue des Moulins* (1895), which shows five prostitutes (plus the madam): they are all sitting about with their signs out, and they have the look of souls in bodies for hire. The atmosphere of the place is, as John Canady comments, one "of stagnant air where the spirit languishes"; the picture is "an image of the desiccation of the human spirit."[21] And surely the sign (*señal*) here is an ironic variation of the signs that Salinas the poet was accustomed to reading in the world around him.

The speaker selects the woman who most attracts him physically ("that one in the tight skirt") and he calls to her, *silbo*. Here he is once more playing on meanings of the verb *silbar* (derived by metathesis from L. *sibilare*, "to hiss"; cf. Eng. "sibilant"), which means both "to hiss" and "to whistle." Hissing in order to draw someone's attention is commoner in Europe and Latin America than in the United States; at the same time it seems to be universally common to whistle for taxicabs. Salinas draws upon both meanings: he hisses ("Psst!") to catch the attention of the taxi dancer, but by his use of *silbar* he maintains the coarse comparison with the taxicab. In either case one is summoning a ride for hire.

In lines 8–9 the speaker's lustful enthusiasm for the lady of his choice becomes apparent: she is a "blonde cloud." Lightly she treads in her tight skirt, and he enjoys watching the lithe gait of those limbs he knows he can possess merely by giving the nod. Here she comes, "his" little blonde cloud—but then something quite unexpected happens to dash any lewd fantasies he may have been entertaining, for his liberal sense of humanity begins to interfere with his libidinal intentions. He has entered the dance hall like any other customer, and with the same intention that characterizes the man seeking a woman for hire, but then he himself begins to feel that isolation that defines the common prostitute. *Caritas* is about to spoil the fun, for loneliness is the one emotion shared by prostitute and client, and the speaker unexpectedly falls prey to this realization.

The anonymous author of *Women of the Streets*, an account of the life led by London street prostitutes points out that one of the two groups of men making up the clients of these women are "men who are lonely, away from home, . . . some of whom want no more than temporary companionship."[22] We may assume that such is the case of the speaker in "Font-Romeu." But he quickly sees that he has come to the very well of loneliness: the woman for hire. Part of this loneliness stems from the ostracized life she must lead, and part of it from the character of her previous life that led her to become a prostitute in the first place.

In *Women of the Streets* we read, concerning the relationship between the prostitute and her pimp, that this "depends largely on the unpleasantness of living in such isolation as the new prostitute experiences. . . . Edith said a girl had so many fellows who meant nothing to her that, when she met someone who did, she hung on to him."[23] And, says Polly Adler, "By becoming a prostitute, a girl cuts herself off not merely from her family, but from such a great part of life. . . . It is not syphilis which is the occupational disease of the prostitute, but loneliness."[24] The pimp is the only man who can offer the prostitute anything like an intimate relationship. The author of *Women of the Streets* quotes another of the women known to her, Alice, who "was highly critical of ponces, but said she understood the girls' need for someone permanent. 'They're so desperate they'll pay a man anything to stay with them.'" Otherwise the feelings that prostitutes entertain for the male animal are understandably negative. The prostitute sees only men's most detestable side. Bessie, one of the London street prostitutes, said: "You don't know the things they do and the things they want. Be all right walking down the street, talk to you ever so nice, but when they get alone with us women, well, some of them are like rats in holes. . . . If a wife knew what her husband was really like she'd never live with him no more. . . . Sometimes a man sits beside me and I shudder away from him, if only people knew what you were like, you awful slimy toad, I think." And of Olive, another London streetwalker, we read that her "physical indifference led men to saying occasionally, 'Put a bit of life into it,' to which she would reply, 'Why should I? It's only your money I want.' " The relationship between prostitute and client is of necessity fraught with hostility. She despises the "John," and he her: "Bella and a friend confirmed that their clients invariably started by asking, 'How can you do this? I'm surprised at your living like this.' Is this a transference of guilt, an establishment of the inferiority of the woman which enables the man to attain dominance in the relationship?"[25]

In "Font-Romeu" the speaker is finally overtaken by the intuition that each woman is "so partnerless" in the kind of life she must lead. If the only partner in life that the prostitute ever gets is the pimp—"He's all she's got to love," observes Polly Adler[26]—this is a violent and degrading relationship that, for the woman, is compounded of fear and necessity. "Neither the ponce nor the prostitute forms the status of the partner."[27]

And so the speaker in "Font-Romeu" was intending to choose a partner, but then he was overcome by the sense of what it means to be partnerless. At this point his original intention gets lost and he awakens in a state of extremity.

This peculiar, and sometimes remarkable state of mind appears not infrequently in the poetry of Salinas; he seems to have been especially aware of it. It occurs when one is on the point of carrying out an intention, only to be unexpectedly frustrated in a way that throws the mind into sudden blankness, or vacancy. The will to act is paralyzed by a dilemma. The relative importance of the intended act has little to do with this extremity, it appears, and even the most trivial circumstance can stimulate it, since the world is in a drop of water. I may be immersed in work at my desk; gradually I become aware that the insistent buzzing of a fly is intolerably irritating. I turn to reach for the fly-swatter—and the fly is sitting on it.[28] At this point either of two things may happen: I may stubbornly seek a substitute ego-solution, ignoring the meaning of the dilemma, or the will to act may drop away, while a nonego intuition *de rerum natura* rushes into the void, and contemplation takes the place of action. Blyth points out the importance to haiku of this extremity, when the mind is in a state of "partial solution": "Such a state of mind, an extremity which is God's opportunity, is perhaps the commonest poetic experience of so-called unpoetic people. Poets and psychologists . . . are accustomed to notice how a dilemma, a lack of outlet for action causes the mind to become abnormally receptive. They are quick to remark on the peculiar meaning of some . . . habitual occurrence."[29]

In "Font-Romeu" the speaker has had the fantasy of choosing from a kind of harem, and he actually does make his choice. At that moment, however, he becomes aware that he is dealing with "plastic" women, and that any relationship with them would also have to be "plastic." Their companionship would be all cheap façade, aluminum and celluloid, because that façade is the peculiar meaning of prostitution. The woman for hire earns a living by selling not only her body, but the charade of a partnership.

This seems obvious enough, a thing not hard to understand, but clearly it is not at all understood by the men who make prostitution the common accompaniment of every civilization. The relationship between prostitute and client has to be rooted in hostility and mistrust; "Gwyneth, always prepared for troublesome customers, clasps a small knife open inside her fist during intercourse."[30] Any woman can peddle her body, but the degree of success with which she does this depends upon how much façade she is able to bring to the transaction.

When the speaker of "Font-Romeu" realizes that the only ones who can make a profession of companionship are precisely those who must do without it, then there is set in motion a movement counter to the will to act: full realization of what it means to be "so alone," "so partnerless." The woman for hire drifts into the market. As Rolph points out, "Very few of us could do this, for our lives are caught up in a network of responsibilities to jobs, families, houses, and our emotions will not allow us to abandon them or to forget places and people."[31] Hence the typical client has the woman where he wants her: merely by beckoning to her and paying her money he can implement fantasies that no "decent" woman would cooperate with. Thus the prostitute is not only his victim, she is also scum. And Salinas sees suddenly that the fly has landed on the fly-swatter.

In discussing this kind of mental extremity Blyth alludes to the adage, "Man's extremity is God's opportunity."[32] By "God's opportunity" he understands the birth of feelings and real intuitions that transcend the limited intentions of ego; this latter is cancelled out and something larger is born into consciousness. In "Font-Romeu" it is the sense of love, *caritas*, born out of a sudden realization that it is loneliness that binds people together. All of us spend our lives working against this isolation, by building up all kinds of durable relationships. This bond, notes the author of *Women of the Streets*, "is not unwelcome, and we seek to reinforce it by self-imposed discipline, membership of groups and organizations, so that we shall never "not belong." . . . It seems that fundamentally we each exist in personal isolation which we are at pains to destroy."[33] It is therefore deeply ironic when a lonely man seeks the companionship of a prostitute, because he has turned to the loneliest person in the world: someone who has had to make a profession out of pretending to be the intimate companion of men she despises. The speaker of "Font-Romeu" intuits suddenly what a prostitute really is, and that "the necessary counterpart to the prostitute is her customer."[34] At this point he very likely turned on his heel and went back to his hotel to write "Font-Romeu, noche de baile."

The speaker in "Font-Romeu" begins by attempting to implement one attitude (the one that leads him to the dance hall in the first place) and ends by succumbing to another. He suffers erotic impotence, as it were, for his will to act is swallowed up by a reality he has contemplated. His own masculine role in an erotic situation is brought into full consciousness, and the emotion is transformed into compassion.

The elements of this kind of transformation within a male ego-consciousness have been theoretically described (particularly by Erich Neumann)[35] as the "lower masculinity" and the "higher masculinity," which is to say masculinity expressed as a primary sexual instinct, and masculinity expressed as a spiritual leavening force; the masculinity of the womanizer on the one hand, and the masculinity that is part of the spiritual climate of, say, the symphonic music of Jean Sibelius. Since the poetic work of Salinas is largely oriented by the higher masculinity, it is appropriate to describe its dynamics and to note how these are related to what happened in the dance hall at Font-Romeu.

The theoretical description of a man's masculinity as lower or higher is determined by his attitude vis-à-vis woman. The lower masculinity is expressed as an instinctual driving force invading, dominating, and even tyrannizing consciousness. But with the integration into consciousness of libidinal energy (a process known as sublimation) the man is no longer the intermittent victim, no longer reduced to the status of phallus-bearer, required to exhaust the drive repetitively as if possessed by a demon that cannot be satiated.

In general, the lower masculinity, the aggressive *machismo*, sees woman as an inferior, alien being; the higher masculinity sees woman as an equal, because she is the flesh-and-blood carrier of one half of the human psyche. For the lower masculine ego the feminine unconscious is repressed and projected unconsciously in the form of a negative image.[36] This results in the masculine feeling of supremacy against which the feminists have long rebelled. For the higher masculinity, one's own psyche is a lifelong evolution of the inner spirit, which means the eventual raising into consciousness of the feminine component of the psyche. We do not speak of effeminacy here, of course, but rather of the so-called male and female principles, the yin-yang. For the lower masculinity, woman is a sex object or the Eternal Mother; for the higher masculinity she is lover and partner.

Introspection eventually produces a realization that the ego-intellect commands very little in the house of the psyche; further introspection tells us that the masculine ego is a culturally determined entity, and that it has been fostered at the cost of repressing those potentialities that the culture considers to be feminine qualities. But once the male ego-consciousness is established, the mature ego comes to admit its subordination to larger forces within, and seeks to integrate certain qualities that the child and adolescent learned to repress. The man is reborn by transforming his previous monosexual ego—what he thought of as his individuality. It is the kind of rebirth recognized by Buber: "Individuality . . . revels in its special being, or, rather, mostly in the fiction of its special being which it has made up for itself. . . . Real knowledge of its being would lead it to self-destruction—or to rebirth."[37] Real knowledge of one's being means transcending the limits of the monosexual ego, which is seen as the illusion that it is—an illusion that need not be slavishly idolized nor allowed to consume much of one's spiritual energies.

Many introspective men of religion, art, and philosophy have intuited this inner rebirth, the marriage of *logos* and *eros*, even if they have not developed any explicit theory about it. Thoreau stated the principle as clearly as any twentieth-century depth-psychologist. Of Chaucer he says: "We are tempted to say that his genius was feminine, not masculine. It was such a femininess, however, as is rarest to find in woman, though not the appreciation of it; perhaps it is not to be found at all in woman, but is only the feminine in man."[38]

The liberation of the feminine into the masculine consciousness is part of the individuation process described by Jung, the shifting of the center of spiritual life from ego to the Self. For the higher masculinity the symbol is the androgyne; for the lower it is the classical don Juan Tenorio.

The literature on the psychology of male supremacy is immense, and there is no need to attempt any kind of résumé within the limits of these pages; those interested may consult H. R. Hays's *The Dangerous Sex: The Myth of the Feminine Evil.*[39] Man's attitude toward woman in civilized society in general, both East and West, has developed along the lines of the lower masculinity with respect to social role-playing. In the arts the male attitude toward woman has evolved along the lines of the higher masculinity, beginning with the Renaissance and the recognition of the anima figure, of woman as the soulmate complementing the male ego-consciousness.

Within the psyche of any man the ambivalent attitude toward woman expresses itself as the struggle between spiritual nobility and overwhelming lust. But the spiritual marriage of the masculine and feminine principles within one psyche is not in itself an erotic fantasy; the *hieros gamos* proclaims spiritual wholeness or equilibrium. That is why the anima figure may appear as a symbolic sister, and not necessarily as a bride. Nor does there enter into the question any Freudian consideration of incest. W. H. Hudson, known particularly for his extraordinary portrait of Rima in *Green Mansions* (the anima as a chaste, jungle-dwelling maiden), was able to identify the anima as his "sister," whom he called Psyche, and who said to him, "not in words but very plainly": "Try to ignore me and it will be worse for you: a secret want will continually disquiet you: recognise my existence and right to dwell in and possess your soul, as you dwell in mine, and there will be a pleasant union and peace between us."[40]

The anima figure makes a chaste appearance, just as the poets consistently portray her, precisely because it is finally not a question of sexuality but rather of the liberation of spiritual potential which the monosexual masculinity was holding in repression. Thus in the fairy tale called "The Glass Coffin," the motif appears in the form of an imprisoned maiden who had always lived happily with her brother. In fact, her description of the relationship is classic: "We loved each other so tenderly, and were so alike in our way of thinking and our inclinations, that we both embraced the resolution never to marry, but to stay together to the end of our lives."[41] The hero liberates her and takes the place of the brother in her life.

In "Font-Romeu" Salinas portrays the man who attempts to approach woman with the possessive attitude of the *macho* and then finds that self-knowledge renders this attitude untenable, for self-knowledge causes his view of the woman to undergo a transformation; the women themselves are transformed before his very eyes. What happens to him in the dance hall is initially effected, perhaps, by a class attitude that produces the kind of male response thought unusual by Polly Adler, the madam who in her day entertained every conceivable type of materially successful male: "It was an odd thing—racketeers frowned on men of their calling who got serious with a prostitute, while men in legitimate business and intellectuals, especially the broad-A group, did not have this attitude and showed far more respect toward a prostitute than did any of the underworld inhabitants."[42] Salinas, had he spoken English natively, would no doubt have impressed Madam Polly as belonging to the "broad-A group." In "Font-Romeu," the man who enters the dance hall in search of a woman for hire is a man on the point of "falling foul of his own soul," as Baynes puts it. The civilized male, he says, "has done the soul an injury in identifying himself exclusively with the ideal and rational aspects of his psychology, because he therewith unloads the unaccepted residue upon the anima. In this way he falls foul of his own soul, identifying her with a witch or demon instead of honouring her as a helpful ministering function."[43] For the lower masculinity the woman may appear as a witch, as Baynes here points out, or as a whore, the despicable creature that so obviously deserves the scorn of the lofty male ego. In the second part of "Font-Romeu" the speaker is liberated from this pose, and sees through the shabby defense erected by a male ego that ought to know better. The egotistic defensiveness crumbles before the veracity of compassion, in the original sense of a suffering with: the higher masculinity has also known what it is to be partnerless, to live beyond the pale of the feminine unconscious.

Chapter Six

THE EROTIC PARTNERSHIP
OF MAN AND WOMAN

ATALANTA

Palabras que estás diciendo
—"cariño... siempre... seguro..."—
con voz lenta en gesto quieto.
Ventanas dobles, vidrieras
cerradas, encortinadas,
guillotinan tentaciones.
(Horizontes, aires, rumbos.)
El cielo es el techo, todo
del color que tú quisiste,
sin constelación ni guía.
Entreabierta alcoba—tuya,
mía—, renuncias desposa.

Pero más allá de todo
¡qué claro se te ve el sino!

Ni ese zapato de cuento,
de cristal, frágil, altísimo,
ni ese pelo ¡qué domado
plano, doméstico, liso!
me engañan. Ya se estremecen
las tierras que estrenarás,
el horizonte que rompas
el cielo por donde subas.
Talón al aire te veo,
aquí tan quieta conmigo,
cabellera suelta al viento
—¡manzanas que te echaría!—
y luego
el mito, ascensor antiguo,
que to sube, allá, a la fábula.

    No. 44, *Seguro azar* (1924–1928)

ATALANTA

Words that you are saying
—"affection . . . always . . . true . . . "—
with slow voice in quiet expression.
Double windows, shuttered,
iron curtain down,
they decapitate temptations.
(Horizons, breezes, routes.)
The sky is the ceiling,
of the color that you chose,
without constellation or guide.
The door to the bedroom is ajar—your
bedroom and mine—and joins our renuncia-
    tions in marriage.

But beyond everything,
how clearly your destiny can be seen!

I am not deceived by that storybook shoe
of glass, fragile, high-heeled,
nor by that hair—how carefully
arranged, domesticated, smooth!
Coming into view
are the lands that you will discover,
the horizon you will reach,
the sky where you will fly.
I see you foot in air,
here so quietly with me,
hair flying in the wind
(the golden apples that I would throw to you!)
and then
the myth, ancient elevator,
that carries you aloft, up there, to the fable.

Ancient Chinese medical treatises and books on sex describe the man's sexual experience by comparing it to fire, while that of the woman is likened to water. Fire easily flares up, but it is also easily extinguished by water; water, on the contrary, takes a long time to heat over the fire but it will also cool down very slowly.—R. H. Van Gulik, *Sexual Life in Ancient China*

As a contrast to "Font-Romeu" we may consider Salinas's poem "Atalanta," which takes up the erotic situation as it exists between lovers, not between customer and prostitute—for the latter encounter is not necessarily even erotic. The customer-prostitute relationship expresses a hostility between the sexes, a basic mistrust, and the confrontation can be mediated only by payment, but the erotic relationship between lovers obviously must be mediated by mutual intuitive understanding of the role that nature herself has assigned to each partner. When this does not happen it probably indicates that the partners are playing roles assigned them by their culture— which is to say that the sexual union may be dominated by a sense of competition wherein sexuality becomes a weapon used to defend one's culturally conditioned self-image.

In the poem "Atalanta" Salinas uses an ancient Greek fable to point up the difference between lovemaking seen as rivalry, and lovemaking seen as a mutual striving. What enables him to make this point is the fruit of that same process of self-integration whereby the ego-intellect recognizes its subsidiary position in the house of the psyche. Just as the unknown master transcends the limits of ego-consciousness; just as the ancient queen is always there within, waiting for her glance to be returned; so is the nature of woman always present, promising a fulfillment. Woman is not there as a prospective conquest—the masculine ego characteristically imagines that it conquers mountains, outer space, and women—but in order to fulfill and to be fulfilled. When this happens it is because the male has learned that the feminine principle is in possession of the secrets of instinctual behavior.

This is nowhere more openly apparent than in the erotic encounter. The mutual gratification to be gotten from sexuality depends crucially upon the male's willingness to bend to and to cooperate with the complexities of the woman's erotic nature, for mutual gratification involves an awakening, an erotic illumination not dissimilar to the illumination that occurs in other forms of nonego experience.

Since the poem shows us woman as Atalanta, the protagonist of a fable, it is necessary that we distinguish between the modern and early meanings of fable—the meaning for ego-intellect as distinct from the meaning for Self. The ego-meaning is the one given by the dictionary (which naturally specializes in such meanings): "a fictitious story meant to teach moral lesson," "a story that is not true."[1] But the etymology often retains the archaic Self-meaning for the self. Thoreau liked to play with the difference between these two meanings, employing the common word with its original, uncorrupted force. When he observes the natural scene before his eyes he writes to himself in his journal: "It convinces me that Nature is still in her youth,— the florid fact about which mythology merely mutters,—that the very soil can *fabulate* as well as you or I."[2]

Fable comes from L. *fabulare*, "to speak," and in the Self-meaning of *fabulare* is the significant speaking to a receptive human awareness, an awareness receptive to the original "I-Thou" union which is dissolved whenever ego-intellect comes into being. When the Japanese poet (for example) writes the simple haiku, it appears as full of meaning to the experienced reader as the original subject of the haiku, because its meaning is the original, natural significance which all things hold for the Self. Everything speaks a surprising language to the nonego awareness. Thus Thoreau: "If I am overflowing with life, am rich in experience for which I lack expression, then nature will be my language full of poetry,—all nature will *fable*, and every natural phenomenon will be a myth. The man of science, who is not seeking for expression but for a fact to be expressed merely, studies nature as a dead language. I pray for such inward experience as will make nature significant."[3]

Thoreau thought of it as melting, this passing in fable from duality into unity, and mentions the human response to music as an instance of it.[4] This melting inevitably puts one in mind of childhood, since that was one's first experience of unity as a fable, when all nature talked, when one experienced naturally the denominator common to nature "out there" and to one's own nature, as yet intact. Thus the poet Jorge Guillén, entranced by the playing of a fountain, is transported again to that virginal world intact, as yet untouched by ego-intellect, and calls his childhood a *fábula de fuentes*, literally a time when the fountains "fabulated."[5] Similarly another twentieth-century Spanish poet, Gerardo Diego, recalls his *fábula de niño*, his "child's fable," the way he saw reality when he was a child.[6] The fable, then, is the unity between the observer and the observed, the magic reality in which "the very soil can fabulate as well as you or I." In the poem "Atalanta" this means the erotic unity of two lovers, each of whom is simultaneously living and being lived.

The poem draws a contrast between the socially oriented ego-personality and the fable-world of the instinctual Self. A man and a woman are sitting, quietly talking, and she is saying something about affection. He has begun to feel amorous, and he is not really paying very close attention to her conversation. They are evidently sitting in the living room, which is the room in the house that conventionally symbolizes the social self, the persona that keeps interlocutors at an affective distance, barring the way to impertinent intimacies.

And so the woman's conversation here, insofar as it allows her social self to play the principal role in this scene, is compared to a locked building that is not easily entered. She seems to be sealed off from erotic intrusions. The very room in which they sit is an expression of her social self, since she is responsible for the décor. The color scheme has been chosen by her, and it expresses nothing about her beyond her sense of social and aesthetic suitability. There is not one sign ("constellation") whereby one could deduce what kind of person she is erotically. But then the speaker's glance strays toward the bedroom door that stands ajar, and "our *renuncias* are joined in holy matrimony." *Renuncia* commonly means "resignation." In this sense it connotes officialdom: an officeholder hands in his *renuncia*. Since for the speaker the bedroom means lovemaking, we can see that what he has in mind is that the two of them should resign from their social role-playing. In the bedroom their mutual act of resigning will be celebrated in erotic union.

This first section of the poem deals, then, with passing from quiet affection over into the world of Venus. But in line thirteen the speaker's thought turns in another direction:

> But beyond everything,
> how clearly your destiny can be seen!

He means her destiny as woman in relation to man. Part of her social identity is supplied, of course, by her manner of dress and grooming: she is carefully coiffured, and also she still wears her high-heeled shoes. The speaker has noted this whole social setting, her social manner of speaking, her fashionable dress, and the domestic surroundings. None of this deceives him, though, he says; through all this he is aware of her own approachable erotic vitality. Already he can see her transformed into an excited partner; already he sees her running in the world of non-*logos*, the world of *eros*; and with that he suddenly thinks of her as being an incarnation of Atalanta.

Atalanta was a beautiful maiden intent on avoiding marriage because an oracle had frightened her ("Marriage will be your ruin."). She did not refuse outright to marry, but said that she would have no man who could not beat her in a foot-race. This decision of hers does not represent absolute obedience to her fear, but rather is an attempt to overcome some matrimonial danger suggested by the pessimistic warning; Atalanta sets as a condition of marriage that the suitor must pass a test. Hippomenes, a handsome youth whom Atalanta loves, decides to race with her, and Venus comes to his aid by giving him three golden apples taken from her own temple. During the race Hippomenes throws them down, Atalanta cannot resist stopping to pick them up, and in this way he wins the race and the bride.

This is a strange tale, if we read it in terms of simple cause and effect. But the real nucleus of any fable is actually its underlying meaning, for which the plot is an excuse; like the shaggy-dog story or the dream it is far-fetched, and so can never be satisfactorily explained in terms of rational causality. The fable is aetiological, in that it accounts for some aspect of reality by concocting a sequence of events which occur by reason of symbolic necessity. Thus we are given to understand that no man could run faster than Atalanta. This is the premise of our story, and it is inacceptable when taken literally, since it requires us to believe that there can be a Wonder Woman whom no man can outrun. Again: Venus helps Hippomenes by giving him golden apples. What does this mean?

The symbological interpretation of the story need not take Freudian overtones, since there is no "disguising by symbols" going on here. The story means what it says, and it does tell us that the goddess of erotic love showed Hippomenes how to win his bride. He could not possibly do this simply by displaying his masculine prowess. And we note that the fable has a happy ending: Atalanta is glad that Hippomenes is successful, not angry that she has been tricked. So the story tells us that woman-as-Atalanta can never be outrun by any man, but that their union can come to fruition if the man has the aid of Venus—that is, if Venus shows him how to succeed with the use of golden apples. Here it is appropriate to consider briefly what these golden apples are.

When we speak of a symbolic apple we probably think first of the forbidden fruit, and we note here that it is popularly given a sexual interpretation, particularly in the Protestant tradition. Again, it is generally thought that this fruit was literally an apple—a Gravenstein, perhaps, or maybe a Roman Beauty or Golden Delicious. But why apple? The King James version of Genesis speaks of a "fruit," just as the Spanish translation by Cipriano de Valera says *fruto*. Traditionally we speak of the "apple of Eden," but of course the word *apple* is an old generic term meaning simply "fruit." This meaning is reflected in formations like "pineapple," "love apple" (tomato), and *pomme de terre* (potato). "Golden apples" are not, then, necessarily apples in the modern sense. The expression means "golden fruit," and the best authorities identify them with the citron or the orange, since these are the "golden fruit" par excellence, identifiable as the sun, the golden orb of life.[7] But tradition has inextricably confused the generic and the specific meanings—particularly in the Spanish (*manzana*).

In any case, the symbolic apple is always the apple of life. In the most general sense the apple of life is interpreted as symbolizing freedom from fear of death, freedom from "fear of passing with the passage of time."[8] That is to say, the life-principle, the life-monad is beyond time, forbidden to the time-bound ego. It manifests itself in the phenomena of temporality, but the vital principle itself is indestructible.

But of course the symbolic apple of life is used widely with a sexual meaning. Thus in one Gypsy tale concerning the Apples of Pregnancy, a wife sees a man pass by with apples. "Whoso eats one of his apples shall conceive. Then she went, and took an apple, and ate the apple, and she conceived."[9] Licht gives a number of European sources as evidence that the apple was sacred to Aphrodite: "Lovers brought apples as a present or threw them to their loved ones, to show their affection."[10] A Scottish Halloween custom "consists in eating an apple before a looking-glass, when the face of the desired one will be seen."[11] In Scandinavian mythology King Rerir and his wife have a child after the goddess Frigg has an apple dropped into the lap of the king: "He shared it with the queen, who not long afterwards bore a son."[12]

Since Venus's apples of love bring about the happy union of Atalanta and

Hippomenes, it appears that the notion of winning the race has to be examined.

The comparison of the sexual act with a race derives from the fact that it consists of a gathering excitement and physical acceleration toward a goal, and that two persons are simultaneously and mutually involved in reaching this goal. The metaphor of the race has some similarity with the traditional comparison of coitus (from *co-ire*, literally, a "going together") with warfare, or with a bodily struggle of any kind. There is an intimate physical contact that will accelerate to a triumphant climax, but of course the activity is accounted most successful, most gratifying, when both partners enter into it in a fully natural spirit—that is to say, when both of them shed their personality roles so that the act is performed like any other natural function, uninhibited by ego-intentions. The battle of the sexes is waged socially, and in it each person seeks advantage by using sexuality to gain leverage and dominance. But the partners in coitus, when they shed their clothes, shed their egotistic social roles as well.

The only way the man could win this race in the competitive sense is to prize egotistic gratification over mutual fulfillment. But the man who sees woman as Atalanta simultaneously sees himself as Hippomenes, and so transcends the timebound exploitation of sex. This means that for him, winning signifies passing the test that every Atalanta sets for her lover.

The fable of Atalanta tells us what has always been known in folklore and myth—that man considers woman to have the greater erotic capacity. To the male multiple coition appears to be something of a feat, a sign of sexual prowess, whereas the woman takes it for granted as part of her natural erotic endowment. Hippomenes passes the test, not by racing more efficiently than Atalanta, but by giving her three times a valuable gift from Venus. He brings to fulfillment her own erotic capacity. If the lover cannot or does not do this then his activity is more appropriately described as autoerotic. Hence "Atalanta" concerns the speaker's realization that the woman is an extremely erotic creature and that he could bring this out if they were to race together—because he, like Hippomenes, is in possession of the secret of Venus: "the golden apples that I would throw to you!"

Mythic stories and fables dramatize the eternal aspects of human behavior. Atalanta and Hippomenes are the ideal sexual partners, and whenever a man and woman make love with full mutual gratification they are realizing a natural potential, an aspect of nature that transcends the particular circumstances of time and place. As the old English expression has it, they are "doing their kind." Thus the ancient fables are always current. It is always possible to reincarnate them by shedding the accidents of fashion in clothing, hairdo, and ego-personality. It is an important aspect of the pornographic novel, which, as we know, is always very weak in characterization. Pornographic literature is repetitive because it depicts a timeless activity.

Here as elsewhere Salinas is stirred by the close physical presence of the woman and senses that the feminine spirit is already in the instinctual realm that he seeks to enter. Popularly it is recognized that the man is more quickly awakened erotically than the woman; he is the fire and she is the water, as we are told in the epigraph from Van Gulik. But the rapid awakening of the erotic impulse in the man is seen as lust; whereas when we say that the feminine spirit dwells more closely to the instinctual realm we mean that she maintains operative a livelier spirit of relatedness, a greater sense of the instinctual realities of life that tend to melt into one another. The *logos*-oriented male bends his energies to ego-goals (winning, conquering) to such a degree that he easily loses contact with the spirit of relatedness. When this is carried to an extreme degree, he is in danger of turning himself into a fanatic.

The man, having been taught to develop his aggressive ego-intellect (the lower masculinity), must subsequently learn to return to his sources (the higher masculinity). If he is very sensitive to this spiritual task, it is then that he comes to realize that the feminine consciousness has never strayed very far from those sources. She is already there, and it is she, as the carrier of the anima projection, who awakens him; she, like Atalanta, who brings him into the race and sets him running. She did it too with Emerson's "rude village boy," who "teazes the girls about the school-house door;—but to-day he comes running into the entry and meets one fair child arranging her satchel: he holds her books to help her, and instantly it seems to him as if she removed herself from him infinitely, and was a sacred precinct. Among the throng of girls he runs rudely enough, but one alone distances him."[13] Atalanta is always distancing man, always ahead of him, and his only hope for successful union with her lies with the fabled secret of the golden apples of Venus.

Chapter Seven

WOMAN AS CARRIER OF THE
ANIMA PROJECTION

OTRA TÚ

No te veo la mirada
si te miro aquí a mi lado.
Si miro al agua la veo.

Si te escucho,
no te oigo bien el silencio.
En la tersura
del agua quieta lo entiendo.

Y el cielo
— tú le miras, yo le miro—,
no es infinito en lo alto:
el cielo
—en su baranda te apoyas—
tiene cuatro esquinas, húmedo,
está en el agua, cuadrado.

No. 3, *Seguro azar* (1921–1928)

ANOTHER YOU

I cannot see your glance
if I look at you here by my side.
If I look at the water I see it.

If I listen to you,
I hardly hear your silence.
In the smooth surface
of the still water I understand it.

And the sky
—you look at it, I look at it—
is not an infinite zenith:
the sky
—you are leaning on its railing—
has four corners, it is wet,
it is in the water, squared.

MARCO

¡Qué cuadrado está el mar!
Tiene
costas inverosímiles,
cuatro lindes de oro.
Su corazón titánico
palpita en un espejo.
Tempestades copiadas
quiebran altas espumas
contra listones frágiles
que lo apaciguan todo.
Entras; y en el azogue
donde
tormenta septembrina
se ciñe, lucha y muere,
claro jirón se abre
al par—otro y lo mismo—
que te miras, sonrisa.

No. 42, *Seguro azar*

FRAME

How squared the sea!
It has
unlikely coasts,
four golden boundaries.
Its titanic heart
beats in a mirror.
Copied tempests
hurl lofty foam
against delicate fillets
that lay all to rest.
You come in; and in the quicksilver
where
the September storm
is bound, struggles and dies,
a patch of blue opens up
just as—different and the same—
you see yourself, a smile.

We have been looking at poems by Salinas concerned with the masculine-feminine relationship in terms of the flesh-and-blood woman—the extraverted form of the union—and now we propose to examine four poems that express its introverted meaning.

The first two of these are simple, direct representations of how the man makes the transition from the beloved to that part of his spirit which she has crystallized. He sees her mirrored reflection and this appears to open up the world on the other side, putting him into contact with it. Ultimately the man may see that there is no difference between his own instinctual nature and Nature herself. Ultimately he may experience the illumination that transcends any specifically feminine form of nature. So it was with Salinas, but as our poems show, the way was prepared by his relationship with the beloved. From the beloved to the feminine unconscious to unity: this is a trajectory that belongs potentially to every man.

The unity of which I speak is visualized sharply and briefly in the poem "Tornasol" ("Iridescence"), by Salinas's close friend, the Spanish poet Jorge Guillén: there he describes how indoors on a hot summer day he sees the shimmering light tremble against the shutters (or matchstick blinds) and suddenly it appears to him that the vast celestial ocean is wanting to be contained within the confines of the window: it wants to be a peaceful, shining lake.[1]

This is the theme of limited consciousness (the mirroring lake) sensing itself to be the incarnation of the limitless ocean surrounding our planet. The mediation of the beloved, leading to the egoless clarity of unconditioned awareness within a shining frame: these are the two themes that appear in the Salinas poems, "Otra tú" and "Marco."

Because these two poems are particularly explicit examples of archetypal material in the work of Salinas, it is well to introduce a specific analogue from folk literature—the Chinese fairy tale called "The Strange Adventure of Liu." The young hero, finding school uncongenial, drops out and decides to become a sailor. Setting sail on the Tung-Ting Lake, he forthwith has a magic adventure: the King of the Lake and his courtiers materialize before his eyes; he falls in love with a beautiful water-sprite who is handmaiden to the Queen of the Lake. The hero writes a poem in praise of the king, who rewards him with two presents: gold, and a carpenter's square made of rock crystal, which has the power to quell storms on the lake. Liu awakens from the vision. When he subsequently establishes himself in the city he calls on a widow who has a beautiful daughter; and the story tells us that when Liu saw her, he thought that she "fulfilled all that Liu had heard of her charms. She held in her hand a carpenter's square, which was identical with his own. Liu felt instantly that they had known each other always, and in fact it seemed to him that he had seen her face somewhere before."[2] She is his dream come true.

In this extraordinary tale we have a traditional and popular form of the symbolic material used by Salinas in "Otra tú" and "Marco." We see that it presents a classic example of the anima motif: the water-sprite who lives at the bottom of the lake. Like all anima fairy tales the story shows how the conscious and the unconscious, the *logos* and *eros* principles, come into harmony, thereby producing a young man who will live happily ever after, meaning that he has successfully passed the ordeal of adolescence. He is ready to embark upon the adventure of maturity without needing to fear the threat of the dangerous regressions that seem characteristically to beset us modern cosmopolitan adults.[3]

In "The Strange Adventure of Liu" the adolescent protagonist is depicted as a dropout. It is too soon in his life to embrace the *logos* principle, because until certain conditions of maturation are met, ego-intellect runs a strong risk of developing lopsidedly. And since this is a typical folktale of how the youth becomes an adult, we see him decide to be a sailor, to turn his back on the land and to give himself willingly to the *eros* principle. This innocent willingness on his part produces a psychedelic experience in which he is vouchsafed a vision of the anima, and it is this that determines the course of his subsequent spiritual development. He learns who he is supposed to be, just as through the vision a man may suddenly raise to consciousness his vocation in life. As a token of this experience Liu is given a magic carpenter's square.

This tool is purely symbolic, since the hero does not become a carpenter; we learn only that he later engages successfully in "business." But it is a curious symbol, because it is so specific. It is not merely a carpenter's square; it is made of rock crystal, and it is not intended to be used in "magic" carpentry at all. Rather, it has the peculiar virtue of quelling storms on the lake. It has all the marks of a typical dream-symbol. Further, it is clearly identifiable as symbolizing the *logos* principle, for the carpenter's square represents the practical application of geometry, one of the means whereby intellect imposes an order of its own on the world it lives in. But fairy tales characteristically concern the union of *logos* and *eros*, not the lopsided development of one or the other. So symbolically it is not difficult to understand the connection between Liu's vision of his Lady of the Lake and the magic square (not dissimilar to Malory's Lady of the Lake, who bestows a magic sword); the square represents the talismanic consciousness that will quell storms, which, psychologically, are symbolic of inner upheavals.[4]

That the square is made of rock crystal is significant, since it is well known that rock crystal itself is a traditional symbol of the *logos* principle. Preintellectuals believe that the crystal comes from heaven. The Australian aborigines hold that Baiame, the Supreme Being, "sits on a throne of transparent crystal. . . . Baiame's throne is the celestial vault. The crystals detached from his throne are 'solidified light.' "[5] Similarly the Dyaks call crystals "stones of light": "Rock crystals, supposedly broken away from the heavenly throne, . . . reflect everything that happens on earth."[6] The vault of heaven, made of glass, lets fall pieces of crystal, and the possessors of these become scryers (diviners with the mirror), since the crystal can show them everything on earth, just as if they were sitting on the celestial throne itself (cf. the Gypsy's crystal ball). Thus the crystal represents a high order of understanding, the *logos* principle raised to an ideal level, which is the level of self-understanding. When we know who we are supposed to be we have the most precious kind of understanding available; and this knowledge comes not from splitting off the intellect from the rest of the self, but rather from integrating it with the instinctual sphere of living. And so Liu has no difficulty at all in recognizing the carrier of his anima; she has a square identical to his own, proving her origin. The anima sensation felt by Liu is classic: he "felt instantly that they had known each other always." It is a variant of the *déjà vu*: "It seemed to him that he had seen her face somewhere before."[7]

By now it is no doubt apparent that our commentary on the story about Liu is applicable to "Otra tú" and "Marco," for in these two poems we see this archetypal material, stripped of all adornment. Both poems concern a form of scrying: the speaker gazes contemplatively at a reflecting surface and experiences the beloved as an image belonging to the inner realm of nonego. In "Otra tú" the image is seen against the reflected sky, at which instant the speaker has the sensation that the sky itself has been squared, that is, brought within the limits of his own consciousness. It is no longer limitlessly distant, but made of the very stuff of his own awareness. In "Marco" a similar episode occurs, except that now the speaker experiences the stormy ocean as squared, and when his beloved's image appears in the mirror the tempest subsides. He sees it contemplatively. The mirror creates the distance between himself and the stormy sea "out there"; the anima image creates the distance between his own tranquil consciousness and the microcosmic upheavals. All storms are quelled by virtue of the protective mediation of the anima, for that is its function.

Chapter Eight

THE FEMININE UNCONSCIOUS
AS A CREATIVE FORCE

UNDERWOOD GIRLS

Quietas, dormidas, están,
las treinta, redondas, blancas.
Entre todas
sostienen el mundo.
Míralas, aquí en su sueño,
como nubes,
redondas, blancas, y dentro
destinos de trueno y rayo,
destinos de lluvia lenta,
de nieve, de viento, signos.
Despiértalas,
con contactos saltarines
de dedos rápidos, leves,
como a músicas antiguas.
Ellas suenan otra música:
fantasías de metal
valses duros, al dictado.
Que se alcen desde siglos
todas iguales, distintas
como las olas del mar
y una gran alma secreta.
Que se crean que es la carta,
la fórmula, como siempre.
Tú alócate
bien los dedos, y las
raptas y las lanzas,
a las treinta, eternas ninfas
contra el gran mundo vacío,
blanco en blanco.
Por fin a la hazaña pura,
sin palabras, sin sentido,
ese, zeda, jota, i...
        No. 28, *Fábula y signo* (1931)

UNDERWOOD GIRLS

Quiet, asleep they are,
thirty, round, white.
Among them
they sustain the world.
Look at them, here in their sleep,
like clouds,
round, white, and within them
destinies of thunder and lightning,
destinies of slow rain,
of snow, of wind, signs.
Awaken them
with dancing touches
of rapid fingers, light,
as one would ancient music.
They play another music:
metal fantasies
hard waltzes, by dictation.
Let them all arise out of the centuries,
all alike, different,
like the waves of the sea
and a great secret soul.
Let them think that it is
the usual form letter.
You, let your fingers
go crazy, and
carry them off and hurl them,
the thirty, eternal nymphs
against the great empty world,
blank white.
Set to the pure feat, then,
without words, without meaning,
s, z, j, i...

With the poet's passing from the beloved herself to contact with the feminine unconscious comes the awakening into creativity, and with this we arrive at the original meaning of *muse*. It is difficult to exaggerate the importance for poets of the woman as muse, and Salinas has two poems which, when taken together, give us a remarkably clear picture of her. The first of these, "Underwood Girls," treats the material in a general way; the second, "35 bujías," treats it specifically. "Underwood Girls" recognizes the creative process as an inner awakening of a kind of collective feminine (cf.

the nymphs of Renaissance pastoral poetry)—an awakening through *musing*, or through the idleness called *Muβe* in German. Musing is associated with the activity known as automatic art, for both let go of the orderly ways of ego-intellect so that something within can be stirred.

"Underwood Girls," like "Madrid. Calle de . . . ," concerns the epistemology of a process. It does not tell what the poet learns, but rather the manner in which awareness is altered. The poem associates the typewriter keys with sleeping women, no farfetched comparison if we recall the history of the typewriting machine and the role it has played in the evolution of twentieth-century society. Indeed, important to our understanding of "Underwood Girls" is the very fact that the title itself is originally in English, not Spanish.

When we look into the history of the typewriting machine we are soon reminded that at least until World War II it was inevitably associated with what is now known to be the beginning of a socially effective women's liberation. In the first three decades of this century, as a matter of fact, the term *typewriter* meant both the machine and its female operator. A typewriter was a woman who made her living by typing, since the machine was used almost exclusively by women in the business world. This means that in those days the typewriter was as feminine an object as the motorcycle was masculine. Thus there existed a vaudeville act known as Gus Edwards' Six Blonde Typewriters, a corps of dancers who "tapped out typewriter rhythm accompaniments for songs and dances." Similarly one of the standard vaudeville jokes—"Who was that lady I saw you with last night?"—produced the following variant:"I saw you and your queen walking down Main Street last night." "Oh, that was not my queen. That was my typewriter!"[1]

In those same years speed-writing contests were popular, and they received newspaper publicity. The typewriting speed-champion was recognized by the press, and a woman usually held the title. These championships were sponsored by the manufacturers of typewriting machines, and each large company had a stable of expert typewriters. A coach was assigned to recruit young talent from the best-known secretarial schools. It is a fact that the Underwood Company dominated the championships for years, to such an extent that rival companies gradually lost interest in the competitions.[2] Since the "Underwood Girls" were given newspaper publicity, it would appear that Salinas's poem was generated by knowledge of such events.

The poet, speaking of his typewriter, refers to the keys as thirty in number. It so happens that the Spanish alphabet has thirty letters—our twenty-six, plus *ch*, *ll*, *ñ*, *and rr*—but of these extra letters only the *ñ* requires a separate character on the typewriter (the numerals require nine more keys in any case). A perusal of catalogs of the history of the typewriter reveals that the number of keys on a machine easily varied from about twenty to well over forty between the turn of the century and World War II. I have not been able to document the existence of an Underwood typewriter with thirty keys, though a Corona portable of the twenties was so equipped.[3] In any case, Salinas is concerned with the alphabet itself.

Salinas himself was a typist.[4] But of course the machine has its characteristic use in the business world, the world of *negocios*, where it is used by the secretary to type business letters—the *fórmulas* of line 23. This is how the signs, or characters of the alphabet are employed by ego-intellect in the world of business activity. But Salinas on occasion would type drafts of poems, and so once again the sacred and secular worlds are in confrontation.

In the beginning of the poem Salinas compares each round, white typewriter key to a cloud. The keyboard of his machine is a sky filled with white clouds, and each one bears a sign; he says that it is the destiny of each cloud to become thunder and lightning and "slow rain." For the poet the destiny of anything at all is that it become transformed, become spiritually significant, and later we shall see how Salinas dwelled considerably upon the sign whereby nature fabulates.

The readers familiar with the fourteenth-century mystical treatise, *The Cloud of Unknowing*, may remember that at the end of the work the author, citing the pseudo-Dionysius, states that "the moste goodly knowyng of God is that, the whiche is knowyn bi vnknowyng." This cloud of unknowing is the blankness of mind, the otiose state of the communicant. To unknow is to abandon ego-intellect, to sink into an intuitive frame of mind. The author of *The Cloud of Unknowing* plays with the two meanings of *know*, the ego-meaning (intellectual, or indirect knowledge) and the Self-meaning (intuitive, or direct knowledge). In "Underwood Girls" the speaker sees each sign of the alphabet as a potential letter in a poem, the sign of intuitive knowledge. In order to pass from the profane to the sacred use of letters he must transcend the purposive activity normally associated with the typewriter. Each key must be seen as a white cloud of unknowing—a cloud out of which may come the thunderbolt and the gentle, fertilizing rain of the "great secret soul." Just as we read in *The Cloud of Unknowing*, out of the cloud comes a beam of light.[5]

Hence the keys of the typewriter, the letters of the alphabet when seen as feminine, are what "sustains the world," which is to say the world reality of the human mind. This reality, the word of the poet (*logos* as symbol, not *logos* as abstraction), is always a becoming, a transformation, never statically conventionalized. It is like the cloud, a part of the perpetual becoming of the water. The clouds of "Underwood Girls," the letters of the poet's alphabet, belong to that same cycle we saw in the poem "Agua en la noche."

With respect to the anima motif we should note that Salinas experiences the alphabet as feminine: the "thirty eternal nymphs" asleep down there; the latent anima function awaiting its awakening out of the "great secret soul," the Self. Here surely we have the closest thing possible to an introverted version of the feminine liberation!

The last ten lines of the poem tell us that the poet is entrusting himself to random activity, as García Lorca would doodle at times when he sensed that he was being led into the forest of nonego,[6] or as Don Quijote would let Rocinante choose the path of adventure. In "Underwood Girls" this random activity becomes a form of automatic writing.

Alan Gauld, in his discussion of automatic art, tells us that the term "means the production of work not consciously directed by the person whose hand executed it. It belongs to, and cannot be sharply separated from, a whole range of phenomena commonly regarded by psychologists as manifestations of layers of the personality which are subconscious or dissociated, cut off from the conscious mind." Since we have been consistently distinguishing between ego and Self, it is of interest to note that automatic phenomena include speaking in tongues and prophecy. Automatic writing "not infrequently develops a 'character' of its own, professing beliefs and opinions which differ from those of the automatist."[7]

In "Underwood Girls" (the name itself, taken literally, suggests the mythic world of the dryads) the speaker, as poet, clearly intends to tap the world of the creative unconscious by imitating the automatists. In lines 24–25 he says to himself, "alócate / bien los dedos." The verb form *alócate* comes from *alocar-se* (based on *loco*), which appears to be a back-formation from *alocado* ("wild, reckless"); perhaps too there is an intentional, implicit allusion to L. *locus*, "place" (cf. Sp. *colocar*, "to put in place"), since the reference is to random touching of keys by (mis)placing the fingers upon them. At any rate he strikes the keys without intentionally attempting to make sense. He will "hurl" the letters—the typebars—"against the great empty world, / blank white." He prepares himself mentally, empties his mind of ego-intentions, and then says, "Por fin" ("Finally"): "Set to the pure feat, then." This "pure feat" has no preconceived meaning, for it is a feat of unknowing. It is similar to the Dadaists' feat of mixing together snips of phrases and selecting them at random, so making a poem without intended meanings. Again, it is not dissimilar to working with the ouija board, a practice regarded as superstitious by the cosmopolitan sophisticate. But of course there is no reason to reject the reality of the phenomenon, even if one is convinced that the writing is not done by ghosts. As Heywood notes in her discussion of the ouija board, "As a rule its productions do not make much sense."[8] In somewhat the same fashion, the poet, by striking typewriter keys in a random sequence, will usually produce a writing "sin palabras, sin sentido" ("without words, without sense"). But Salinas has faith in such an experiment, because it is simply one more way to seek contact with unconscious contents. These contents are pure in the same sense that the mirror of "Crepúsculo" is pure—they are preintellectual and filled with primal innocence.

Chapter Nine

THE ANIMA FIGURE AS HELPMATE

35 BUJÍAS

Sí. Cuando quiera yo
la soltaré. Está presa
aquí arriba, invisible.
Yo la veo en su claro
castillo de cristal, y la vigilan
—cien mil lanzas—los rayos
—cien mil rayos—del sol. Pero de noche,
cerradas las ventanas
para que no la vean
—guiñadoras espías—las estrellas,
la soltaré. (Apretar un botón.)
Caerá toda de arriba
a besarme, a envolverme
de bendición, de claro, de amor, pura.
En el cuarto ella y yo no más, amantes
eternos, ella mi iluminadora
musa dócil en contra
de secretos en masa de la noche
—afuera—
descifraremos formas leves, signos,
perseguidos en mares de blancura
por mí, por ella, artificial princesa,
amada eléctrica.

No. 27, *Seguro azar* (1924–1928)

35 CANDLE POWER

Yes. When I wish,
I will release her. She is prisoner
here above, invisible.
I can see her in her transparent
glass castle, and she is guarded by
—a hundred thousand lances—the rays
—a hundred thousand rays—of the sun. But
at night,
with the windows closed
so that she cannot be seen by
—winking spies—the stars,
I will release her. (Press a button.)
Down she will fall, entire, from above
to kiss me, to enfold me
in grace, in transparency, in love, pure.
In the room just she and I, eternal
lovers, she, my illuminating
docile muse, despite
assembled secrets of the night
—outside—
we will decipher buoyant forms, signs,
pursued on oceans of white
by me, by her, artificial princess,
electric beloved.

He . . . decided that he felt like a smashed light bulb.—Peter S. Beagle, *A Fine and Private Place*

We have within us the Lamp of the World; and Nature, the genie, is Slave of the Lamp, and must fashion life about us as we fashion it within ourselves.—George William Russell (Æ), *The Candle of Vision*

"35 bujías" is particularly striking for its portrayal of anima as muse, the image of the beloved whose purpose is to guide the masculine consciousness across the inner ocean on a voyage of discovery. In the spiritual sense the poem is not dissimilar to "Atalanta," since the concern is with a kind of mutual arrangement: the poet liberates the feminine within—awakens her to life, as it were—but by so doing alters his own consciousness and awakens himself to an extended awareness. In "35 bujías" the figure of the beloved is presented as pure fantasy, and the speaker's enthusiasm for her benign role leads him to develop a complex conceit grounded in the fairy tale. His attention is addressed to a clear light bulb that will mark the poet's embarkation upon a quest. He thinks of himself as a hero who will rescue a princess held captive in a glass castle, whereupon the two of them will join in loving union and go traveling across the sea.

The principal motif of this modern fairy tale will be familiar to readers who remember the story called "The Glass Coffin" (Grimm, No. 163, "*Der gläserne Sarg*"). The hero, a tailor's apprentice, goes traveling, enters a great forest, and loses himself. He suffers from a "painful solitude" as night falls, and spends several hours in the darkness, until he sees the glimmering of a light that guides him to a small hut. Its inhabitant, a surly little old man, allows him to spend the night there. In the morning the hero is awakened by the sounds of a violent battle between a stag and a bull, and he sees how the bull is eventually slain. The victorious stag carries the hero to a magic cavern-hall whose walls are covered with "unknown signs" (*unbekannte Zeichen*; in Spanish, *signos misteriosos*). He hears a voice instructing him: "Step on the stone which lies in the middle of the hall, and great good fortune awaits you." This magic elevator carries him to a subterranean hall that appears to be a museum filled with clear glass containers and two large glass showcases. The clear bottles contain a colored *Spiritus*, as the German text has it, or smoke. One of the large glass cases displays a marvelously wrought miniature village centered around a castle; in the other, the glass coffin of the story's title, the hero can see imprisoned a beautiful maiden lying as if asleep. She suddenly opens her eyes and cries out, "My deliverance is at hand! Quick, quick, help me out of my prison." In order to accomplish this all the hero need do is simply push back the bolt of the glass lid. He does so, whereupon the maiden tells him her story of how she had been enchanted. She and her brother had been inseparable friends. When a stranger came to woo her, she rejected him, and he spitefully transformed the brother into a stag and by enchantment set the maiden into the glass coffin. There she had a dream that the hero would come to set her free. When he arrived she opened her eyes and the deed was accomplished. Her story done, the glass bottles all open themselves, and the imprisoned world of the maiden is delivered. We learn that the bull slain by the stag was the villain—the stag being, of course, the maiden's own brother. And so "on the self-same day the maiden . . . gave her hand at the altar to the lucky tailor."[1]

The reader will note that the story of the glass coffin is a classical example of the anima motif, the activation of the feminine unconscious, and that it corresponds closely to the poem "35 bujías," set in the place we may identify as somewhere east of the sun and west of the moon. For these are the two principal ideas behind the poem: the quest beyond the sun and the moon (and stars), and the encounter there with the beautiful maiden. The speaker expresses the belief that he and his muse will join in loving union to go "decipher signs" only after both the light of day and the lights of night have been shut out.

The fairy tale characteristically begins with the formula, "Once upon a time," "Es war einmal", "in illo tempore," which is the time before time began. It is the preintellectual period, "in the days when wishing was still of some use."[2] The preintellectual epoch is the time that precedes the development of ego-intellect; it is the world of the Self, inhabited by a small child. Every creative act entails a return to that world and the concomitant falling out of sidereal time, the clock-time measured by the stars (L. *sidus, sideris*). It is the return to the timeless moment, the whole world of myth—that unseen world which the Australian aborigines call their Dreamtime, or The Dreaming: "once upon a time," "in the Beginning."

The hero of "35 bujías" describes how he intends to liberate a princess held captive in a clear glass container. The essential condition of this undertaking is the exclusion of the light of the sun and stars. By day the sun measures the seasons of our years, and by night the stars are his spies; even though by night the hard light of the sun does not flood our world, nevertheless clock-time, measured by the stars, continues to run on. In the world of sidereal time there is no functional difference between day and night, for the round of clock-time keeps us on a twenty-four-hour shift except when we drop out of it altogether by going to sleep—by entering into the Dreamtime of our mythic oneiric fantasies. There, sidereal time is quite excluded, except as one more symbolic entity (cf. the anxiety dream of being late by clock-time).

The hero of "35 bujías" likens his journey with the maiden to the union of lovers (the *hieros gamos*, or sacred marriage, of consciousness and the unconscious), for mythic time is also that world into which lovers enter when in the privacy of their chamber they surrender to each other. There the entire notion of clock-time ceases to have meaning in the passionate context of their union, and there too, the poet opens the floodgates of his creative unconscious and enters into union. Like the hero of "The Glass Coffin" he will release his beloved. All the tailor's apprentice had to do in order to accomplish this was to push back a bolt—and likewise the hero-poet: "I will release her. (Press a button.)."

We should note that the motif of the Sleeping Beauty refers to a mutual awakening. The world of the Self is a repressed world, and the fairy-tale enchantment or bewitching symbolizes this repression. The princess imprisoned is always the Sleeping Beauty, who remains as if dead until the hero can make his way across the barrier of repression (the hedge of thorns, the Glass Mountain, a wide river, a portal guarded by lions), whereupon he kisses her, awakens her, and by this act is himself awakened. It is just as John Collier has observed in his story "Sleeping Beauty": "It is the fate of those who kiss sleeping beauties to be awakened themselves."[3]

Salinas calls this captive maiden an "artificial princess," which involves a play on words. In Spanish *artificial* and *arte* are semantically closer than their English cognates are. The princess is artificial in the sense that she belongs to the world of artifacts, the artful libido of civilized people, and she is literally artificial in that she is created in a particular form by the art-making capacity of the metropolitan poet. Civilized poetry, just like civilized painting and civilized music, is artificial, not natural in the sense that primitive artifacts are natural, but rather the product of a highly apperceptive ego-consciousness clearly separated from the surrounding world.

"35 bujías" alludes to the privacy of introspection that we have discussed with respect to meditation. This turning inward to the world of the self in the grateful solitude and silence of the night is described at some length in Salinas's essay in praise of reading, "Defensa de la lectura." By *reading*, Salinas (one of the great omnivorous readers of his time) means reading as a meditative act, not as a way of killing time, and the optimum condition for this kind of meditation over the word is what he calls *el conticinio*. The conticinium (based on L. *taceo*, "to be silent;" cf. Eng. "tacit") is the "silence in the dead of night," the ideal setting for the modern reader who enjoys the privilege of the incandescent light bulb. The reading lamp creates this silence, and Salinas fondly describes that moment of evening's solitude when the reader can pass from the daytime world of noise and *negocio* to the silent circle of the armchair and lamp: "There is a moment of unequaled pleasure for many of us. It is when the body gratefully sits down, welcomed comfortably by the armchair, without impertinent pressures, and a simple flick of the finger awakens the precious miracle of light out of its invisible, crystalline dream, so that by its warmth the imperishable flower of the book may open up." It must not be an overhead light, he says, because what one requires is an *ámbito*, an ambit, or private circle, an intimate, subjective inner zone. "I see it . . . as an act of withdrawal," he says, using the word *recogimiento*—a high-frequency word among the Spanish mystics; for it indeed means "meditation." The reading lamp is the creator of solitude, lighting an area for but one person, so that one may receive the "beloved reading which has waited till one came to awaken it, like a Sleeping Beauty lying in her bed of dense lines."[4] Here again we note the motif of the Sleeping Beauty, lying now in the poetry of the book, the captive princess that some other meditative writer has brought into being in the secret signs of a book that awaits deciphering.

In general we can see that Salinas is playing with the idea of libido—psychic energy—as the driving force that gets the job of poetry-making done, and that he turns this into a psychological projection. He projects his libido outwardly onto a light bulb. The symbol of the light bulb is natural enough, since libido is easily thought of as the specifically human form of electricity. We need only recall the psychoanalytical use of the term *cathexis*, used by analogy with the electric charge: an accumulation or concentration of energy in a given direction. *Cathexis* means "interest"; to become interested in something is to "cathect" one's electricity, one's psychic energy upon it.[5] So the poet turns on his thirty-five-candle-power lamp and embarks on an ocean voyage with his muse:

> we will decipher buoyant forms, signs,
> pursued on oceans of white
> by me, by her, artificial princess,
> electric beloved.

This much had already been stated by the English poet, George Russell, in *The Candle of Vision* (1918). Just as Salinas points to the deliberateness of fostering the conticinium ("Yes. When I wish, / I will release her"), so does Russell tell us that one must "heighten the imagination and intensify the will." Then—and here we have another poet's prefiguration of "35 bujías"— "the darkness in you will begin to glow, and you will see clearly, and you will know that what you thought was but a mosaic of memories is rather the froth of a gigantic ocean of life, breaking on the shores of matter, casting up its own flotsam to mingle with the life of the shores it breaks on. If you will light your lamp you can gaze far over the ocean and even embark on it."[6] Russell's and Salinas's symbolic contexts are nearly identical, but of course this does not imply that Salinas, for all his polyglot reading, knew Russell's book; what it does imply is that both Russell and Salinas were equally familiar with this aspect of symbolic realities. Russell's book is certainly more mystical than Salinas's playful poem, but eventually Salinas too will be led to a transcendental experience of the cosmos at play. In *El Contemplado* the ocean is an object of deep contemplation, where one goes far beyond the limits of the projection fantasy.

At the beginning of this discussion there is a pair of epigraphs that employ the idea of the lamp as metaphor for libido. In the first, a man's ghost, contemplating the freshly dug grave where its body lies buried, compares itself to a smashed light bulb, and in the second, psychic energy is a microcosmic lamp, the Lamp of the World. These appear to be exactly analogous, in a curiously personal way, to the notion developed in "35 bujías." Salinas's poem appears in *Seguro azar*, a book containing pieces written in the years 1924–1928, which allows us to deduce an interesting bit of symbolism underlying the poem. Salinas was born in 1891, which means that he was thirty-five years old in 1926. It therefore appears rather likely that 1926 was the year in which he composed "35 bujías." Not that this year really matters otherwise, but one may surmise that the title of the poem points to a probable coincidence: the size of the light bulb and the age of the poet. It is he who is the "35 Candle Power," he who allows his thirty-five-year-old psyche to cast its private ambit of light. The enjoyment of the loving ministrations of the feminine creative unconscious is brought about by "turning on."

Part Three

Reading Signs from the Unconscious:

The Poet as Seer

Chapter Ten

THE CREATIVE MEANING OF
THE SUPERSTITIOUS IMPULSE

In my introductory pages I presented material documenting that general state of awareness called unified consciousness, in which the so-called environment ceases to be experienced as such. One reads a new meaning (actually the primordial meaning) in it, and I say "reads" advisedly, since in self-transcendence the world is seen to have a spiritual significance in somewhat the way a written text does; it appears to be a language that one has just learned to read, a code that one has just deciphered. Poets and contemplatives alike frequently speak of signs in the world, signs through which one raises to consciousness the transcendental human awareness.

I have previously recalled that the rise of civilization means the rising power of secular ego-consciousness. *Secular* refers to the loss of contact with the magic of signs, so that the world presents itself simply as an object to be manipulated, but in no way intimately a part of one's own spirit. With the increasing dominance of the secular viewpoint—ultimately the fruit of civilized education—the sense of the world as a magic text falls into disrepute and, generally speaking, it is the less educated person who continues to find any means of communication with it. Eventually this communion, this reading of the signs, comes to be degraded as superstition. The superstitious folk are those who themselves have long since lost the transcendent experience of what a sign actually means, and of how it can function creatively.

Salinas saw all the way into signs, from the simplest and most immediate experience of them to the illumination in which the entire world is a swarming mass of signs all pointing to unity. Because he was so successfully adapted to metropolitan existence it is all the more unusual that he should be as much a transcendentalist as, say, Thoreau, who spent the better part of his time out in the fields alone among the signs. But in the signs lies part of the meaning of self-integration for the cosmopolite.

The successful city-dweller's specialized ego-intellect is much more professional (that is really the best word) about reality than is the amateurish, run-of-the-mill human consciousness at large. Its goals are more clearly perceived and it demands discipline in the pursuit of them. It has to be this way, because the urban reality is a dense tissue of practical commitments, and sloppy mistakes can be costly in terms of profit and loss. Ego-intellect represents the necessary means of adapting to life in the city. Human consciousness at large down through the ages has taken a more generalized view of things and is capable of seeing pretty far in two directions: both "out there," into the environment, and inwardly, into the microcosm, where matters of interest like the forms of religion and art first begin to take shape.

By custom the cosmopolite seeks the spiritual riches of life indirectly, as spectator or as audience, obtaining spiritual enrichment by consuming the sophisticated artifacts produced by artists. But the spiritual riches enjoyed by simple folk appear to be directly accessible, or intrapsychic. The country bumpkin and the primitive do not go the the opera or to the art gallery, but they see ghosts and they live committed to the vagaries of superstitious beliefs. While this does not sound like any sort of compensation for living beyond the pale of metropolitan sophistication, we must recognize that facile intercourse with numinous contents of the unconscious lies even at the heart of all great artistic inspiration. The creative artist seeks to keep open the lines of communication with the Self, and when this artist is a city sophisticate the art may even appear to be a stubborn affirmation of primitive modes of symbolic reality.[1]

Students of Jungian psychology are very familiar with Jung's idea that an important function of the unconscious is that of serving consciousness in a corrective or compensatory capacity. When ego-consciousness exaggerates in one direction—let us say ego-inflation—the unconscious produces material (e.g., a dream) dramatizing this hubris. Overweening pride may be compensated for by a numinous dream, which is to say that ego-consciousness, confronting a numen within, is humbled—a symbolic reprise of the ancient Greek tragedy. Cosmopolites, with their lopsided, secular ego-image, seek protection against reproaches from the Self within, whereas primitives and simple country folk alike tend to pay serious attention to transpersonal knowledge supplied unconsciously. The most ancient manner of doing this is through divination, and this mode of subjectivity exerted a strong attraction on Pedro Salinas. He, the city sophisticate, found a compensatory spiritual path via the superstitious mode of divination, the superstitious belief, what we may call the superstitious emotion.

The etymology of the word *superstition* cannot be accounted for. Philologists recognize, of course, that it is a combination of *super* and *stare*, but the semantics behind the combination must be guessed at. The *OED* gives *superstare*, "to stand upon or over," and then explains: "The etymological meaning . . . is perhaps 'standing over a thing in amazement or awe.' Other interpretations . . . have been proposed, e.g., '*excess* in devotion, over-scrupulousness or over-ceremoniousness in religion' and 'the *survival* of old religious habits in the midst of a new order of things'; but such ideas are foreign to ancient Roman thought." We can see that the etymological explanations given above include both the point of view of ego-intellect and that of the Self—the objective and the subjective approaches to superstition. Objectively considered, superstition can be explained as a historical phenomenon, "the survival of old religious habits in the midst of a new order of things." Superstition is thus seen as a phenomenon within the historical evolution of civilization.

For the Self, "superstitious" emotion is to be understood as deriving from a weak ego-grasp of reality: "standing over a thing in amazement or awe." Now this general description of an attitude applies with equal force to the poetic point of view. The work of lyric poets derives from the fact that they experience a certain degree of amazement and awe vis-à-vis the things of this world; nothing is to be taken for granted. They see "signs." The poets seem spontaneously to subscribe to the so-called doctrine of signatures, which means that all visible things in God's creation carry an invisible significance—a signi-ficance—showing how the visible world and the invisible world are related. In this country we have long been familiar with this notion as it was manifested in the Transcendentalist movement. In the poetry of Pedro Salinas it appears in several important forms, beginning with what is perhaps the most amusing, the least transcendental, and probably the most universally practiced form of superstition: what we may call the subjective self-bet, concerned with the simplest form of taking the auspices, of seeking auguries and omens.

The subjective self-bet is a form of spontaneous fortunetelling, and it is something that probably all of us do occasionally, even those of us who have no truck with popular superstition as such. It is a form of private fantasy that sometimes flashes so rapidly into consciousness and out again that it may even remain subliminal, hardly noticed unless we have reason to think about it searchingly. Perhaps it seems so childish that we choose not to give it a second thought. Eric Maple, in his *Superstition and the Superstitious*, gives us a good example. He cites the case of a lady "who disclosed . . . that she felt it imperative to turn away from the television, where she had been watching a Wimbledon match, and to begin cutting the hedge, saying to herself as she did so: 'If only I can finish this job in ten minutes they must win.'"[2] This is a spontaneous fantasy on the part of a civilized Englishwoman. Though it is clearly related to superstition, it suggests that whatever it is we call superstitious goes beyond merely entertaining traditional folk beliefs. The fantasy, because it is spontaneous, suggests no superstitious belief as such, but rather the impulse whereby such belief comes into being. The vulgar superstition is to be eschewed—but what about the impulse itself? "She felt it imperative." This impulse is closely connected with the notion of chance (in Spanish, *azar*), of which Salinas makes so much in his poetry.

Jahoda, in *The Psychology of Superstition*, makes a connection between the self-bet, divination, and chance occurrence: "Some of these actions partake of the nature of divination ('If I manage to hit the tree three times with a stone, my wish will be fulfilled'). Again, it may be a specific sign that is looked for to determine whether or not a given outcome is likely to be propitious; I find this happening sometimes to myself, and recall an occasion when the thought obtruded itself 'if the signal light changes from red to green before disappearing from view behind the house, things will work out all right.'"[3]

This experience perhaps typically happens without even being put into words at all; one notes two unrelated chance phenomena and spontaneously relates them, thus bestowing an arbitrary significance, as in my case: "If I walk to the next corner before five cars pass me, I win; if not, 'they' win." This is comparable to the traditional forms of divination, such as haruspicy (taking the auguries from the entrails of animals): "if the present situation coincides with a certain appearance of the entrails, then it is propitious, and 'things will work out all right,' i.e., we win; if not, they win."

This is a form of creating. What one creates is an event out of a nonevent; two things not at all related previously are given a symbolic meaning—they constitute an event. What the event is, and what the nature of its significance, is up to the self-bettor, but when it is an impulse that is involved, then the significance is established unconsciously. Two things happen to be simultaneously in the same field of perception (they are there "by chance") and the significance attached to them is the sign. That some unconscious impulse leads one spontaneously to take notice is ipso facto a sign that the impulse is present. We shall see that for Salinas this sign vouchsafed him is the sign that the poetry-making impulse is alive and well.

The connection between this kind of natural divination and the making of poetry is suggested by one of the forms taken by Dada collage, already briefly mentioned. Words and phrases are snipped out of a text, mixed up in a hat, and then drawn out at random to be pasted on a sheet of paper. This constitutes the possibility of a new poem "by chance." Things are thrown together in one field (the hat) and thereby made to coincide in an unprecedented combination. One can use the resultant text as the basis for making a poem, for like the Rorschach test, the chance text stimulates free association, and one seeks to discover the sign. Nonpoets who undertake the experiment are often surprised to find out that they can actually come up with convincing poems. And in the same general sense the subjective self-bet is a kind of mental collage creating an unprecedented, significant context where one wins in terms of the signs given.

The notion of signs (*signos*) looms large in the poetry of Salinas. His first book of poems is entitled *Presagios*. The *presagio* is a sign in the divinatory sense; the Royal Academy even calls it an *adivinación*, which is not very different from *divinación*. The "presages" of Salinas's first book of poetry were the signs that he had been reading in the process of writing the poems that make up that book. After *Presagios* comes *Seguro azar* ("Dependable chance")—a title expressing the trust that the poet places in that impulse that produces the signs. His third book of poetry is *Fábula y signo*, the "sign" being the indicator that a "fable," or mythic element, is accessible to the poet-as-seer. Then after two books of love poetry comes *El Contemplado* ("The One Contemplated"), in which the poet reads the largest sign of them all: the ground of reality in the two forms of the Sea and the Self of Pedro Salinas. These coincide, with a cosmic significance.

The reader of signs knows that the gods put these signs on earth. The augur is the skilled interpreter of them, but only the gods can bring the proper things together in order to create a new event. Perception of the event comes via nonego consciousness, the Self that is known by being thus experienced even as the beloved is experienced, one kiss at a time, one poem at a time. For Salinas the fascination with the way this intuition of becoming manifests itself turns him into his own seer—his own fortuneteller.

The Poet Tells His Fortune

Seguro azar begins with the poem "Cuartilla" ("Blank sheet of paper"):

Invierno, mundo en blanco.
Mármoles, nieves, plumas,
blancos llueven, erigen
blancura, a blanco juegan.
Ligerísimas,
escurridizas, altas,
las columnas sostienen
techos de nubes blancas.
Bandas
de palomas dudosas
entre blancos, arriba
y abajo, vacilantes
aplazan
la suma de sus alas.
¿Vencer, quién vencerá?
Los copos
inician algaradas.
Sin ruido choques, nieves,
armiños, encontrados.
Pero el viento desata
deserciones, huidas.
Y la que vence es
rosa, azul, sol, el alba:
punta de acero, pluma
contra lo blanco, en blanco,
inicial, tú, palabra.

Winter, a blank world.
Marble, snow, feathers,
whites rain down, they erect
whiteness, they play at white.
Most delicate,

slipping away, high,
the columns support
roofs of white clouds.
Flocks
of doves, hardly seen
among so many whites above
and below, hesitant
invoke
the full strength of their wings.
Win—who will win?
The snowflakes
begin catapulting.
Noiselessly, colliding, snowflakes,
ermines, swirling about.
But the wind falls
suddenly.
And the winner is
rose, blue, sun, the dawn:
steel point, pen
against blank white,
you, the first word.[4]

The poem describes a winter snowscene in the city. Snow is falling and the observer, sitting indoors at his writing table, looks out upon a tour de force of whiteness. The columns of large buildings appear to be holding up white clouds. He sees doves flying about—at least he thinks he does; among so many whites it's hard to say, at first. They find it difficult to fly in the swirling winds, and they invoke the greatest wing-power possible. This setting of the scene carries us halfway through the poem. The poet, sitting before a blank sheet of paper, has scanned the scene outside his window, has noticed the struggle with which several doves are flying, and then he asks all of a sudden, "Win—who will win?" He is suddenly seeing the scene as a contest, and is saying, "If the doves manage to fly to such-and-such a place (perhaps up to their roosts in the eaves of that building), then 'they' (we) win; if they don't then 'they' (we) lose." The birds get caught in a snow-flurry, but then this dies down and the flakes fall more slowly; their trajectory is extended out more perpendicularly. Silence ensues, but then there are flurries again. In the end his side wins. The auspices were favorable, and so creation was born: a new creation, a re-creation, or *renovatio* ("rose, blue, sun, the dawn") which is, of course, an inner springtime. The whiteness and silence of the mind allowed entrance to new poetic material.

Actually this new material is the poem we have just read, so it has an ironic twist: when we get to the beginning of the poem just born (last line: "you, the first word") we are at the end of it. The theme of the poem is what we have just read. The very first word is the very last word.

The poem is entitled "Blank Sheet of Paper," which is the sheet that contains the poem, of course, except that it is no longer blank, precisely because it was able to be blank in the first place. It let itself be blank, like the mirror on vacation in "Madrid. Calle de. . ." By impulse (the thought "obtruded" itself), the poet took the auspices (from L. *auspex: avis*, "bird" + *spicere*, "to see"): he observed the flight of birds in order to see if the omens were favorable, to see whether he, as poet, was winning or losing. He immediately perceived the relationship between his white sheet of paper and the whitening, emptying process going on "out there." This is the instant in which the new material is raised to consciousness, for in order to see that relationship his mind already had to be "otiose" and white.

"Cuartilla" is appropriately placed at the beginning of *Seguro azar*, because it shows dependable chance at work. Chance is dependable, of course, only when you feel like taking the auspices. Feeling like it is the original sign that the divine will, or creative unconscious, manifests a need to be consulted. This kind of divination is the sure one, the legitimate one; it is dependable because it is a self-fulfilling prophecy. Here we have the amorphous beginnings of inspiration: one senses the need to let go, to empty the mind of whatever *negocios* happen to be cluttering it up.

The blank sheet of paper in this poem is analogous to the blankness of mind in *zazen*, the Zen meditation in which one sits before a blank wall. Inside (blank mind) and outside (blank wall) cease to be a duality, so that one is prepared for the reception of new contents from below the threshold of immediate consciousness, whether illumination (*satori*), or a new poem. Normally our secular attention is focused "out there" in a sequence of time; the blank wall/mind establishes a context of nonsequence. The mind falls out of time, and the symbol as an experience (cf. the dream) becomes possible.

The hypnagogic state itself immediately precedes the passage into the symbolic reality of the dream, and this appears to be related to the threshold of poetic inspiration. The poet's experience of flying doves becomes inwardly significant at the moment he crosses the threshold of "Win—who will win?" and at that instant the dividing line between objective and subjective reality is erased. An inner dawning takes place; the birds "out there" turn into a reality enhanced by the same power that enhances the fictitiously objective reality of the dream. The doves are then no longer opposed by the wind (the *spiritus*, or breath of life).

Nature mystics and people who have experienced psychedelic states are well aware of what it is to take the auspices naturally or spontaneously—how easy it is, and how convincing the signs are! The world suddenly shines with significance (literally, "sign-making"), and is no longer secular. Reality is suddenly an exalted kind of winning, because it is filled with a sacred meaning. It is a sacramental reality—indeed, Saint Augustine called signs by the name of sacraments. When the world is full of signs, it becomes obvious to the seer that the significance of his own aspirations is identical with the significance of how things appear "out there." If they embrace your aspirations, you win; if not, you lose.[5] Nowadays this is called being "turned on," and the poet is the person who "turns on" spontaneously. Salinas "turns on," and the flight of doves is seen to be exactly what it is: the externalization of the way his mind is going at that moment. The upward flight of unconscious contents hovers a moment on the threshold. Who will win?

   We won—and here's the poem to prove it: "Cuartilla."

Chapter Eleven

THE CREATIVE MEANING

OF DIVINATION

"Cuartilla" showed us the basic mode of the sign, which is a self-evident demonstration that contact has been made with the creative unconscious. The result is a new poem. But this is a very limited example of a process that can have consequences for the evolution of one's entire consciousness, because the new content raised up can be much more than a new poem. It can be nothing less than the discovery—or confirmation—of a vocation. One is silent, and hears a calling, the calling of Someone within, that "unknown master" in the guise of the Self. The evocation of a sign suddenly teaches how the visible world and the invisible world are interdependent. If the vocation is a creative one it may consist in ringing the changes on this interdependency, recognizing that life itself gives the chance to fulfill the life of the Self, the world of the spirit made manifest in the world of our own time and place in history.

At bottom, the calling proclaims that there is no discontinuity in the nature of reality: the visible and the invisible worlds are identical, and so reality takes on a new, illuminated appearance. Every thing that is, manifests the very same Presence that underlies the observer's own consciousness. A species of vibration is evident—what Thoreau called a fine effluence: "The ultimate expression or fruit of any created thing is a fine effluence which only the most ingenuous worshipper perceives at a reverent distance from its surface even. The cause and the effect are equally evanescent and intangible. . . . Only that intellect makes any progress toward conceiving of the essence which at the same time perceives the effluence."[1] Here we find what appears to be the primary intuition underlying the old doctrine of signatures. In its most superstitious form this doctrine is nothing more than folk medicine, but it is rooted in the conviction that divine beneficence is known to us through the signs stamped on all things. As folk medicine, the doctrine of signatures is ultimately the cure of the sickness brought on by the "doctrine of duality"; duality obliterates the effluence, because duality is sophisticated, not ingenuous. For the ingenuous, the significance of each created thing consists of its role as mediator between the microcosm and the macrocosm.

Hence the poet as well as the diviner has always been recognized as a seer, for, like the diviner, the poet sees the will of the gods by observing the signs of nature. The diviner may err, practically speaking, but the underlying doctrine can no more be considered erroneous than a poem can be said to be a mistake. On the other hand, the grave mistake that ego makes is to grant an ultimate ontological validity to the doctrine of duality, thereby blinding itself to the significant presence, the ground of reality. Eliade has described the quality of preintellectual consciousness (Thoreau's "ingenuous worshipper"), which needs to dwell "in a rich and significant Cosmos; rich not only in food . . . but also in significance. . . . this Cosmos reveals itself in a cipher; it 'speaks,' it transmits its message by its formation, its states of being, its rhythms. [One] 'hears'—or 'reads'—these messages and consequently behaves towards the Cosmos as towards a coherent system of significance. . . . This cipher of the Cosmos . . . concerns para-cosmic realities."[2] Such are the "signs," the "ciphers," the "clues," and the "evidence" scattered throughout the poetry of Salinas the seer. But Salinas was not only a seer in the manner of all poets. He was a diviner, even a *haruspex*, similar to those of the pre-Christian era, as can be appreciated by studying his remarkable poem "Crepúsculo" ("Twilight"), number thirty-eight of the collection appropriately entitled *Presagios:*

Crepúsculo. Sentado en un rincón
siento en el alma el poso de este día.
Aquí a mi lado,
firme pupila la ventana abre:
lo que ella ve de afuera
lo repite en el fondo de la estancia
un viejo espejo familiar, ingenua madre
que la luz y la vida nos trasmite
pura y sin mancha.
En el espejo la mirada hundo
y en lo que veo en él: como en entraña
palpitante del mundo,
la sangre del ocaso hacia él afluye
y por encima, las iniciaciones
de vagas ilusiones estelares
y el signo del apóstata —mas no la cruz—
y el "vencerás conmigo,"
clave de todo el arco.
¿Será posible? Acaso...
Me lanzo a la ventana. Miro:
cada cosa en su sitio, como siempre;
la montaña, el poniente y la estrella primera,
otra vez me confirman esa orden
que al nacer entendí, sin nada nuevo.
¿Y lo que yo esperaba?
Miro al espejo y sólo a mí me veo
—ya se borró el crepúsculo indeciso—
en la estampa de mí que me da el rostro.
De lo demás, allí en los ojos algo...

A mi rincón me vuelvo. Que la vida
se muera lentamente en el espejo.

Twilight. Seated in a corner
I feel in my soul the sediment of this day.
Here at my side,
a steady eye opens the window:[3]
the view outdoors
is repeated in the back of the room
by an old domestic mirror, the ingenuous mother
who conveys to us light and life,
pure and spotless.
I plunge my glance into the mirror
and into what I see in it: as into the quivering
gut of the world,
there comes an afflux of sunset blood,
and above, the beginnings
of vague stellar illusions
and the sign of the Apostate—but not the Cross—
and the "You shall conquer with me,"
keystone of the entire arch.
Can it be possible? Perhaps . . .
I rush to the window. I look:
each thing in its place, as always;
the mountain, the west and the first star
again confirm for me that order
that I understood at birth, with nothing new.
And what of my expectations?
I look at the mirror and see only myself
—the fleeting twilight has faded—
in the picture of me that my face gives back.
Of the rest, something there in the eyes . . .
I go back to my corner. Let life
die slowly in the mirror.

The classic work on divination is Cicero's *De divinatione*. Though Cicero wants to debunk this ancient art, his essay nevertheless takes the form of a dialogue between two speakers, an attacker and a defender. As it turns out, the attacker represents the practical voice of ego-intellect, whereas the defender speaks in favor of the invisible world of the spirit. Quintus, the voice of the Self, so to speak, tells us: "The human soul [*animus*] is in some degree derived and drawn from a source exterior to itself. Hence we understand that outside the human soul there is a divine soul from which the human soul is sprung." No creative artist would want to argue with this premise. Quintus states what to him is obvious, inevitable. Therefore it follows, he says, that "there are gods . . . [and] they give us . . . signs; and if they give such signs, it is not true that they give us no means to understand those signs—otherwise their signs would be useless." The logic is inescapable. But disagreement arises when ego-intellect assumes that all this talk is couched in its own vocabulary, when, as a matter of fact, religious notions that spring from the belief in the "I-It" duality end up with the grossest kind of superstitious anthropomorphism. Thus is born the image of God as a patriarch. From the point of view of the Self, God is immanent, an indwelling experience. The Self is always experienced as numinous, as teeming with numina, and when any aspect of it is raised into consciousness one begins to grasp what it means to be poet, prophet, mystic—or insane. One begins to grasp what it means to speak of a continuous (i.e., not discontinuous) reality. Thus argues Quintus: "Since the universe is wholly filled with the Eternal Intelligence and the Divine Mind, it must be that human souls are influenced by their contact with divine souls." If ego-intellect will but concede the existence of the Self ("a divine power which pervades . . . our lives") then "it is not hard to understand the principle directing those premonitory signs which we see come to pass." If one could be aware of all events, one would be omniscient, "but since such knowledge is possible only to a god, it is left to [the human being] to presage the future [*futura praesentiat*] by means of certain signs which indicate what will follow them."[4]

Naturally, there is no point in obscuring the issue by debating the secular, self-seeking application of divination, and anyone is a fool who believes that the flight of birds will, in some automatic and objective way, predict a win or loss tomorrow. But the principle of divination is psychologically sound enough when one seeks to know the meaning of one's own spirit. We know that people of destiny are not infrequently awakened to their genius through witnessing a numinous sign that guided their steps and showed them the path marked out for them. Such persons are not being superstitious; rather, they are recognizing a sign pointing to their own specific means of being effective in their lifetime—effective in all the reality of their individual, entire Self. This is what we call a vocation, a calling of some voice that is not the voice of ego.

Whence comes that voice? And how did it make itself heard? The only way for Self to reach the realm of consciousness is through the sign. It cannot write consciousness a letter, cannot put through a long-distance telephone call,[5] cannot arrange for a formal debate. It can only flash up like a thunderbolt from below the threshold of consciousness. Ego-awareness is struck with amazement at the tremendous energy that the psyche can accumulate in a certain direction, and so takes this in itself as a convincing sign that this is the direction in which it ought to allow the spiritual energies to flow. The calling comes from within, but is easily projected onto reality "out there" in the form of a vision, as happened with Constantine, who realized that the sign *in hoc signo vinces* was raising to consciousness his inner drive toward conversion to Christianity. If we choose to say so, we may say that he hallucinated a vocation—which is not to say that he saw something unreal, but rather that he was enabled to grasp the most real fact about his own spirit. When the young man falls in love at first sight, he numinously experiences the unknown woman to be wearing a sign that reads, "*In hoc signo vinces.*" As in the self-bet, the sign tells you whether you win or lose.

In the poem "Madrid. Calle de. . . ," we saw how Salinas came to understand the epistemology of symbolic activity: the passage from ego to Self involved a passage from *negocio* to *ocio*, whereupon images were liberated from the bondage of ego-intellect, and the world "out there" joined the world "in here." Now this experience with the mirror is described again in the poem "Crepúsculo," except that here the speaker is concerned not with how, but rather with what. He reads natural signs as reflected in a mirror, and sees what they signify for him. It is, in effect, a poem resulting from scrying, or crystal-gazing: the use of a reflecting surface or speculum for the purpose of raising into consciousness transpersonal contents.[6]

When we set up a mirror so that it can reflect the world of nature outdoors, our contemplation of the image leads us in a transpersonal direction. This kind of mirror-gazing can be an ambiguous exercise in consciousness, as the reader can easily experience personally, for one is never quite sure what kind of reality is being represented in the looking-glass world. Of course a meditative look at world reality itself can breed the same doubts, but long custom has taught us faith in the simple subject-object dualism. The mirror-world, however, has a private depth to it; it frames itself to your eyes and it is your solitary view.

To contemplate a mirrored landscape, then, almost guarantees the inducement of the meditative spirit, for a specular landscape, being nonmaterial, is perfectly spiritual. One cannot do anything with it, and if one undertakes to contemplate a mirrored landscape for even fifteen minutes, one becomes well aware of its persistent spirituality. It sits there and asks of you the only thing it can ask: to be contemplated. It is perfectly nonfunctional. The scryer is literally a spectator, a gazer into a speculum, a looker and not an actor, a contemplative and not an active, beyond karmic involvement. Hence the mirrored landscape points to pure being. Or, to put it another way, the world when seen in a speculum insists upon showing itself to us under the aspect of pure being, the world in its suchness.

The relationship between specular divination and the world of the Self finds its classic expression in the experience recorded by the German mystic Jacob Boehme, who one day, like Saul of Tarsus, was struck blind. That is, the phenomenal reality suddenly disappeared, to be replaced by the intuitive realization of unity, and this happened by means of a speculum: "He . . . had one illumination, on Trinity Sunday, 1600, whereby he was 'enraptured . . . by means of an instantaneous glance . . . cast upon a bright pewter dish' and thus 'introduced into the innermost ground or centre of the . . . hidden nature.' "[7] Boehme himself attempted to explain the phenomenon of scrying: "In crystal or mirror-gazing, the Tincture radiates from the eyes of the gazer and collects on the surface of the crystal or mirror, and there forms a sensitive film in which the Astral scenery reflects itself; and thus reveals occasionally past, present, or future events."[8] As a scientific explanation this is of course fantastic. But we should note the significant reference to astral scenery reflecting itself, for here is where we reach the notion of a transpersonal image of nature both within and without: astral scenery is spiritual scenery (cf. the occultist use of the term *astral body*), the scenery that is continuous with the spirit of the gazer.

In "Crepúsculo" the speaker crosses the threshold and enters the astral landscape of the looking glass. Here we should recall that the twilight (like the sunrise) is itself a magic threshold, and so contributes to the specific conditions which Andrew Lang described as optimum for scrying: "It is best to go, alone, into a room, sit down with the back to the light."[9]

The room in this poem is called a *rincón*, actually the nook or corner of a room, and by extension *rincón* means "private place"—a *lugar retirado*, as the Royal Academy says—a place of withdrawal. The speaker says further that he feels in his soul the *poso* of the day, which translates as "sediment." *Poso* is cognate to "repose," and is to be contrasted to "excitement." In other words, *poso* is symbolically synonymous with *ocio*. Seated before a mirror the speaker thus finds prepared a path leading out of dualistic reality, even as Kojisei (Ming Dynasty) has written: "Water not disturbed by waves settles down of itself. A mirror not covered with dust is clear and bright. The mind should be like this. . . . Happiness [i.e., unity] must not be sought for; when what disturbs passes away, happiness comes of itself."[10]

Now the speaker sees that the view outdoors—the setting sun—is reflected in the mirror, which he calls

> the ingenuous mother
> who conveys to us light and life,
> pure and spotless.

For "spotless" the original Spanish text has *sin mancha*, "without a stain." *Mancha* is a corruption of L. *macula* (a piece of ordinary knowledge to Spanish intellectuals) and is cognate to *inmaculado*. Thus one speaks of the Immaculate Virgin, the Virgin without *mancha*, morally spotless. Here it is important to remember that *mancha*, like sin, belongs to the world of ego-consciousness. The unconscious is innocent, immaculate, does not enter into the question of moral guilt (we say, for instance, that a person is not morally responsible for any "sinful" dreams). Again, we recognize that the mirror-image seen by the scryer is really a symbol for microcosmic images born out of the unconscious. Therefore Salinas is speaking literally when he says that the mirror is an "ingenuous mother" conveying to us "light and life / pure and spotless." The scryer's speculum, like the Virgin, is the Immaculate Mother of us all, because the feminine unconscious is the matrix out of which ego-consciousness has been "fragmented." This notion of the magic mirror as the Ancient Mother of us all finds an analogue in the Orient, for, as Besterman notes, "when Amaterasu [the sun goddess] sent her children out to rule the world she gave them a mirror into which they could always look to see their mother's face and 'in consequence to find the truth.' "[11] Similarly, Budge tells us that crystal itself "was held in high esteem by the early Christians, who regarded it as a symbol of the Immaculate Conception."[12] Glass and crystal are ideally pure and unblemished, and so are the images they reflect to the selfless spectator.

The poet tells us that his attention is diverted from the real sunset to the specular image. He plunges his glance into that reality "as into the quivering / gut of the world," and sees a visceral microcosm, then a transpersonal sign: "the sign of the Apostate."

Julian the Apostate (331–363), the nephew of Constantine the Great, turned away from Christianity (which Constantine had begun to naturalize) because of his devotion to the earlier gods of the Romans. He had been educated in Athens into the ancient pagan religion. He was a sincere practitioner of the old rites, an initiate into the pagan mysteries, and was himself a *haruspex*. In Gibbon's *Decline and Fall of the Roman Empire* we learn how Julian, who had actually been initiated into the Eleusinian rites, had consecrated his life to the worship of the gods. A man involved with public life, he was extraordinarily aggressive, above all as a courageous general; at the same time, however, he devoted himself regularly to private worship. Throughout his short career he continued to sacrifice to the gods. Gibbon tells us, "While the occupations of war, of government, and of study, seemed to claim the whole measure of his time, a stated portion of the hours of the night was invariably reserved for the exercise of private devotions."[13]

Julian never undertook political enterprises without consulting the gods, which is to say, their omens: "Amidst the . . . crowd of priests . . . it was the business of the emperor to bring the wood, to blow the fire, to handle the knife, to slaughter the victim, and, thrusting his bloody hands into the bowels of the expiring animal, to draw forth the heart or liver, and to read, with the consummate skill of an haruspex, the imaginary signs of future events."[14] "The imaginary signs," says Gibbon. But obviously to Julian these signs were not imaginary in the sense that Gibbon means the word.

Now in "Crepúsculo" the speaker says that he sees in the mirror "the sign of the Apostate," which is something of an interpretive problem, since Julian is not known to have had any one particular sign. Throughout his career he had several signs. His uncle Constantine, on the other hand, is famous for the sign by which he would win: the Cross. Salinas says that when he himself looked into the mirrored sunset he saw "the" sign of the Apostate *and* the sign of Constantine—but not the Cross. Evidently we are dealing with "sign" in the generic sense: communication from the Self.

The explanation for this vision seems to lie in the nature of the poetic vocation itself. The poet is the human being who discovers a special calling transcending the common task of getting on in the world, and this is, that the individual consciousness is to be an instrument whereby the Self is made manifest. This may be seen as a sacrifice of the integrity of ego-identity so jealously guarded by the common lot of us. Ego-identity—selfishness—is regularly or occasionally sacrificed to the task, which suggests why the French poet Albert Giraud characterized poets as crucified victims: "Beautiful verses are great crosses / Whereon the poets bleed."[15]

Salinas tells us that he experienced the specular image of the flaming sunset as a *haruspex* might do: he saw it as the "quivering gut of the world," as an "afflux of sunset blood." This clearly parallels the experience of Julian the Apostate who, in search of omens, would "slaughter the victim," thrust "his bloody hands into the bowels of the expiring victim," and "draw forth the heart or liver" in order to read the signs.

Constantine's sign was allegedly in the form of an illuminated scroll about the Cross. Salinas says that when he looked into the sunset reflected in the mirror he saw the *in hoc signo vinces*, "but not the Cross." He senses that the numinous sign vouchsafed him is a triumph ("You shall conquer with me")—but it is free of the Cross.

On the most obvious level we could read "but not the Cross" as a rejection of conventional Christianity, but this seems unnecessarily tendentious when attributed to a person of Salinas's spiritual and intellectual sophistication. There is a better interpretation to be made in the light of the *ocio/negocio* dialectic. Salinas knew that he had the poet's vocation; and when one possesses a strong vocation that cannot possibly make one's fortune the question naturally arises: to what extent is one willing to sacrifice ego-pursuits to that vocation? The creative vocation, like the religious, poses the problem: how much *otium* and how much *nec-otium*? In the United States this question came to have considerable importance for two very successful insurance executives, Charles Ives and Wallace Stevens. The latter expressed the *otium/nec-otium* problem with his gentle irony: "I have no life except in poetry. No doubt that would be true if my whole life was free for poetry."[16]

In "Crepúsculo" Salinas sees that the auspices are favorable; the poet will out, he will win. But the speaker will not set his whole life free for his art, just as Ives and Stevens would not. The supreme sacrifice is not called for: "not the Cross." I have already quoted Robert Graves to the effect that being a poet involves "a particular mode of living and thinking." As T. S. Eliot put it, "The progress of an artist is a continual self-sacrifice, a continual extinction of personality."[17] "Beautiful verses are great crosses / Whereon the poets bleed."

Salinas rejects the supreme sacrifice, then. He may seek unity, he may even be mystically inclined, but he is not a mystic nor even yet a poet-mystic inclined to sacrifice himself on the cross of the poetic obsession. He is one of those "others" described by St. Augustine, who distinguished between the mystic (the sacrificer of self, the selfless one) and the mystically inclined: "Some of the least ones, who yet perseveringly walk in the path of faith, come to that most blessed contemplation: while others who have knowledge of what invisible, unchangeable, incorporeal nature is, but refuse to follow the path leading to the abode of such happiness, which seems folly to them, viz. Christ crucified, are not able to come to the shrine of that quiet, although their mind is already, as at a distance, touched by the ray of its light."[18]

R. C. Zaehner notes in *Mysticism Sacred and Profane* that a chasm separates the theistic mystic from the natural mystic. "Mystical religion proper . . . shows that the mystical state at which the religious [person] aims is the reverse of the natural mystical experience: it is the cutting off of one's ties with the world, the settling in quietness in one's own immortal soul, and finally the offering of that soul up to its Maker."[19] This is why Salinas, as a poet inclined to natural mysticism, as a Spaniard with a strong background of institutionalized religion, and as a scholar with a sound knowledge of the Spanish mystic tradition, must sense the line that divides his own kind of spiritual quest from that of the self-sacrificing seeker, whether this be a theistic mystic or a mad poet. He was powerfully drawn in two directions, those of secular involvement (ego-realization), and of Self-realization. An existential struggle develops in which the demands of the Self, that "unknown master," appear as an unreasonable sacrifice—the very Cross. It is the sacrifice that had been known throughout the Renaissance as the "madness of the Cross," the madness that required "human reason to abandon its pride and its certainties in order to lose itself in the great unreason of sacrifice."[20]

In "Crepúsculo" Salinas states that the motto "You shall conquer with me" is the "keystone of the entire arch." Within the context of the Romans Julian and Constantine the arch is of course the Arch of Triumph. Within the context of heavenly phenomena and omens, a second meaning emerges: the vault of heaven. The keystone is the central support of the arch, and so Salinas's statement equating the motto and the keystone is actually a truism. To undergo the numinous vision in the zenith of the heavenly vault is in itself the triumph of which he speaks, not only a promise of future proximity to the "other side," the world of the Self, but in itself the sign that it has happened. It is an illumination, an initial enlightenment, the raising of the

Self into consciousness. To maintain this as a living force in one's life is to attain to the way of unity. But this is not the path of Salinas.

He is rightly amazed by this illumination, by realizing, in a flash, what *triumph* actually means. "Can it be possible?" he thinks to himself, and rushes to the window to compare empirical reality with the vision he has seen in the mirror. The illumination has passed; all he sees is "each thing in its place, as always."

"As always"—back to the secular world-order "that I understood at birth." Salinas was not one to dwell, like Wordsworth, on the magic of his own childhood. For him the child is someone in the process of learning to cope with the world of *logos*, of civilized reality; someone who, by virtue of innate intellect, is already beyond the brute consciousness of the dumb animals. And so in "Crepúsculo" the poet awakens from his illumination to find himself again in the same old world that he has always known, "with nothing new."

He turns to the mirror, this time treating it as a cosmetic glass (it is no longer on vacation) and he sees what he calls "only myself," the individual who negotiates his own world reality. He perceives a vestige of the illumination ("something there in the eyes"), and it sends him back to his corner. "Let life / die slowly in the mirror."

This line is ambiguous, and must be interpreted from context. Since the return to his corner is linked with life's dying in the mirror, we can only surmise that by "life" he means karmic involvement—*negocio*. He is in the immediate aftermath of an illuminating experience, and settles back into the meditative posture. In the final thought expressed the key word seems to be *lentamente*—which in a meditative context we take to mean "in its own good time." That is to say, in *ocio* there is nothing to be pursued, no motivated effort. In meditative unity the effort of acting must be relinquished.

This is the attitude expressed forthrightly in an early poem, "Quietud" (No. 14 of *Seguro azar*), in which the poet, setting aside all intention, says:

> Me llama un ocio, un quehacer
> de no hacer nada, de estarse
> como agua pura, ni río,
> ola ni torrente, agua
> quieta esperando que pasen
> por arriba alas o nubes,
> las almas que tengo fuera.
>
> An *ocio* calls me, a task
> of doing nothing, of just being
> like pure water, neither river
> nor wave, nor yet a torrent; still
> water awaiting the passage

above of wings or clouds,
the souls I have out there.

Again we find the speaker expressing the technique of how to take a
vacation, how to sit vacantly, how to let life die slowly in the quiet mirror of
the mind, even as Miguel de Molinos taught his Quietists: "Quietude of the
spirit, indispensable for attaining interior peace, can be obtained only by
calming it, by isolating it from life, until it is emptied of sensations and
affects. Meditation must be the means."[21] Isolate the spirit from "life." That
is, from karmic involvement. Let ego-intentions die slowly in the mirror.
The way of poetry is not qualitatively different from the way of Quietism; but
the dream of Salinas the poet will not be actualized in a self-sacrificing way of
the Cross.

Chapter Twelve

WORLD-AS-MIND

LOS SIGNOS

¿Ya te cansa, mundo, ser
enorme sueño indistinto?
¡Tantos espacios ofreces,
invitación, a los signos!

De día y de noche, playas,
páginas de lisa arena.
Las cubren olas y olas,
de curvas coplas concéntricas.

¡Qué cargada de iniciales,
de corazones y fechas,
la corteza del aliso,
cronista de amor agraz,
historiador de parejas!

Frescos pliegos, extendidos
céspedes, en la pradera.
Sol, ramas, hojas y sombras,
en ellos cuentan historia
de trémulas peripecias.

Pendolista, la mañana
sobre lámina de alberca
se inclina, y en trazos finos
de viento marcero, apunta
esdrújulas agudezas.

Aspero riscal, ¡qué blando
a escrituras, cuando nieva!
Penígeros, luna y sol
con letras de oro y de plata
lo convierten en leyenda.

A ese cándido papel
aun el candor se le aumenta,
si siente posarse el verso
que del vacío le salve
y a inmortalidad le ascienda.

¿Qué esperanza de ser fábula
mantiene al mundo rodando?
Abierto y sin prisa espera,
tan en blanco,
que sus más ocultas glorias
al fin se le vuelvan poema.

From *Confianza* (1955)

SIGNS

Are you getting tired, world, of being
an enormous, vague sleep?
You hold out so many places,
as an invitation, to signs!

By day and by night, beaches,
pages of smooth sand.
Wave after wave covers them
with curved concentric ballads.

How loaded with initials,
with hearts and dates,
the bark of the alder tree,
chronicler of young love,
historian of couples!

Like fresh sheets of paper, wide
lawns in the meadow.
Sun, branches, leaves and shadows
relate there the story
of tremulous peripeties.

A copyist, the morning
leans down upon the sheen
of the pool, and in the fine hand
of March wind, notes down
witty proparoxytones.

Rude crags, how you yield
to writing when it snows!
On wings moon and sun
with letters of gold and silver
transform you into legend.

Even that white paper
grows whiter yet
if it feels the verse alight
which might save it from the void
and elevate it to immortality.

What hope of being fable
keeps the world turning round?
Open and unhurried it hopes,
so blank,
that its most hidden glories
may at last turn into a poem.

Salinas found that his vocation to be a poet was confirmed by a sign, meaning that the vocation itself was to consist in reading the signs of reality, the "fine effluence," the "vibrations," the auras in which the natural world is steeped. Strangely enough auras as such can at present be photographed by means of the Kirlian technique; but it is one matter to document their existence scientifically and quite another to experience them.[1] The Kirlian photographer builds a better mousetrap and with it captures the auras in spite of themselves, but the value of experiencing the "fine effluence" lies in the kind of spirit required to do the thing: a spirit at one with instinct so that the natural world is indeed one's home, the outward expression of what one is as a terrestrial being, the kind of being who experiences the self as part of the world fable.

In a late poem, "Los signos," Salinas goes beyond the reading of signs in any specialized sense. He considers the plain fact that everything constitutes a *signo*, and that a world without signs ipso facto has no significance. "Los signos" returns to the idea behind the title of 1931, *Fábula y signo*, for the natural world appears as seeking to become a fable (line 34), which means it awakens in the unified consciousness of the seer.

We have noted in passing that this is common to the Transcendentalism familiar to Americans, for it is a kind of ecology of the spirit that Thoreau characterized as follows: "What is the relation between a bird and the ear that appreciates its melody . . .? Certain they are intimately related, and the one was made for the other. It is a natural fact. If I were to discover that a certain kind of stone by the pond-shore was affected, say partially disintegrated, by a particular natural sound, . . . I see that one could not be completely described without describing the other. I am that rock by the pond-side."[2] The human being is evidently the only creature on the face of the planet that can apperceive the natural world as spirit. Such being the case, Transcendentalist and poet alike find it easy to believe that this spiritualization of the world is the final cause for the existence of the human mind. When one perceives the "ecology of the spirit," the nonmaterial network that binds us to nature, one does it by reading the signs that have been set everywhere. George Russell's credo expresses this concisely: "I believe of nature that it is a manifestation of Deity, and that, because we are partakers in the divine nature, all we see has affinity with us; and though now we are as children who look upon letters before they have learned to read, to the illuminated spirit its own being is clearly manifested in the universe even as I recognise my thought in the words I write."[3]

When Rainer Maria Rilke (1875–1926) received illumination and thereafter wrote the *Duino Elegies*, he declared the poetic task in the Ninth Elegy, which begins with the question, Why *have* to be human?

Not because happiness really
exists. . . .
Not out of curiosity, not just to practise the heart . . .[4]

Why then, have to be human? His answer is, in effect, In order to be Here Now. The *Hiersein*, being here, is of the utmost importance for Rilke,

> . . .because being here amounts to so much, because all this Here and Now, so fleeting, seems to require us and strangely concerns us.   (ll. 11–13)

The Here and Now is unified consciousness in the Eternal Present, which is the only place spirit is to be experienced. It is spiritual ecstasy, and Rilke, after the manner of the mystics, uses the erotic analogy:

> Is not the secret purpose
> of this sly earth, in urging a pair of lovers,
> just to make everything leap with ecstasy in them?   (ll. 36–38)

The erotic ecstasy of the lovers fulfills libido, the vital force, and in the same way the poet's consciousness is consummated in the word of Here and Now:

> Are we, perhaps, here just for saying: House,
> Bridge, Fountain, Gate, Jug, Olive tree, Window,—
> possibly: Pillar, Tower? . . . But for saying, remember,
> oh, for such saying as never the things themselves
> hoped so intensely to be.   (ll. 32–36)

This spiritualization of reality means turning reality into the spirit:

> Earth, isn't this what you want: an invisible
> re-arising in us? Is it not your dream
> to be one day invisible? Earth! invisible!
> What is your urgent command, if not transformation?   (ll. 68–71)

The transformation into the spirit is what Thoreau calls "translation," using the word in its earlier sense of "conveying to heaven" (Heb. 11:5, "By faith Enoch was translated that he should not see death"). "I have a common-place-book for facts and another for poetry, but I find it difficult always to preserve the vague distinction which I had in my mind, for the most interesting and beautiful facts are so much the more poetry and that is their success. They are *translated* from earth to heaven. I see that if my facts were sufficiently vital and significant,—perhaps transmuted more into the substance of the human mind,—I should need but one book of poetry to contain them all."[5] Here Thoreau comes very close to using "heaven" and "human mind" interchangeably, since both heaven and the human mind (in the state of nonego) are equally the abode of the spirit, or perhaps we could say that when the human mind experiences unified consciousness it is in a state of grace and the spirit fills it.

In "Los signos" Salinas brings us back to the fable. Fable is, as we have seen, the natural world speaking or "fabulating" to us, and it does this through signs. In our nightly dreams we are aware that our instinctual self is speaking to us with signs, images, or symbols. This awareness expresses itself in the quality taken on by the dream; if a dream-image creates an anxiety state, that anxiety itself is the intuitive understanding of the symbol. And in similar fashion the quality of consciousness in the midst of a fabulous world grasps that things are turning into signs, being "transmuted into the substance of the human mind." The metaphor of reading signs is not, then, a mere comparison made for sake of clarity; like the numinous dream the sign-reading is an actual spiritual experience. Fitz Hugh Ludlow, after his illumination, drew the contrast: "I looked abroad on fields, and water, and sky, and read in them a most startling meaning. I wondered how I had ever regarded them in the light of dead matter, at the farthest only *suggesting* lessons."[6] Ludlow emphasizes *suggesting* here, indicating that he was suddenly cured of thinking that all talk of signs was nothing more than simile. To the same end George Russell insists, through repetition, on the experiential reality of reading signs: "The visible world became like a tapestry blown and stirred by winds behind it. If it would but raise for an instant I knew I would be in Paradise. Every form on that tapestry appeared to be the work of gods. Every flower was a word, a thought. The grass was speech; the trees were speech; the waters were speech; the winds were speech."[7]

Here we have the meaning for the Self of Saint Paul's definition of faith as "the evidence of things not seen" (Heb. 11:1). The ego-meaning has it that one ought to take the matter on faith—even on something called blind faith. But to unified consciousness the invisible signs are simply the evidence of themselves; they are Self-evident—what Spanish translations of Scripture give as the demonstration or proof of things not seen. Faith is not based on the demonstration; the demonstration is faith showing itself.

The first strophe of Salinas's poem "Los signos" asks:

Are you getting tired, world, of being
an enormous, vague sleep?
You hold out so many places,
as an invitation, to signs!

The second line of the original Spanish says, "enorme sueño indistinto." *Sueño* (from L. *somnus*; cf. Eng. "somnolent") means both "sleep" and "dream"; here I prefer the former meaning, since the contrast is between the initial "tired of being a *sueño*," and the final "hope of being *fábula*." The world as apprehended by secular consciousness lies in a dreamless sleep, whereas the poet awakens to dream reality, which is to see it and therefore experience it as if in a dream. In the dream we do not simply see things; we

live them. They are Earth arising invisibly within us. This is how the poet
dreams reality while wide awake, seeing the surfaces (*espacios*) as carriers of
signs, at which point spirit is perceived to be the obvious presence that it is.
At this level of discovery all poets tend to speak alike; Denise Levertov
(b. 1923), on observing the flight of birds, writes in her poem "The Open
Secret":

My sign!
    —yours, too—
anyone's—
    aloft in the coppery
afterglow, gulls or pigeons,
    too high to tell. . . .

She closes by repeating the message:

   . . . —a sign
if I look up—
    or you—
anyone.[8]

The open secret of the fabulating signs is an open invitation to all. Unified
consciousness knows that it is experiencing something universal, not
idiosyncratic ("if I look up— / or you— / anyone"), just as Salinas, in his
poem "Vocación" (No. 4 of *Seguro azar*), says the poetic task consists in
bringing an unfinished world into being:

un mundo sin acabar,
necesitado, llamándome
a mí, o a ti, o a cualquiera. . . .

an unfinished world,
in need, calling
to me, or to you, or to anyone. . . .

After the initial strophe, the poem "Los signos" catalogs the world as a vast
series of blank surfaces that get written upon. In the second strophe water
writes on the beach; in the third lovers write on the tree trunk; in the fourth
the sun writes on the meadow; in the fifth the wind writes on the water; in
the sixth moon and sun write on the snow; and in the final strophes the poet
writes on the paper.

Apparent throughout the poem is the distinction between *natura na-
turans* and *natura naturata*: nature as a vital force that is constantly cre-
ating, and nature as the phenomenal world of things. The distinction goes
back to antiquity, as does the notion that the universe is composed of four

elements: earth, air, fire, and water. These elements do not represent four analogous categories, however, since the element earth contrasts in many ways to the other three. Earth means form, stability, and repose. The other three elements are unstable; they are motion, change, and formlessness, and were grouped together of old as the *volatilia*, the volatile elements.

The element earth, moreover, is the material with which the other elements work. The mysterious and dynamic phenomenon called life comes to pass in earth as a result of the never-ceasing metamorphoses of light, air, and water. Thanks only to these can earth be something more than inert mass, something more than a heap of stones—organic life, and not rocks. The three elements come down to earth to perform their labors, and then they escape again into the infinite, into the unknown. This Earth of ours is only a stone fallen into a maelstrom of vitalizing metamorphoses, and one day, when it goes forth from that maelstrom, it will return to its original state of inertia.

Earth, in short, is the historical element. An infinite number of times it comes forth out of the unknown, out of the formless; it lives out a life, and then sinks back into darkness. Heraclitus said that the principle of the universe was fire, and perhaps he was right. Earth came forth from fire, and she will perish in it, and one day she will be no more than a dying ember in our flaming universe—and then, a handful of cold ashes. But fire, air, and water are eternal, not historical; they fructify and destroy and fructify anew. They are change; earth is that which is changed.

Readers who know the romantic poetry of Gustavo Adolfo Bécquer (1835–1870) will doubtless recognize in what I say here the principle of his *Rimas*, dwelling on the *volatilia*. *Rima* XXIV has the catalog form that characterizes so much of Bécquer's work:

Two tongues of fire
curled on a trunk, approach;
and when they kiss
they make a single flame.

Two notes as one
are plucked upon the lute;
they meet in space,
and fuse in harmony.

Two waves advance
to die upon the shore;
they break together,
crowned with shining crest.

Two wisps of vapor
rise from off the lake,
and in the sky
they form a silver cloud.

Two thoughts spring up together;
Two kisses sound as one;
Two echoes intermingle:
Our two souls.[9]

The lovers are not *like* the volatiles; they *are* the volatiles in human form. It is this message that is repeated in Salinas's "Los signos," where all "writings," as the fruit of self-transcendence, are equally significant, and so the lovers are included in the catalog. It appears to be a modern continuation of Bécquer's poetic intuition.

In the seventh strophe of "Los signos" we note Salinas's use of *vacío* ("void"), and the idea of salvation. Here we must avoid the animism that has proven attractive to a number of Salinas's critics. The white sheet of paper is one more surface; the void is here negative, and corresponds to the dreamless sleep of the first strophe. The void and the signs are not "out there" in the world, obviously; they always have reference to the quality of human consciousness, and it is this latter that is saved through unity, through awakening. Said Ludlow, using the metaphor of sleep: "What a world of symbols, then, lies sleeping in expectancy of the approaching times which shall bring some translator to their now unnoticed sermons, and bid them speak of unconceived beauties and truths!"[10] The translator is the poet, of course, and all the writing that goes on in the Eternal Present—the sudden events, the "tremulous peripeties" of the fourth strophe—all this writing is being done on one surface: the poet's own mind. The poet is the one who is literate, the one who can read and translate.

Hence "Los signos" is not to be characterized as an elaborate conceit, or many-sided allegory. It tells us in greater detail what the poem by Ikkyu tells us:

The mind,—
What shall we call it?
It is the sound of the breeze
That blows through the pines
In the indian ink picture.[11]

The human mind is here the *pneuma*, the *spiritus* that creates the picture, and it is perceived in the painting, but it is the same force that created the real pines "out there," and unified consciousness perceives it there too.

Thus the poet is engaged in penetrating the significance of the world. Without the human mind in unity, the world has no significance and lies in a dreamless sleep, but with the arrival of the poetic imagination the volatiles suddenly begin to write the poem. The poet is the savior, just as Rilke says:

These things that live on departure
understand when you praise them; fleeting, they look for
rescue through something in us, the most fleeting of all.   (ll. 63–65)

Rilke says literally that these things look to us for *ein Rettendes*, from *retten*, "to save, rescue, deliver, preserve." This is not a poet bragging of his elite vocation. The poet means all of us—you, myself, anyone; he means the human mind that penetrates the surface of things, the mind that apprehends Mind in the world, that sees something more than an "environment." It is this that makes the white paper—*cándido papel*—of the seventh strophe whiter yet—greater in candor, just as Thoreau spoke of how only the most ingenuous worshiper could perceive the "fine effluence" of reality. Unified consciousness strongly suspects that this is why we are here, that the human mind was evolved so that Spirit could contemplate itself in the spirits of men and women.

Hence it seems to Salinas that the poetic feat is the realization of a hope always latent in the reality that lies sleeping. It turns into a poem, which is the tremulous Here at last furnished with words.

Chapter Thirteen

PENETRATING THE ILLUSION
OF WORLD REALITY

FIGURACIONES

Parecen nubes. Veleras,
voladoras, lino, pluma,
al viento, al mar, a las ondas
—parecen el mar— del viento,
al nido, al puerto, horizontes,
certeras van como nubes.

Parecen rumbos. Taimados
los aires soplan al sesgo,
el sur equivoca al norte,
alas, quillas, trazan rayas,
—aire, nada, espuma, nada—,
sin dondes. Parecen rumbos.

Parece el azar. Flotante
en brisas, olas, caprichos,
¡qué disimulado va,
tan seguro, a la deriva
querenciosa del engaño!
¡Qué desarraigado, ingrávido,
entre voces, entre imanes,
entre orillas, fuera, arriba,
suelto! Parece el azar.

   No. 2, *Seguro azar* (1924–1928)

FANTASIES

They look like clouds. Sailing,
flying, canvas, feather,
to the wind, to the sea, to the waves
—they look like the sea—of the wind,
to the nest, to the port, horizons,
they go straightaway like clouds.

They look like charted courses. Craftily
the breezes blow on the bias,
south mistakes north,
wings, keels, they trace lines
—air, nothing, foam, nothing—,
there is no "where." They look like charted
   courses.

It looks like chance. Floating
in breezes, waves, caprices,
how furtively it goes,
so sure, drifting along,
homing in on deceit!
How uprooted, weightless,
among voices, among magnets,
between edges, outside, above,
loose! It looks like chance.

With the poem "Figuraciones" we find ourselves on the verge of discussing unity exclusively, for this piece lies right on the threshold between the experience of the world-as-sign and the overwhelming illumination of unified consciousness. Here the speaker talks of forms in the world "out there," and of the ambiguity of their meaning for human awareness. Things are not what they seem; he realizes this. But if things are not what they seem, why is this so, and how is it that they seem like anything at all in the first place?

But he speaks not only of things—multiple reality—"out there," and of what they may or may not seem to be. In the third section of the poem the discourse suddenly shifts to the singular, an unidentified "it." "It looks like chance." Since in Spanish there is no need to use the subject pronoun, it is as if one ventured to observe colloquially in English, "Looks like chance, doesn't it?" What then is the implied subject? The entire poem is concerned with the activity going on out there in the world, and any purpose for it seems to elude the observer. Further, in the last section of the poem the speaker puts forth the notion of furtiveness, of deceit. In what sense may we say that the immense activity of the natural world has anything to do with deception? This relates to our idea of reality in the world. Normally our secular view of the real is not to be called into question. But in the state of altered consciousness this secular view is seen to be nothing more than that: a limited point of view that serves only practical ends. How can it be so wrong? How can one live for many years taking for granted a gross misconception of reality? If this can be, it must be because whatever it is that is deceiving us is a virtuoso in deception.

But it is possible to awaken, to realize that there is indeed a deception going on all the time. The normal illusion of the world reality that we accept has long been identified as such by the Hindus, who call it *maya*, which can be variously translated as "illusion, trick, artifice, deceit, deception, fraud, jugglery, sorcery, witchcraft."[1] The term *maya* is generally applied by the Hindus to our everyday world of duality, of mind-body, of "I-It." The underlying unity, the ground of reality, churns forth myriad forms that are illusions—a notion strongly resisted by the Western mentality, because we misunderstand what is meant. We occidentals give an ego-meaning to the term, and reply that anything that actually affects us (such as a bomb dropped on us) can hardly be called an "illusion." But when the Hindus speak of *maya* they are not concerned with our cause and effect. "Illusion" is from L. *ludere, lusus*, "to play," and the world of duality is like the playing of fountains. If we fall into the fountain we get wet—that is no illusion in our sense of the word—but that is not to deny that the fountain is indeed playing. The word *maya* expresses awareness that the world of duality is secondary, not primary—something that mystics, sensitives, and artists know and take for granted. When ego drops away from consciousness one perceives that duality, no matter how much it affects one, is a kind of smoke screen behind which there lives quite another reality.

Because unified consciousness is an experience, not mere speculation, my exposition must constantly include testimony, and with respect to *maya* the following seems cogent. One young American experimenter, E. Robert Sinnet, saw that in unity his "perceptual constancies" were an illusion, because they were now perceived to be "an oversimplification of the sensory world." By way of explanation he remarked, "The best analogy I can make is that after once seeing the set for the Bonanza show on location, I have found the illusion of the Western adventure somewhat fragile and harder to maintain than it was prior to visiting the set, where the illusion-creating implements were visible and obvious."[2] The words *visible* and *obvious* are important here, and I will return to them in my discussion of the poem "Figuraciones." For the moment, however, I would like to quote another observation on the illusion of routine reality. "How much depends upon the way things are presented in this world can be seen from the very fact that coffee drunk out of wine-glasses is really miserable stuff, as is meat cut at the table with a pair of scissors. Worst of all, as I once actually saw, is butter spread on a piece of bread with an old though very clean razor."[3] Profane reality itself is the result of "the way things are presented in this world," that being the way of duality, which Salinas, like other poets, is constantly overcoming in his poems. One must see through the way things are presented in this world. Coffee in a wine-glass is no different from coffee in a mug; nor is Self in a psyche different from Self in a tree.

Alan Watts, experiencing unity and the "cosmic *joie de vivre*," looks at the ordinary American neighborhood around him and sees through the illusion of reality pretending to be secular: "—nothing around here but just us folks! I can see people just pretending not to see that they are avatars of Brahma, Vishnu, and Shiva, the the cells of their bodies aren't millions of gods, that the dust isn't a haze of jewels. How solemnly they would go through the act of not understanding me if I were to step up and say, 'Well, who do you think you're kidding? Come off it, Shiva, you old rascal! It's a great act, but it doesn't fool me.' But the conscious ego doesn't know that it is something which that divine organ, the body, is only pretending to be."[4]

Just so, in his poem "Figuraciones" Salinas is concerned with revealing to the world at large the trickery underlying the primary illusion called *maya*. We think that everything depends upon the dualistic reality of ego-intellect, and yet it is really the splendid show being put on by a prestidigitator who is also deceived by the show. The poem is dominated by the verb *parecer*, "to seem," "to look like." "They look like clouds," he begins; "they look like the sea"; "they look like charted courses"; and "it looks like chance." But these forms only *look* like that. A master magician is deceiving us, but the speaker is not fooled. Like Alan Watts, he is in on the trick.

When one sees beyond duality one sees that everything is inevitable, that there is no such thing as chance. But to deny the existence of chance—what is this a denial of? What does the word *chance* actually mean, after all? Webster defines it as "the apparent absence of cause or design," and the operative word here is *apparent* (from L. *apparens*), cognate to the verb *parecer* Salinas employs throughout his poem. Even the breezes that blow are only apparently blowing in random directions. The breezes, frequently used as the symbol of fickleness and capricious changeability appear to be acting at random, casually, just as the prestidigitator wants to convey the impression that his "patter" and moving about are casual, while all the time he is practicing the elemental art of diverting our attention from what is really taking place.

Now, it is banal to say that "nothing happens by chance," that Fate is always at work, etc. It is one of those spurious ideas used to introduce a homily on Providence or Destiny. But Salinas is not simply saying that chance is apparent. He is trying to reveal an ontological point of view concerning the one ground of reality and the illusion of multiplicity that appears to overlay it and hide it. The multiplicity of forms, of figures scattered against the background of the One, produces the optical illusion that takes place when concentrated attention causes an alternating leap back and forth between figure and ground. To apprehend the one and the multiple in this way is to see that dualism is an "illusion-creating implement" suddenly become "visible and obvious," like the off-camera trappings of a television show—our Western Adventure, to use Sinnet's words in the largest sense. One is in on a secret, and the secret is not that nothing happens by chance, but rather that one's customary point of view (ego-intellect) is seen to be a kind of magician creating the illusion that the figures we see have no ground. But the visual penetration by nonego consciousness of these figures normally monopolizing our field of vision suddenly opens up interstices, as it were, and the more one concentrates on these the wider they open until they are like yawning chasms, while the previously solid figures are no more than the merest shadows that sometimes look like the charted courses of ego-intellect and sometimes look like random movement. Then when the visual leap is made back to customary reality the ground fades away. But one is left with the conviction that "reality" is a piece of mighty trickery.

The first two sections of the poem are concerned with the multiple play of *maya*, the figures. In line 13 the speaker switches from figure to ground; not now "they look like," but rather " *it* looks like." In line 7 Salinas has already used the word *taimado*, which means "sly, slick, crafty," or (as the Royal Academy puts it) "bellaco, astuto, disimulado y pronto en advertirlo todo," which is to say, "cunning, astute, underhanded, and quick to take note of everything." *It* is very foxy, indeed. Subsequently, in line 15, Salinas uses *taimado*'s synonym, *disimulado*, meaning "crafty, dissembling, pretending to be other than it is":

> ¡qué disimulado va,
> tan seguro, a la deriva
> querenciosa del engaño!

> how furtively it goes,
> so sure, drifting along,
> homing in on deceit!

Querencioso is derived from *querencia* (and this from *querer*, "to love, to want"), meaning "one's favorite haunt," and is applied both to human beings and animals, as a homing-pigeon is said to have its *querencia*, the place to which it will always return. *Querencia* is what we consider to be our territory. So when Salinas, in defining "it" for us, says that its movement toward deceit is *querenciosa*, he is saying that "its" main movement, the whole idea behind "it," is to deceive us. It is foxy, like the master illusionist, and most important to its foxiness is to give the appearance of casualness. Indeed, without this wonderful ease with which the illusionist performs, the show would be a failure. Amateur magicians, beginners, never quite manage to hide their effort, and without the urbane and casual concealment of course there is no magic effect at all. Hence Salinas sees "it" as "dissembling," *a la deriva*, just "drifting along"—or in the words of Alan Watts, "nothing around here but just us folks!"

Since this poem appears in the book *Seguro azar* ("Dependable chance") it is noteworthy that Salinas here applies the word *seguro* to "it," not to chance:

> It looks like chance. Floating
> in breezes, waves, caprices,
> how furtively it goes,
> so sure . . .

In this context *seguro* must be given the appropriate shade of meaning: not simply "sure," but "self-assured," "self-confident." "It" is quite confident of its ability to put on a marvelous display of entertaining deception, to play masterfully upon our willingness to be deceived. But when we see behind the scenes, we react accordingly: "It's a great act, but it doesn't fool me." One sees that "it looks like—appears to be—chance," which means only that "it" deceives us into thinking that "it" is not there at all. We see that "it" is "uprooted," which is to say that it has no roots in the forms of multiplicity, the normally solid-seeming reality in which we think everything is rooted.

Being nameless, "it" is never named in the poem. Only that which exists in duality can be named. What Salinas says of "it" indirectly is similar to the circumlocutions of Lao Tzu. Salinas tells us that the forms of *maya* seem to be charted courses, appear to be on the way to somewhere, but if you attempt to follow these courses they will never lead you to any destination, because there is no "where." Just so, Lao Tzu says at the beginning of the *Tao Te Ching*, "There are ways but the Way is uncharted."[5] It cannot be named, for "nameless indeed is the source of creation." It is not a part of *maya*, says Salinas, for it is "loose," it is free and unencumbered. So says Lao Tzu:

> Something there is, whose veiled creation was
> Before the earth or sky began to be;

So silent, so aloof and so alone,
It changes not, nor fails, but touches all:
Conceive it as the mother of the world.[6]

"It looks like chance," but *chance* is a secular term that refers negatively to the possibility of knowing "it" rationally. Speculation is futile, but experience divulges the secret.

Part Four
Unified Consciousness

Chapter Fourteen

THE GROUND OF REALITY

¿QUÉ PÁJAROS?	WHAT BIRDS?
¿El pájaro? ¿Los pájaros?	The bird? The birds?
¿Hay sólo un solo pájaro en el mundo	Is there only one single bird in the world,
que vuela con mil alas, y que canta	that flies with a thousand wings, and that sings
con incontables trinos, siempre solo?	with myriad trills, always alone?
¿Son tierra y cielo espejos? ¿Es el aire	Are earth and sky mirrors? Is the air
espejeo del aire, y el gran pájaro	a mirage of the air, and does the great one bird
único multiplica	multiply
su soledad en apariencias miles?	its solitude in thousands of appearances?
(¿Y por eso	(And so for that reason
lo llamamos los pájaros?)	we call it "the birds"?)
¿O quizá no hay un pájaro?	Or perhaps there isn't one bird?
¿Y son ellos,	And they are
fatal plural inmenso, como el mar,	a necessary, immense plural, like the sea,
bandada innúmera, oleaje de alas,	an innumerable flock, a tide of wings,
donde la vista busca y quiere el alma	where the eyes seek and the spirit tries
distinguir la verdad del solo pájaro,	to distinguish the truth of the single bird,
de su esencia sin fin, del uno hermoso?	of its unending essence, of the beautiful one?
From *Confianza* (1955)	

In *I and Thou*, Martin Buber seeks to explain the difference between living in the world in an "I-Thou" relationship and living in it in an "I-It" relationship. For the reader who already knows by experience what Buber is talking about, there is no problem in understanding. But for the ingenuous reader who attempts intellectually to penetrate the meaning of "I-Thou" the book appears to be a conundrum without an answer. This is so because when we speak of the "I-Thou" relationship ego-intellect naturally cannot help but think that a relationship is involved. *Relationship* presupposes a tie between two separate entities; whereas Buber wants to articulate the difference between a relationship and a fusion, in which there are no longer two entities in relation at all.

The distinction between "I-Thou" and "I-It" can be clarified by analogy with our dream-life. When we dream of an object it is not simply an object that we see in the dream; the object is experienced as a projection of our consciousness, and it has the power to turn the dream into a joyful experience or into a nightmare. This quality of the dream is not accounted for by saying that the dreamer is being affected by an object, since the oneiric object is a projection of the dreamer's own psyche, and so belongs to that psyche from its very inception. It is a kind of hallucination, enabling the psyche to experience itself in the form of an object that seems to be perceived objectively. The oneiric image seems to be experienced in a kind of relationship, but there is no "I-It" relationship of course, because in the dream the mind is experiencing itself. True, it creates a hallucination in order to accomplish this end, but the dream cannot be realistically assessed as a relationship between two different entities. The dream represents a fictitious "I-It" relationship, but it is affectively experienced for what it is: an "I-Thou" situation, which is no relationship at all, but a unified experience of the mind contemplating itself.

In waking life we interact in an "I-It" relationship with what we call empirical reality; this is the illusion from which one may awaken into unity, where there is no breach of continuity between the observer and the observed. The poets and contemplatives dwell on this. When they awaken in unity the first thing they notice is that reality is not a matter of any kind of relationship. This is because unified consciousness is a state in which one awakens to the obvious fact (the open secret) that the separation between ego-consciousness and the reality "out there" is purely instrumental; we need that duality in order to function practically in the world. We behave *as if* the mind were a subject acting on an object.

That is why the oriental teachers are constantly saying that ego and empirical reality are illusions. They do not deny the real existence of cause and effect, but liken cause and effect to the playing of waves on the ocean of being, whose existence is not determined by the playing of those waves. The poets and contemplatives tell us that ego is an illusion, in the sense that it is not autonomously separate from the rest of creation, even though its existence is predicated upon such a belief. This is nothing more than a truism, for indeed, how could ego be a separate entity standing apart? One might as well say that canine consciousness and feline awareness are qualitatively different from the rest of creation.

Human consciousness is remarkable, not because it has ego-intellect, but because it is the bearer of the spirit that can contemplate itself in the mind. When this occurs the individual knows instantly that *this* (so simple, not subtle at all!) is what people have been calling illumination for all these centuries; the Buddha-nature "out there" is identical to the Buddha-nature within; Atman is Brahman and Brahman is Atman; "yet not I, but Christ liveth in me."

Ego does not live within one in the same sense that potential illumination does. Ego takes up time and history, takes up most of one's life. But ego is only provisionally alive, because it is subject to the ravages of time. Nevertheless there is One that lives within one, and this One is no illusion. It has lived throughout the history of the human race, and it will continue to live because it is out of time. It is this One that is implied, and eventually spoken of, in the poetry of Salinas. Such is the case with the work of all poets who have a vocation, a calling—for who, after all, called them in the first place?

"¿Qué pájaros?" is not dissimilar to "Figuraciones" in that it concerns the ontological question, What kinds of reality does human consciousness establish for itself, and how are they to be distinguished? But "¿Qué pájaros?" treats specifically of one form of reality, and so we will have to consider the symbology of bird-flight. This subject is cognate to the material treated in "Agua en la noche," since in either case we have to do with the poetic task apprehended as a feat of spiritualization. In our discussion of "Agua en la noche" we have already seen how the serpent-principle is mythologically transformed into the spirit of flight, how the river-serpent ascends transfigured as the cloud that brings to us the gift of fertilizing rain. The vision of spiritual flight has also been intuited universally as instinctual energy (libido) soaring aloft in the form of bird-flight, and this grasp of the dynamic earth-reality belongs to the seer, the *vates*, and the poet; it cannot properly be called a metaphysic or a philosophy, since these terms connote a view of reality that is elaborated intellectually.

"¿Qué pájaros?" is concerned with distinguishing between the metaphysical and the poetic view of reality. Specifically, the first ten lines of the poem recapitulate the Platonic theory of Ideas, the main points of which may be given here in résumé. George Henry Lewes says that the Platonic realists, "finding The One in The Many, . . . abstracted these *general* characteristics from the *particular* accidents of individual [beings], and out of these characteristics made what they called *Universals*." These are the Platonic Ideas, "the constants or *noumena* of which all individual things [are] the variables of *phenomena*." Our notion of the world reality, then, is composed of *noumena*, or intelligibles, and of phenomena, or sensibles. We imagine that "sensible objects" participate in the Ideas, and hence can, according to Aristotle, be classified intellectually as genera. "The phenomena which constitute what we perceive of the world (i.e., the world of senses) are but the resemblances of matter to Ideas. In other words, Ideas are the forms of which material Things are copies; the *noumena*, of which all that we perceive are the Appearances (phenomena)." The phenomena are thought to be inexact copies of their models, and so the question arises, How to ascertain the truth, if phenomena are not exact copies of *noumena?* Here enters the Platonic theory of recollection. Since the soul dwelled in heaven before becoming incarnate on earth, when its earthly senses perceive this world, "the sensation awakens recollection, and the recollection is of Truth; the soul is confronted with the Many by means of Sense, and by means of Reason it detects the One in the Many." Lewes subsequently quotes a passage from the *Republic* in which Plato explains himself by means of a comparison. Socrates asks, "Shall we proceed according to our usual Method? That Method, as you know, is the embracing under one general Idea the multiplicity of things which exist separately, but have the same name." Socrates gives as examples the "multiplicty of beds and tables," noting that the carpenter can make only many beds and tables, but not the Idea of beds and tables. There is, however, one artisan who can do this—has done it—and that is the maker of the universe. Then comes a striking analogy:

> "Do you think that in one sense any one could do all this . . .? Could you not yourself succeed in a certain way?"
> "In what way?"
> "It is not difficult; it is often done, and in a short time. Take a mirror and turn it round on all sides: in an instant you will have made the sun and stars, the earth, yourself, the animals and plants, works of art, and all we mentioned."
> "Yes, the images, the appearances, but not the real things."

In the same sense, argues Plato, the carpenter "does not make the Idea of the bed, he makes nothing real, but only something which represents that which really exists. And, if any one maintain that the carpenter's work has a real existence he will be in error." The phenomena are "reflections" in the mirror of the maker.[1]

This synopsis of the Platonic theory of Ideas puts us in a position to examine the first half of "¿Qué pájaros?" which says:

The bird? The birds?
Is there only one single bird in the world
that flies with a thousand wings, and that sings
with myriad trills, always alone?
Are earth and sky mirrors? Is the air
a mirage of the air, and does the great one bird
multiply
its solitude in thousands of appearances?
(And so for that reason
we call it "the birds"?)

In the opening line Socrates' usual method can be recognized: "the embracing under one general Idea the multiplicity of things which exist separately." "The bird? The birds?" We are given a dialectic between the one and the many, the *noumenon*—Bird—and its "thousands of appearances"—the phenomena.

When Salinas asks if earth and sky are mirrors he brings us round to the analogy used by Plato. One can, "in a certain sense," create things by holding up a mirror to the world, which is to say that one is imitating the original creative act. The reflections in the mirror are insubstantial appearances, and so we may understand that the phenomenal world itself is like the mirror of the Maker. Salinas the augur observes the birds in flight, but then the metaphysical question of reality is allowed to intrude, and he makes a certain point of doubting the substantial existence of these phenomena: "Are earth and sky mirrors?"[2]

That these are all insubstantial, phenomenal reflections is expressed more clearly in the Spanish text, since the word used for *mirage* is *espejeo*, a close derivative of *espejo*, "mirror." And because the birds are flying in the air, the second question particularizes the first:

Are earth and sky *espejos*? Is the air
an *espejeo* of the air . . .?

This is not the symbolism of the mirror as it is used in "Madrid. Calle de. . ." There, the glass reflecting the "astral scenery" is like the clear mind of the contemplative consciousness. In the Platonic sense the specular image is adduced as an example of insubstantiality: all that an *espejo* gives us is an *espejeo*. Such is the literal, not the symbolic, meaning of the mirror when viewed by ego-intellect.

The second part of "¿Qué pájaros?" begins with the word *or*, and gives us the alternative notion of reality. Having shown us the meaning of Platonic realism, Salinas now proceeds to look at the matter differently:

Or perhaps there isn't one bird?
And they are
a necessary, immense plural, like the sea,
an innumerable flock, a tide of wings,
where the eyes seek and the spirit tries
to distinguish the truth of the single bird,
of its unending essence, of the beautiful one?

Before looking into this alternative vision we will cite a prose analogy to it. J. B. Priestley once had a numinous dream of unity in which it seemed to him that he was standing at the top of a tower, "looking down upon myriads of birds all flying in one direction. . . . But now in some mysterious fashion the gear was changed and time speeded up, so that I saw generations of birds, watched them break their shells, flutter into life, weaken, falter, and die." This cosmic rhythm impressed him at first as a "gigantic meaningless biological effort," but then everything speeded even faster, as in time-lapse photography, until he saw only "an enormous plain sown with feathers." It was alive, however, for "along this plain, flickering through the bodies themselves, there now passed a sort of white flame, . . . life itself, the very quintessence of being." At this point he was illuminated: ". . . and then it came to me, in a rocket-burst of ecstasy, that nothing mattered, . . . because nothing else was real, but this quivering and hurrying lambency of being. . . . It left nothing to mourn over behind it; what I had thought was tragedy was mere emptiness or a shadow show; for now all real feeling was caught and purified and danced on ecstatically with the white flame of life."[3]

What Priestley experiences finally is the living ground of reality that dances in the perpetual play of *maya.* Theodore Roethke experienced it too:

> A flame, intense, visible,
> Plays over the dry pods,
> Runs fitfully along the stubble,
> Moves over the fields,
> Without burning.[4]

With the word *or*, the second half of "¿Qué pájaros?" begins by rejecting the Platonic *noumenon*, Bird. Rather, it says, the birds are necessarily plural, "like the sea." The image of the mirror has been exchanged for the image of the ocean. The multiple phenomena are now no longer "inexact copies" of one model, but rather are like the myriad waves of the sea, what Priestley saw as an enormous, living plain of wings, ultimately not birds at all, but an illusion created by the upward-flashing life-force. Observing the ocean we speak of this wave and that, but at the same time we never really fool ourselves into thinking that the great watery plain is busy producing distinct entities called waves that could somehow be detached from the ocean.

But if we apply this notion to seemingly detached phenomena such as birds or human beings, we may see a new, non-Platonic way in which these are illusory. They *are* phenomena, to be sure, but not in dialectical opposition to *noumena*, because they do not correspond to any models. They are incessantly churned forth out of the oceanic unity, just as the waves unendingly rise up out of the ocean; but the ocean is a force, an urge, and not an Idea of which each wave is an inexact copy. "Life is but earth translated into force," as poet Ignatow puts it; "we are only earth transposed into force, just as coal is formed into flame and heat by the transmutation process applied to it."[5] From the static, Platonic point of view each genus appears to us as multiple phenomena (many birds, many horses, many trees), and we perceive great numbers of genera. But from the alternative standpoint the whole notion of many genera is but one more illusion of multiplicity. All material phenomena are myriad manifestations not of a lesser number of genera (a few abstract Ideas), but of one force—only one.

This is the idea underlying Vedanta, of course, but there is no evidence that Salinas was a student of the *Upanishads.* He had experienced unity, and the vision of the one force, busily engaged now, always now in churning up the world of phenomena is the first notion that thrusts itself upon unified consciousness. When Aldous Huxley experienced unity he immediately comprehended the metaphysical chasm separating Platonic realism from the vision of Brahman: "Plato seems to have made the . . . mistake of separating Being from becoming and identifying it with . . . the Idea. He could never . . . have perceived that what rose and iris and carnation so intensely signified was nothing more, and nothing less, than what they were—a transience that was yet eternal life, a perpetual perishing that was at the same time pure Being, a bundle of minute, unique particulars in which, by some unspeakable and yet self-evident paradox, was to be seen the divine source of all existence."[6] Thus Huxley ends his thought as Salinas does in "¿Qué pájaros?" He has gone from Platonic dualism to a unified vision of the spirit: "the divine source of all existence," the "unending essence of the beautiful one."

Salinas's use of the word *esencia* ("essence") deserves comment, for it is as vague a word as *idea*, and can be understood only in context. The context in this case is the symbolic ocean forever manufacturing phenomena, *maya*. The One becomes the many, and unified consciousness, witnessing this, cannot understand how these many keep exfoliating out of the One. The One is alive, God knows, and so it is always becoming. That is why *maya* is a "necessary, immense plural"; the One cannot become One, since the statement itself is a mere toying with words. It must become more than One; it must become multiple.

Salinas says that "the eyes seek and the spirit tries to distinguish the truth of the single bird, of its unending essence." Plato wanted to distinguish the truth of the "single bird," which he called the *noumenon*. But if we reject this intellectual theory we have only one other choice: "the beautiful one." Does "the beautiful one" mean "bird" here? Is Salinas saying, "the truth of the single bird, / of its unending essence, of the beautiful bird"? The answer cannot be Platonically "yes"; it is both yes and no, because the alternative to dualism is unity, and in unity no such clear-cut choices are possible. In speaking of *El Contemplado*, the poem-cycle in which Salinas "trips out" on the ocean, the reader may ask, Is "the one" here the ocean—or is it something else? This is the same unanswerable question, rephrased; the *One* contemplated is unity itself, Atman-as-Brahman and vice versa. Yes, the One contemplated *is* the ocean—and also anything else that we are contemplating when we suddenly awaken in unity, because this is an indivisible state of awareness.

And the essence of the bird of *maya* is unending, because Brahman, the ocean of life, is always magically creating the world right now. In the traditional Christian view God created the world once, and then time began. In the Hindu view the world is our necessary plural always pouring into being now.

"¿Qué pájaros?" portrays the two alternatives, then, but not polemically. No reader of *El Contemplado* can doubt that Salinas himself believes in his

heart of hearts that the second alternative represents for him the true picture
of the nature of reality, but his rejection of the Platonic realism is in the end
not so much a rejection as it is the description of a static theory that suffers
by comparison with the dynamism of real experience.

That Salinas chose to use the flying birds in order to express his meaning is
no doubt connected with the universal notion of spiritualization, for they are
the prime symbol of it. Plato himself said, "It is the nature of wings to lift up
heavy bodies toward the habitation of the Gods; and, of all things which
belong to the body, wings are that which most partakes of the divine. The
divine includes the beautiful, the wise, the good, and everything of that
nature. By these the wings of the soul are nourished and increased; by the
contraries of these, they are destroyed."[7] The human spirit is the microcos-
mic bird, and so it was that "in the medieval bestiaries and volucraries, and
in collections of fables, a distinction was made between beasts and birds, the
beasts representing the passions of the flesh, while the birds represent those
of the spirit."[8] The shamanistic birdman/birdwoman, who, entranced, enters
the world of the gods, is discussed and documented at length by Eliade in his
Shamanism: Archaic Techniques of Ecstasy. Of the bird as psychopomp he
says: "Becoming a bird oneself or being accompanied by a bird indicates the
capacity, while still alive, to undertake the ecstatic journey to the sky and
the beyond." The shaman is the one who can become a bird, which is to say,
awaken in the "spirit condition."[9] Thus Jack Lindsay, who characterizes
Aristophanes' play *The Birds* as "a vivid storehouse of Greek ideas about the
mantic and sacred nature of birds," says that that play "is in a sense a great
shamanist fantasy."[10]

In our own cultural tradition we call the hybrid human-bird by the name
of angel, the mediator between God and us. The angel is the human being in
the spiritual, or flying aspect, the realization of the "spirit condition,"
sharing both in the instinctual earthly body and in the nonphysical life of the
spirit. Says Meister Eckhart: "An angel is nigh unto God and matter is nigh
unto him."[11] Sir John Mandeville explains tree-burial in terms of spirituali-
zation; he describes a literal instance of human transformation into birds. Of
certain primitives he says baroquely that "they have a custom that, when
their friends are grievous sick, they hang them upon trees, that they may be
worried and eaten with fowles; for they say that it is better they be eaten
with fowles, which are angels of God, than foully to be eaten in the earth
with worms."[12]

Of course the connection between seer, *vates,* and poet is age-old. The
poet, when inspired, is a mantic individual whose libidinal energies take
flight, as in the myth of Pegasus, the winged horse upon whom the poet is
traditionally said to ascend. Here the heroic steed, our most striking and
powerful symbol of libido, sprouts wings and bears the spirit aloft. Thus
Delmore Schwartz calls poetry "the consummation of consciousness"; Theo-

dore Roethke, assaulted by the poetic fury, declares, "This flesh has airy bones"; and David Ignatow writes:

> All comes to sunlight.
> A bird stirring its wings.
> In the air it has the shape of a dream.
> It too is perfect off the ground,
> I follow its flight.[13]

Ignatow has described graphically the flying sensation associated with the spirit of creation: "It has always been interesting to me how I am able to work up to a poem by simply writing around it. . . . For example, I have discovered that the action of a plane racing down the field to gather speed for . . . take-off is similar . . . to working in prose until the emotions and ideas have meshed and are ready with their accelerated heat and energy to take flight, circle around the landing field and fly off."[14]

Carl Sandburg characterized the human tendency toward spiritualization in his definition of poetry, "the journal of a sea animal living on land, wanting to fly in the air." The major Latin-American poet of Modernism, Rubén Darío, portrayed his own vocation in a poem entitled "Augurios," and saw his spirit variously as eagle ("Give me the strength, / in the human slime, to feel myself / with wings"), owl, dove, falcon, and nightingale.[15] And of course Salinas himself, in the poem "Cuartilla," identified the writing of a poem with the upward striving of a flock of birds.

Hence there is good reason for Salinas to conceive of the process of spiritualization as the life force of unity that is incessantly becoming spirit, and further, that the necessary plural should always have as its unending essence the beautiful One. For the single bird is the single principle of spiritualization, the single force that creates "a sea animal living on land, wanting to fly in the air." When the seer undertakes fight, the ascension gives an overview of reality that is seen as one, not as multiple—and certainly not as Ideas. Blyth, speaking of Robert Burns, says, "[He] was a poet. By this we mean that he saw the Life of life." Similarly Gerhart Hauptmann defined poetry as "the art of causing the Word to resound behind words."[16] "The Life of life," the "Word behind words"—this is what Salinas is calling "the Bird of birds." It is not a static *noumenon*, but the living, dynamic symbol, the upward-gathering of spiritual power in which the poet's spirit "tries to distinguish the truth of the . . . beautiful One."

Chapter Fifteen

THE EXPERIENCE OF UNITY

TEMA

De mirarte tanto y tanto,
del horizonte a la arena,
despacio,
del caracol al celaje,
brillo a brillo, pasmo a pasmo,

te he dado nombre; los ojos
te lo encontraron, mirándote.
Por las noches,
soñando que te miraba,
al abrigo de los párpados
maduró, sin yo saberlo,
este nombre tan redondo
que hoy me descendió a los labios.
Y lo dicen asombrados
de lo tarde que lo dicen.
¡Si era fatal el llamártelo!
¡Si antes de la voz, ya estaba
en el silencio tan claro!
¡Si tú has sido para mí,
desde el día
que mis ojos te estrenaron,
el contemplado, el constante
Contemplado!

VARIACIÓN III: DULCENOMBRE
  (fragmento)

Desde que te llamo así,
por mi nombre,
ya nunca me eres extraño.
. . . .
Si te nombro, soy tu amo
de un segundo. ¡Qué milagro!

THEME

From watching you so long,
from the horizon to the sand,
slowly,
from the seashell to the cloudscape,
shimmer by shimmer, astonishment by aston-
  ishment,
I have given you a name; my eyes
discovered it for you by watching you.
At night,
dreaming that I was watching you,
in the shelter of my eyelids
it matured, unbeknown to me,
this ringing name
that descended to my lips today.
And they speak it, amazed
at how long they took to speak it.
Why, it was inevitable to call you so!
Why, before the voice, it was already there,
in the shining silence!
Why, you have been for me,
since the day
my eyes first saw you,
the contemplated one, the immutable
One Contemplated!

VARIATION III: SWEETNAME (excerpt)

Ever since I gave you
a name of my own,
you have not been alien to me.
. . . .
If I speak your name, I am your master
for a second. What a miracle!

El Contemplado, a cycle of poems consisting of a theme with fourteen variations, represents in the poetry of Pedro Salinas the culminating experience of the enlightenment of unity. In the early forties Salinas was a member of the faculty of the University of Puerto Rico, and it was then that he lived by the Sea of San Juan and discovered the contemplative act in what was for him its fullest sense. It was this experience that produced *El Contemplado*, where the general theme is the enlightenment itself, while the variations concern different aspects of the phenomenon. In the present study I do not attempt to examine all fourteen variations, but rather concern myself with the main theme, seen as one more text in the universal literature of enlightenment—what Aldous Huxley called the Perennial Philosophy, the world view produced by knowledge of the transcendent ground of reality.

Salinas contemplated the ocean, and at some point, with a sudden start, he realized with numinous clarity that he was in the presence of cosmic being. To live through this is to know experientially the one reality that is both inside and outside one's person. What the Hindus call the Atman is the ground of being apperceptively experienced, and the Brahman is the ground of being experienced "out there." Enlightenment consists in experiencing that the Atman is Brahman within, and that Brahman is the Atman "out there," and "the last end of every human being is to discover the fact, . . . to find out Who [one] really is."[1] Clearly this is no oriental idea in any but a linguistic sense. It is the universal experience of mystics and poets alike.

We are of course concerned with a poet, and so before we cite any mystical parallels to *El Contemplado* perhaps we should recall that Percy Bysshe Shelley, in his *Defence of Poetry*, speaks from his own acquaintance with unified consciousness. He speaks of poetic insight as recognition of the subliminal self—a transport of nonego. He says that poetry "is the record of the best and happiest moments of the happiest and best minds,"[2] meaning quite the same thing James Wright meant in the poem that I have already cited, "Today I was Happy, So I Made This Poem." Shelley goes on to tell us that poetry "is as it were the interpenetration of a diviner nature through our own," and uses here a cosmic metaphor that reminds us of *El Contemplado*: "Its footsteps are like those of a wind over the sea, which the coming calm erases, and whose traces remain only, as on the wrinkled sand which paves it." "Poetry redeems from decay the visitations of the divinity."[3]

And later Shelley implies the distinction between what Robert Graves called "a particular mode of living and thinking" and "a technical mastery of words."[4] The poetic experience is the living of symbolic reality given by unity, and the resultant poem has as its substance the symbols born therein. If not, then the poem is merely a technical mastery of words, and that is why Shelley satirically lumps together the drunkard, the flatterer, the coward, the madman, the peculator, the libertine—and the poet laureate.[5] The poet laureate is the one whose works speak for the collective consciousness of the secular society, whereas Shelley knows that the poetic experience is a return to unity, to the primordial obviousness of nondual reality. Salinas, in "Tema," says his lips were amazed at how long it took them to get around to speaking the word of unity, and that it was inevitable that they should do so. Just so, Gerard de Nerval wrote, "How, I said to myself, have I been able to exist so long outside Nature, without identifying myself with her?"[6] Soshi observed that "people all over the world try to know what they do not know, instead of trying to know what they already know."[7] And so Shelley: poetry "compels us to feel that which we perceive, and to imagine that which we know."[8] We already know it, because we do not discover unity; we only return to it. Each natural object is a variation on the theme of the ground of being. We give each thing a name, but unified consciousness transcends all such names. Presently I will treat of how this matter of naming comes to be an ironic function of *El Contemplado*.

The treatment of multiple reality as variations on the theme is a high-frequency motif in classical haiku, where it is characteristic to view an object or phenomenon as being the carrier of the Buddha-nature—an insight made possible only when the haiku poet is looking with the eyes of the Buddha-nature. That is to say, Buddha within contemplates Buddha without, just as the Atman watches Brahman. Blyth brings this out specifically in his commentary on Shiki's haiku:

> Turning my back on the Buddha,
> How cool
> The moonlight!

The Buddha here is a temple statue being contemplated by the poet, who turns to look at the moon. But Shiki knows that it is ironic to speak of turning one's back on the Buddha, since all things are in the Buddha. Reality is the Buddha *in rebus*, as it were. Blyth goes on to comment (citing similar haiku by Shiki) that when we turn our back on the Buddha in one form, there it is again, perhaps in the form of a crab, or in the form of clouds. We may see it "through the aperture of the stone lantern," and of course it is also to be seen in the ocean contemplated by Salinas. "In all these verses what Shiki perceives, with absolute clarity and conviction, is the Buddha; but he [says] 'a crab,' 'white sails,' 'the sea.' "[9] Here Blyth emphasizes for the benefit of the Western reader what the experienced haiku reader knows: that the poet is speaking of a real, apperceptive occurrence which we may with equal aptness call either mystical or poetic; in either case both the nature mystic and the poet have gone beyond the usual esthetic appreciation of nature; beyond a mere belief in her harmony. "One may hold that the real is an undifferentiated One, but some further stroke of insight is needed to turn this into a mystical conclusion. This insight is the discovery that the mystic . . . is one with what [is known], and, since [this] is reality itself, we may say that [the mystic] has discovered what it means to be real."[10] Thus in *El Contemplado* the poet does not sing the praises of the sea because he "holds" that it is divine; he expresses his own personal experience of the Self in the form of the sea, and he appears to name the unnameable.

What's in a Name?

In "Tema" Salinas sets forth the occasion of his enlightenment. It was preceded by long meditation at the beach, the emptying of the mind of its *negocios.* He sat "otiose" and quiet, watching slowly, and at length a name rushed up into consciousness. As he puts it, a name descended to his lips. When he found himself in the "shining silence," then something was given to him and his lips spoke of their own accord, saying, "El Contemplado." He writes that it was *fatal* ("inevitable") that this *nombre* ("name") should at long last reach his lips. And so we find ourselves confronted by a problem in analysis, since unified consciousness lies beyond all naming.

The usual meaning and function of the name, or noun, has elsewhere been clearly defined by Salinas himself. In the spring of 1944 he delivered the commencement address at the University of Puerto Rico, and his subject was language—more specifically, *lenguaje*, or language used colloquially. This address appears in the collection of essays by Salinas, *El defensor* ("The Defender"), under the title "Defensa del lenguaje" ("Defense of Language").

Since the address was composed for an academic occasion, we might naturally expect it to be appropriately intellectual. Salinas discusses the role of language and intellect in the formation of the educated, civilized human being, and he places special emphasis upon the valuable role played by *logos*, the word, as a differentiating force. The *logos* function, the capacity to distinguish clearly between oneself and the surrounding world, the ability to construct an abstract notion of reality—this is what makes it at all possible to build up an effective consciousness. Salinas describes the awakening of this capacity in the small child who says its first words: "This is a great moment! The moment when the human being begins to enjoy . . . the essential faculty of intelligence: the capacity to distinguish, to differentiate among things, to distinguish oneself from the world."

Then he relates an anecdote to illustrate this dramatic event. An acquaintance of his once took a little girl to the beach. She had never seen the ocean before, and in great excitement, with eyes like saucers, she simply looked and exclaimed, "¡Mar, el mar!" Thanks to this abstraction, says Salinas, the child avoids being swallowed up by the immensity of the ocean: she "affirms her own person, her own little person in its first stages . . . by virtue of the word. She stands facing the sea, telling it, 'You are the sea, and I am a girl who calls you that.' "[11] He is, of course, describing the word as used by ego-intellect in order to establish the "I-It" relationship with the world. It is *logos* as abstraction, and is not to be confused with *logos* as symbol. The one differentiates, the other fuses. The one lies at the basis of dualistic thinking, the other springs from unity.

In *El Contemplado* the poet is not a little child awakening to the miracle of ego-consciousness; rather, he is the adult plunging back into unity. But still he tells us that a name was vouchsafed him. This event, signalizing sudden realization of one's encounter with the divine, has produced names in the past—names that are evidently tautological. Moses looked upon a numinous bush and asked for a name: "Behold, when I come unto the children of

Israel, and shall say unto them, The God of your fathers hath sent me unto you; and they shall say to me, What is his name? what shall I say unto them?" (Ex. 3:13). The Divinity obligingly gives him a name to repeat, a truism: I AM THAT I AM (in the Spanish, YO SOY EL QUE SOY). This is not qualitatively different from the *tat tvam asi* of the Hindus, discussed by Aldous Huxley in the first chapter of his *The Perennial Philosophy*. "The doctrine that is to be illustrated in this section belongs to autology rather than psychology—to the science, not of the personal ego, but of that eternal Self in the depth of particular, individualized selves, and identical with, or at least akin to, the divine Ground. . . . This teaching is expressed most succinctly in the Sanskrit formula, *tat tvam asi* ("That art thou")."[12] By the same token the name Buddha means nothing more than "the awakened one" (p.p. of Sans. *budh*, "to awake, know"), even though the Westerner may think of it as part of somebody's full name—Buddha Jones, perhaps.

Contemplatives characteristically tell us that the transcending of intellectual categories is ineffable, since what they have seen cannot be named, by definition. But in order to talk about it, in order to allude to it, they produce a functional label that is nothing more than a truism. Thus Lao Tzu wrote in his *Tao Te Ching* (Tao meaning "the way"):

> I know not its name
> So I style it "the way."
> I give it the makeshift name of "the great."
> Being great, it is further described as receding,
> Receding, it is described as far away,
> Being far away, it is described as turning back.

Or, in another translation:

> I do not know its name;
> A name for it is "Way";
> Pressed for designation,
> I call it Great.
> Great means outgoing,
> Outgoing, far-reaching,
> Far-reaching, return.[13]

Even though the critics like to praise the fact that Salinas, with his "technical mastery of words," hit on the "exact name" for the ocean ("just like the girl in the story," says one critic, thinking of the Salinas anecdote cited above[14]), we can see that the One Contemplated is no more a name in the ego-meaning of the term than is Buddha—or Lao Tzu's *Tao*. Like Lao Tzu, Salinas sees it as "receding" and "turning back," as ebbing and flowing, and realizes that he is at last seeing what he is seeing. And that is its name: the One Contemplated. As Blakney says in his commentary on the *Tao Te*

Ching, "No word or name can disclose nature's deepest secret." "Nature's secret, the constant, normative Way from which no event is exempt, is disclosed only to those who can be rid of personal wishes or prejudices about it. . . . Prejudiced eyes are stopped cold at the surface."[15] This constant, normative Way is what Salinas identifies at the end of "Tema" as *el constante / Contemplado,* "the immutable / One Contemplated."

And to find the Way is to *be* the Way: *tat tvam asi.* "The One Contemplated" is simultaneously the ocean and the poet. This notion is set forth succinctly in a haiku by Issa. As a wayfarer he once stopped to ask a peasant for directions. The peasant was pulling turnips at the time, and this is what happened:

> The turnip-puller
> Points the way
>   With a turnip.

Blyth comments: "The man who is pulling up the turnips is so much one with them that he uses a turnip as his own finger, to point the way. And see! the man points the Way with a turnip, of all things!"[16]

This is really the ancient, simple secret of what the old missionary mentality conceived to be savage idolatry. Bruno Spaccio's observation, written in 1584, applies as well to *El Contemplado.* "Thus crocodiles, cocks, onions and turnips were never worshipped for themselves, but the gods and the divinity in [them]. . . . One simple divinity which is in all things, one fecund nature, mother and preserver of the universe, shines forth in divers subjects, and takes diverse names, according as it communicates itself diversely. You see how one must ascend to this One by the participation in divers gifts."[17] Perhaps we Westerners, with our ego-consciousness as large and as sturdy as the Monastery of the Escorial, require something grandiose to point the Way, something on the order of the Atlantic Ocean. But when we find it, we need not call it *Tao* or say that we have glimpsed the Buddha-nature; we need not appeal to any historical names at all, because we ourselves are our own sufficient documentation. By the Sea of San Juan Salinas found his own name for it, and this turned out to be authentically meaningless. As he might have said subsequently, "You'll never imagine what I saw today on the beach: I saw what I was truly seeing! I saw what I was contemplating!" And what was that? "Why, the One Contemplated, of course!"

"If I Speak Your Name, I Am Your Master for a Second"

The poet has told us in "Tema" of his discovery that the macrocosmic and microcosmic oceans have an identical significance: unified consciousness experiences that it is all and that all is it. Nevertheless, in the third variation there occurs the strange passage reading, "If I speak your name, I am your master for a second." We say the passage is strange, because in the midst of unity it seems to speak of a dual relationship: one is master over another. But because the poet is speaking within unity, we may rest assured that no merely logical or literal meaning can be appropriately attributed here, though this has been done by several critics.

It appears that the published criticism on *El Contemplado* seems consistently to have proceeded along the lines of logical analysis, using words with their usual ego-meanings, but this tends to lead to prefabricated conclusions. Benjamin Paul Blood put the matter neatly when he criticized the use of a secular viewpoint for talking about unity. Blood was concerned with the mystery of the Eternal Now, which "keeps exfoliating out of itself, yet never escapes." How "explain" it? "What is it, indeed, that keeps existence exfoliating? The formal being of anything, the logical definition of it, is static. For mere logic every question contains its own answer—we simply fill the hole with the dirt we dug out."[18]

Now, no critic has treated our Salinas passage (or the idea behind it) as if it had other than a secular meaning—which is to imply that the passage may be interpreted from the viewpoint of dualistic thinking. On that view, the passage seems to mean that the poet, by giving the sea a name, possesses it. Here are some typical comments.

The act of naming "brings him into complete possession [*posesión perfecta*] of things" (Feldbaum).

The poet "will be able to take possession of it [the sea]—even though it may be but for a second—by the very fact of naming it" (Correa).

"Upon pronouncing [the name] *Contemplado*, the poet possesses [*a prise sur*] the sea and unites with it in spite of itself" (Dehennin).

"The contemplated is the possessed" (Matos Paoli).

"At times the poet goes forth to possession of the infinite by escaping from the finite" (Lewis de Galanes).

"The finding of the name has abolished distances, has given to the contemplator total possession of the object" (Arce de Vásquez).[19]

So much for the literal meaning of the passage. Now we should ask ourselves what it means to read it literally, since a moment's consideration ought to tell us that in such a reading we are filling the hole with the dirt we dug out. The poet says he possesses the sea, and there's an end on it. But if this were the case, then Salinas himself would be mistaken about the reality of his own situation, since possession requires control. In this sense the English Navy once "possessed" the ocean—but no contemplative poet ever did.

Salinas has not written here, however, that he "possesses" anything. The passage reads, "If I speak your name, I am your master for a second." *Amo de un segundo*, literally "master of a second," is a single idea, a "one-second master," not merely a noun that happens to be modified. We have seen above how one critic has handled the interpretive problem here by saying that the poet "will be able to take possession of it—even though it may be but for a second—by the very fact of naming it." But to interpret the passage by adding "even though" is not critically valid, since Salinas does not say, "I am your master, *if only* for a second."

We have quoted this passage along with "Tema" because it carries one step farther the peculiar notion of "naming" it. Correa praises "El Contemplado" as being the "exact name," but I have already gone to some lengths to show how it is *not* exact at all. The exact name for the sea in Spanish is *mar*. El Contemplado is the "makeshift name" alluding to the phenomenon of altered consciousness we call unity. When one truly sees reality there is no way of coming up with an exact name for what one is seeing, since names have as their function the expression of our instrumental view of reality, and the things "in" reality. Names are part of the way we conduct our business in the world, our karmic activity. But the contemplative is not interested in doing anything with reality, not interested in *negocios*; it is a matter of finding out who one is. And Salinas, in a state of *ocio*, did not find out a new name for the ocean; he found out how to see Who he is. This process has been explained in simplified form (as if for children) by Alan Watts, who uses the metaphor of hide-and-seek. Reality is God playing hide-and-seek; but since there is nothing outside God, God solves the difficulty by pretending to be us, but does it so well that God as Self appears to forget the hiding place: you and I as God in disguise. This is, of course (as Watts notes), the reality of the *Upanishads* and of unity; the concept of God is clearly not that of a king of the universe ("the Absolute Technocrat").[20] Unity in egolessness is awakening from the "I-It" illusion of duality. Anyone who awakens in this fashion may be called a mystic or a poet, depending upon how one chooses to live thereafter. Salinas, as a poet, had always lived on the brink of awakening, as do many. Compare Roethke:

I was always one for being alone . . .
At the edge of the field, waiting for the pure moment.[21]

When Salinas at last experienced the great breakthrough, he naturally began to speak in the fashion of unified consciousness. Hence the opening poem of *El Contemplado*, which we may now examine as a *manifold*.

Characteristics of Unified Consciousness in "Tema"

The psychological characteristics of unified consciousness can be listed and described, but of course it is central to the issue that unity is not a discontinuous reality. Analysis treats it as divisible, as if it were not what it is. Nevertheless it is true that the experience ebbs and flows, and that a variety of feelings and modes of comprehension present themselves. A number of these are fully present in "Tema," and it is now my task to attempt their description.

First, one is sure that the experience gives understanding, and not simply "gorgeous feelings." As Clark puts it, "It is necessary to emphasize that the mystical consciousness is not primarily an emotion; it is a *perception*. Furthermore, this perception is not hazy, vague and confused. It is . . . remarkably simple, cogent and clear." Or, to quote Tennyson: "By God Almighty! there is no delusion in the matter! It is no nebulous ecstasy, but a state of transcendent wonder, associated with absolute clearness of mind."[22] "Tema," as a whole, is a declaration of clarity. The watch by the sea has culminated in the understanding of the one simple fact, the truism of unified consciousness: It was there all the time. I simply had not perceived it, and now I do.

Second, one is struck by the quality of suddenness in the experience. The light strikes in a flash; it is not a gradual dawning. Contemplatives like to use the metaphor of dawn because they come into a new world, but not because the awakening was gradual. Hence Delmore Schwartz, in "The First Morning of the Second World" begins, "Suddenly. / Suddenly and certainly," "Sudden and overwhelming," "Certainly and suddenly, for a moment's eternity."[23] Basho's haiku tells us:

> How admirable,
> He who thinks not, "Life is fleeting,"
> When he sees the lightning flash![24]

The ego-meaning of "lightning" is "brief"; its Self-meaning is "sudden illumination." And so Salinas all at once finds that the name, the experience, has rushed into consciousness. For a long time it must have been elsewhere, maturing, ripening, and then all at once, "today," it leaped full-blown into consciousness.

Third, one sees that one has somehow stumbled onto the obvious answer to a cosmic riddle. This is the open secret. "Nothing whatever is hidden; / From of old, all is clear as daylight."[25] "When Buddha attained the enlightenment, it is recorded, he perceived that all beings non-sentient as well as sentient were already in the enlightenment itself."[26] This is what Salinas himself says: "Why, before the voice, it was already there, / in the shining silence!" When children remove their Halloween disguises, they are not different—they were there all the time. Enlightenment removes the disguise, and then one sees that nothing has changed; reality is what it is, and it was already there. It is impossible to escape the sensation that one has been let in on a cosmic joke. As the Zen Buddhists like to put it, "Before enlightenment, carrying wood and fetching water; after enlightenment, carrying wood and fetching water." Nothing changes; one simply perceives that it was here all the time.

Fourth, one realizes the true meaning of *enthusiasm*. The ego-meaning is, naturally, dualistic: one waxes enthusiastic over something ("I-It"). But the Self-meaning of *enthusiasm* is "in God" (*en* + *theos*)—a very exciting place to be. It is no wonder that Salinas ends "Tema" with a series of exclamations. To exclaim, "Now I understand that what I am seeing is what I am seeing!" is natural to the true enthusiasm, and one might as well cry out, "Now, at long last, I am indeed enthusiastic!"

Fifth, there is a flooding sense of at-one-ment. Ego-intellect long ago disguised this word by calling it "a-tonement," and even invented a back-formation, "to atone," which of course requires dualistic circumstances in order to take place. Through "a-tonement" we and God are reconciled, like subjects and king; not unified, not one, but reconciled, like old enemies. The old cosmic tyrant is now a benevolent monarch. This is a sectarian doctrine, of course, whereas the awakening into unity is not a religious event and may occur without benefit of clergy, as any number of poets have shown us. Thus Salinas tells us in "Tema" that suddenly he awoke to discover that the ocean "out there" was also the ocean within—using the notion of sleep as preawakening:

> At night,
> dreaming that I was watching you,
> in the shelter of my eyelids
> it matured, unbeknown to me,
> this ringing name . . . .

Now, Salinas was no mystic, since being a mystic implies leading a certain kind of life; but *El Contemplado* does tell us that he found out by his own personal experience that the inner and outer oceans are the two aspects of the one reality. Of Brahman, Heinrich Zimmer writes: "Every being dwells on the very brink of that infinite ocean of the force of life. We all carry it within us."[27] To awaken to this fact (and not merely to believe it) means to be at one with it. Enlightenment is the original atonement.

And finally, unity is egoless, and consciously so. One who awakens from duality suddenly realizes inner identity, and perceives that ego is a very late arrival on the scene of reality. One has spent a whole lifetime thinking that human egos are in charge of reality, and that human intellects represent the greatest capacity for initiating activities that nature has ever evolved. Ego-intellect has the illusion that it takes things into its own hands, and that it would never get any place at all unless it did something about reality. But enlightenment means suddenly realizing that reality is the busiest place imaginable, and that ego's own personal business is something like that of a nervous mongrel ceaselessly barking as the circus parade goes past. When enlightenment happens to us, we are completely aware of precisely that: it has happened *to* us; ego-intentions had no part in it. Ego was the obstacle unable to get out of the way. Illumination is perfectly gratuitous, and so Salinas says that the name simply "descended" to his lips. His lips spoke of their own accord. If this was possible it is because there was an "otiose," vacated consciousness ready to be filled—the shining silence of line 18. When the *logos* function ceased its activities a silence fell, and then it was possible to hear the name that is no name. The egoless silence is part of the shining void, because words are the constant accompaniment of ego-intellect. The ego-meaning of *silence* is "absence of conversation," just as the ego-meaning of *solitude* is "absence of companionship." But one must clear the mind both of idle words and idle images if it is to be truly cleared.

That silence is part of the path to egolessness is a point that evidently ought to be made. One study of Salinas, *La luz no usada*, is devoted entirely to a literal study of the void (*nada*) in Salinas's poetry—but omits discussion of *El Contemplado*, since this cycle is not concerned with the theme of the void![28] But *El Contemplado* could not even have been written without the *silencio tan claro*, the "silence so clear" of egolessness. And *El Contemplado* is the poet's maximum expression of what that void can produce.

The silence of egolessness is exactly as described by Thoreau, the solitary "worshiper" who ought to know: "Silence is the communion of a conscious soul with itself. If the soul attend for a moment to its own infinity, then and there is silence. She is audible to all, . . . at all times, in all places, and if we will we may always hearken to her admonitions."[29]

"Tema" is appropriately the poem of awakening, and the "Variaciones" that follow build on the complexity of the poet's astonishment. Unified consciousness presents a variety of characteristics not specifically touched upon in "Tema"—the Eternal Now, the pleroma, the *renovatio*, synaesthesia, consciousness as bliss—and these can be illustrated elsewhere in *El Contemplado*.

For the present I shall return to the passage from "Variación III" that says, "If I speak your name, I am your master / for a second," for it may be that by now it is possible to interpret the Self-meaning of it for the self. To recapitulate briefly: the crucial event of *El Contemplado* is the awakening, which Salinas describes as the discovery of a name. But since he has awakened out of duality, his words no longer retain their secular ego-meaning. When the mind is filled with unity one exclaims, "This is Reality! Reality is exactly what I am seeing!" All is one and is the One Seen, the One Contemplated." We may call it so, hence that is its name.

Now in "Variación III" Salinas says, "If I speak your name, I am your master / for a second," which we may paraphrase as follows, so as to ease our understanding out of its dual channels: "When I realize unity, when I exclaim, 'The One Contemplated!' I have the momentary conviction that I am in charge."

Here we have to distinguish between the ego-meaning of *I* and its Self-meaning. The poet is in the state of egolessness; therefore *I* means "this enlarged consciousness aware of itself." There is no ego, but one is more fully Self-conscious than one ever thought possible. The whole experience is shot through with a sense of triumph—triumph at having been allowed to solve the cosmic riddle; triumph because reality has burst into Self-consciousness. When we awaken to the truth that the One Contemplated is our "own" Self, the sense of having mastered the riddle of the universe is inescapable. The mystic poet, Juan Ramón Jiménez, gave expression to this by exclaiming, "Everything is mine now, everything!—I mean, nothing / is mine anymore, nothing!"[30] Similarly, Thomas Traherne (1637?–1674), experiencing unity, wrote: "The dust and the stones of the street were as precious as gold, the gates were at first the ends of the world. . . . Boys and girls tumbling in the street, and playing, were moving jewels. . . . Eternity was manifest in the light of day. . . . The streets were mine, the temple was mine, the people were mine. The skies were mine, and so were the sun and moon and stars, and all the world was mine, and I the only spectator and enjoyer of it."[31] This mastery of reality can occur only in the Eternal Now, in the pure moment. That is where everything belongs to one, because everything is identical to one's consciousness here and now. Hence Salinas, ending "Tema," asserts, "If I speak your name—contemplate with the eyes of unity—I am your master in the Eternal Now."

When we have discovered the secret, it flashes on us like lightning. Whenever we return to it we find it eternally there, lighting up the heavens of consciousness. Then we are no longer facing reality, we *are* reality, the master or mistress of it; not master in the sense of controlling it or possessing it (since there is no one to do the controlling and possessing), but in the sense of being the central figure. Egolessness can admit this, for after all, isn't reality the central figure of reality?

Chapter Sixteen

THE SELF AS

HUMAN CONSCIOUSNESS

"Shall I unharness you," asked Dorothy, "so you can come in and visit?"

"No," replied the Sawhorse. "I'll just stand here and think. Take your time. Thinking doesn't seem to bore me at all."

"What will you think of?" inquired Betsy.

"Of the acorn that grew the tree from which I was made."—L. Frank Baum, *The Scarecrow of Oz*

PRESAGIO, VARIACIÓN XIII

Esta tarde, frente a ti,
en los ojos siento algo
que te mira y no soy yo.
¡Qué antigua es esta mirada,
en mi presente mirando!
Hay algo, en mi cuerpo, otro.
Viene de un tiempo lejano.
Es una querencia, un ansia
de volver a ver, a verte,
de seguirte contemplando.
Como la mía, y no mía.
Me reconozco y la extraño.
¿Vivo en ella, o ella en mí?
Poseído voluntario
de esta fuerza que me invade,
mayor soy, porque me siento
yo mismo, y enajenado.

PRESAGE, VARIATION XIII

This afternoon, facing you,
I feel something in my eyes
that watches you and it is not I.
How ancient is this glance,
watching in my present!
There is something, in my body, another.
It comes from a distant time.
It is an impulse, a longing
to see again, to see you,
to continue contemplating you.
Like my glance—and not mine.
I recognize myself in it, and it is unfamiliar.
Do I live in it, or does it live in me?
Possessed voluntarily
by this force that invades me,
I am greater, because I feel myself to be
I myself, and estranged.

SALVACIÓN POR LA LUZ, VARIACIÓN XIV

Este afán de mirar es más que mío.
Callado empuje, se le siente, ajeno,
subir desde tinieblas seculares.
Viene a asomarse a estos
ojos con los que miro. ¡Qué sinfín

de muertos que te vieron
me piden la mirada, para verte!
Al cedérsela gano:
soy mucho más cuando me quiero menos.
. . . .
¡En este hoy mío, cuánto ayer se vive!

SALVATION THROUGH THE LIGHT, VARIATION XIV

This longing to look is more mine alone.
A silent impulse, it can be felt as nonego
rising up through the age-old darkness.
It comes to look out of these
eyes with which I look. What an endless number
of the dead who saw you
ask me for my glance, so as to see you!
Upon yielding it to them, I am the gainer:
I am much more when I love myself less.
. . . .
In this today of mine, how much yesterday lives!

Ya somos todos unos en mis ojos,
poblados de antiquísimos regresos.
¡Qué paz, así! Saber que son los hombres,

un mirar que te mira,
con ojos siempre abiertos,
velándote: si un alma se les marcha
nuevas almas acuden a sus cercos.
Ahora, aquí, frente a ti, todo arrobado,
aprendo lo que soy: soy un momento
de esa larga mirada que te ojea,
desde ayer, desde hoy, desde mañana,
paralela del tiempo.
En mis ojos, los últimos,
arde intacto el afán de los primeros,
herencia inagotable, afán sin término.

Posado en mí está ahora; va de paso.
Cuando de mí se vuele, allá en mis hijos
—la rama temblorosa que le tiendo—
hará posada. Y en sus ojos, míos,
ya nunca aquí, y aquí, seguiré viéndote.

Una mirada queda, si pasamos.
¡Que ella, la fidelísima, contemple
tu perdurar, oh Contemplado eterno!
Por venir a mirarla, día a día,
embeleso a embeleso,
tal vez tu eternidad,
vuelta luz, por los ojos se nos entre.

Y de tanto mirarte, nos salvemos.

El Contemplado (1946)

Now we are all alike, here in my eyes,
inhabited by most ancient returns.
What peace, thus! To know that human beings are
a looking that looks at you,
eyes always open,
keeping watch over you: if a spirit departs
new ones join the ranks.
Now, here, facing you, utterly entranced,
I learn what I am: I am a moment
of that long looking that eyes you,
from yesterday, from today, from tomorrow,
parallel with time.
In my eyes, the latest ones,
burns intact the impulse of the earliest ones,
an inexhaustible inheritance, unending impulse.
Now it perches here before flying on.
When it takes wing it will go to pause
in my children, the slender branch I offer,
and in their eyes—mine—
I, absent but here, will continue watching you.
A look stays on though we pass.
May this most faithful glance contemplate
your duration, oh eternal Contemplated One!
Through coming to watch it, day by day,
entrancement by entrancement,
perhaps your eternity,
transformed into light, may enter us through our eyes.

And from watching you so, we may attain salvation.

To be shaken out of the ruts of ordinary perception, to be shown for a few timeless hours the outer and the inner world, not as they appear to an animal obsessed with survival, . . . but as they are apprehended, directly and unconditionally, by Mind at Large—this is an experience of inestimable value to everyone and especially to the intellectual.—Aldous Huxley, *The Doors of Perception*

We have been speaking of self-transcendence principally as the means whereby God or Brahman or It is revealed to human consciousness by becoming human consciousness. But we are dealing with nature mysticism, in which the state of self-transcendence does not come to dominate entirely the life and works of the worshiper. It is a withdrawal from the world and a return to it. A Zen master has been quoted as saying that "we must live with an empty heart, to let the world fill it,"[1] and this world is the world of life itself. In unity one experiences the "consummation of consciousness," and one knows immediately that this is what thousands of others have experienced. One has been initiated into the one literally selfless human society.

In "Presagio" and "Salvación por la luz" Salinas meditates on the Self in its specifically human manifestation, sensing that this is probably the only real way in which we are all one family, because it is in this fashion that all people may see and hold this world in common. To take part in a deeply experienced world-reality is the basis of true compassion. *Caritas* is a simple and natural result of self-transcendence, because it comes as a real experience, and has little to do with dutiful obedience to a publicly recognized moral law. In the state of nonego the individual becomes not altruistic, but selfless, that is to say, without regard for the wearisome task of playing ego. Of this selflessness Huxley said: "I was now a Not-self, simultaneously perceiving and being the Not-self of the things around me. To this newborn Not-self, the behavior, the appearance, the very thought of the self it had momentarily ceased to be, and of other selves, its one-time fellows, seemed not indeed distasteful, . . . but enormously irrelevant."[2]

When the world of one's own ego comes to appear "enormously irrelevant," one is the whole human race, the spirit of humanity momentarily liberated from the bonds of time. For the present one is Man and Woman, not just a man or a woman. In "Presagio" Salinas writes:

> This afternoon, facing you,
> I feel something in my eyes
> that watches you and it is not I.

We have translated "it is not I," but the Spanish reads "no soy yo," which will admit of two meanings simultaneously. The usual meaning is the one we have given; but the second meaning is peculiarly appropriate to the context. It is that meaning intended by García Lorca in his "Romance sonámbulo," where he has one of the speakers say, "Pero yo ya no soy yo, / ni mi casa es ya mi casa,"[3] which means, "But I am no longer myself, / nor is my home my own any more." And it is really difficult not to sense this meaning in the context of "Presagio":

> This afternoon, facing you,
> I feel something in my eyes
> that watches you and I am not myself.

"I am not myself" is a paradox, but the statement is perfectly comprehensible, since it corresponds to living experience, which will impose itself upon language with or without logic. By the same token Salinas tells us in "Presagio" that his transcendental glance upon the world is his—and not his

("Como la mía, y no mía"); similarly, in "Salvación por la luz" he says that one day his eyes will be simultaneously absent and present ("ya nunca aquí, y aquí," "here nevermore—and here"). The question arises in "Presagio" (as it always will in unity), Do I live in it, or does it live in me? And the thirteenth variation ends with the paradoxical "I feel myself to be / I myself, and estranged." The Spanish says, "me siento / yo mismo, y enajenado," using reflexively the verb *sentir*, "to feel" ("me siento alegro," "I feel happy"); hence "me siento yo mismo" means "I feel myself (as) I myself." At the same time the speaker is *enajenado* (derived from *ajeno*, and this from L. *alienus*, "alien"). The speaker is alienated from ego—it is "enormously irrelevant" right now—because he is filled with the *yo mismo*, which translates as "I myself," or "the very I."

This is the state that brings with it the nonego meaning of human salvation, and it is that with which "Salvación por la luz" is concerned. The light in this poem is, of course, the light of contemplative consciousness, the true seeing, which is liberation. Salinas puts as one of his epigraphs at the head of *El Contemplado* the lines from a poem by his friend, Jorge Guillén: "The light, that never suffers, / guides me well."[4] Unified consciousness does not suffer, because suffering is a function of ego. This is the basic notion underlying the Buddhist intuition that all suffering arises from ego-desires, and that the goal of consciousness is liberation from suffering through liberation from ego. Full consciousness beyond ego is "the light that never suffers," and is ipso facto experienced as salvation. All egos suffer, but mind simply *is*. The "salvation through the light" is experienced as *ajena*, which we have translated as "estranged," but which could be more appropriately translated "I feel myself to be I myself, and nonego," though the diction is not very attractive.

In "Salvación por la luz" Salinas hits upon a way of describing this second world of self-transcendence:

> Now, here, facing you, utterly entranced,
> I learn what I am: I am a moment
> of that long looking that eyes you,
> from yesterday, from today, from tomorrow,
> parallel with time.

The speaker has actually learned what it means to be here, now—that is, in the Eternal Present. Richard Alpert speaks of this kind of learning in his book, *Remember: Be Here Now*, the story of his own quest for self-transcendence. When he visited India he became the disciple of an ascetic with whom he eventually intuited the meaning of here-now. Alpert wanted to be friends with him, have conversations, but "he wasn't the least bit interested in all of the extraordinary dramas that I had collected. . . . He was the first person I couldn't seduce into being interested in all this. He just didn't care. And yet, I never felt so profound an intimacy with another being. It was as if he were inside of my heart. And . . . everywhere we went, he was at home."[5] Whenever Alpert wanted to trade anecdotes about the past, whenever he wanted to talk about his hopes for the future, the ascetic would tell him, "Just be here now."

And so one discovers that the here-now, the Eternal Present, is actually an entirely other world that is always running alongside the world of sidereal time, or, is, as Salinas puts it, "parallel with time." It is in the here-now that he finds out that "we are all alike," just as Alpert discovered that one human being can be at home inside the heart of another. It is self, experienced under the aspects of varied consciousnesses.

Salinas senses too that this kind of self-transcendence is "most faithful," for it never deserts the human race. Only the otherness of the dualistic world deserts us, and it is there where we find what Santayana melodramatically called "this great disaster of our birth."[6] Buber characterizes the "I-It" world as evil, because it is based on a presumption of present being: we think we are here now, but we live in the past and future. If one "lets it have the mastery, the continually growing world of *It* overruns [one] and robs [one] of the reality of [the] *I*, till the incubus over and the ghost within whisper to one another the confession of their non-salvation."[7] Ego, in an access of self-pity, laments its own mortality, while the ghost within approaches to say its life is ruined.

We recall that in "Tema" Salinas has written:

> From watching you so long
> . . . .
> astonishment by astonishment,
> I have given you a name;
> . . . .
> the contemplated one, the immutable
> One Contemplated.

And now, in the closing lines of the cycle we read:

> Through coming to watch it, day by day,
> entrancement by entrancement,
> perhaps your eternity,
> transformed into light, may enter us through our eyes.
>
> And from watching you so long, we may attain salvation.

The two passages are substantially identical, and since they are concerned with salvation, it is appropriate to contrast the ego-meaning of the term with its Self-meaning.

The ego-meaning of salvation is personal survival in heaven, after death; *eternity*, which for ego means a dwelling in clock-time "forever." This is the ego-eternity described in the Grimm tale, "The Shepherd Boy," where the protagonist is asked to tell "how many seconds of time are there in eternity." This is his answer: "In Lower Pomerania is the Diamond Mountain, which is two miles high, two miles wide, and two miles deep; every hundred years a little bird comes and sharpens its beak on it, and when the whole mountain is worn away by this, then the first second of eternity will be over."[8]

Such is the manner in which secular consciousness approaches the problem of what eternity is. It must be time without end—sidereal time, in contrast to Chan Sei Ghow's "Forever is / but a moment aware. / How foolish to think Eternity is numbered."[9] For Self, eternity is no-time, and unified consciousness is immediately aware of this. There is no death because death, like birth, happens in time.

Hence the salvation of which Salinas speaks at the end of "Salvación por la luz" can come about only by watching, by contemplating until unity is achieved:

> From watching you so long . . .
> astonishment by astonishment . . . ("Tema")

> entrancement by entrancement . . .
> from watching you so . . . ("Salvación por la luz")

It is only by "watching so long" that ego is transcended. It "dies" and is replaced by a higher consciousness which is ipso facto salvation: "The ego death is . . . followed by the sense of rebirth, . . . 'redemption,' or 'salvation,' spoken of in scriptural passages; or the achievement of 'illumination,' 'ekatvan,' 'nirvana,' 'satori,' or whatever the term used in some of the non-Christian traditions."[10]

The Eternal Now produces a paradoxical sense of strangeness coupled with familiarity ("I recognize myself in it, and it is unfamiliar"). One knows immediately that this has always been here, doing what it is busy doing—"exfoliating" out of itself—and yet because one has lived for so many years identified with the ego-personality the shock of recognition is inescapable. Thus Sir William Ramsay, in the bosom of the Eternal Now, wrote, "Everything has occurred before. . . . Trace of beginning sense of having been here before . . . feeling of recurrence, e.g., table, mantelpiece, etc., having been *always* there." In quoting this, Nicoll observes, "The main feeling is that everything has happened before and that in some way everything always is."[11]

Thus the Eternal Now is a kind of enormous *déjà vu*, and it may well be that the normal *déjà vu* has its deepest explanation right here.[12] When the *déjà vu* occurs there seems to be a momentary egolessness, and everything seems to be hanging suspended out of time; words being spoken by anyone reverberate with a significance that has nothing to do with their immediate meaning. One suddenly senses that a kind of new space has opened up, and this appears to be the first inkling of unified consciousness: a split-second loss of ego-orientation so subtle that it is rarely recognized for what it is.

Very well, then; one of the characteristics of this cosmic *déjà vu* is what we may call experiencing people as Self. The Self is identical in all human consciousness, and when the historical and geographical ego-personality drops away (cf. the etymology of "secular"), one not only realizes that one is Self, but also perceives it quite clearly in everybody else. Everyone around seems always to have been there; it has all "happened before." When George Russell experienced unity he wrote:

> all I thought of heaven before
> I find in earth below:
> A sunlight in the hidden core
> To dim the noonday glow.
> And with the earth my heart is glad,
> I move as one of old. . . .[13]

One realizes that human consciousness is always exfoliating out of the one Self, and that the myriad historical kinds of cultural consciousnesses have always been merely a thin overlay of what the human spirit is always busy doing, whether we are aware of it or not. Watts describes this as follows when, experiencing the unity given him with LSD, he was sitting with friends: "At some time in the middle of the twentieth century, upon an afternoon in the summer, we are sitting around a table on the terrace. . . . We seem to have been there forever, for the people with me are no longer the humdrum and harassed little personalities . . . we are all pretending to be. They appear rather as immortal archetypes of themselves without, however, losing their humanity. It is just that their differing characters seem . . . to contain all history; they are at once unique and eternal, men and women but also gods and goddesses. For now that we have time to look at each other we become timeless."[14] Watts says here of the Eternal Now that "we have time to look at each other," meaning, of course, the timeless present in which one has an eternity to do anything at all, because the one doing it is reality, already complete, and therefore not looking into the future, at which time some imagined goal of completion may be reached. It is the complete Self "exempt from the enchainment" noted by Robert Powell in *Zen and Reality:* "The You which is Not You is timeless, ambition-less and without desire. It is the undifferentiated and fundamental life within us which has not been entirely malformed and riveted by the iron domination of personality. It is part of the universal consciousness still exempt from the enchainment in the [secular] Self-consciousness which is a special attribute of each separate personality."[15] This is the very "chain of iron" recognized by Salinas himself in the poem placed at the beginning of these pages. By contrast, that "unknown master" is the you which is always here, and which impresses the individual as a cosmic homecoming free of death. Delmore Schwartz realizes that he knows

> at last that death is inconceivable among the living . . .
> Hearing the thunder of the news of waking from the false
>   dream of life that life can ever end.[16]

The ego-personality will die, we say to ourselves, shuddering along with Unamuno; but in unity the ego-personality already *has* died, and one realizes that it didn't hurt a bit. Hence the sense of knowing finally what real, experiential salvation is.

This is the burden of Salinas's "Salvación por la luz," for there he expresses his knowledge that whenever the Self leaps into one's eyes, it is "Mind at Large" in its specifically human form of awareness. It is all people at once and the speaker is looking with the eyes of the human race. *It* has passed through the living spirits of every generation of human beings. In the poem "¿Qué pájaros?" it was identified as the "beautiful one," the "single bird," and the symbol recurs in "Salvación por la luz."

> Now it perches here before flying on.
> When it takes wing it will go to pause
> in my children, the slender branch I offer,
> and in their eyes—mine—
> I, absent but here, will continue watching you.

"I" means "you," and "you" means "I." Secular mentality can never accept this salvation through ego-death, since secular mentality cannot conceive of what it means to be completely conscious without benefit of ego. But for the speaker of *El Contemplado* it is the salvation that he devoutly wishes for us all.

Chapter Seventeen
TRUE SEEING

VER LO QUE VEO

Quisiera más que nada, más que sueño,
ver lo que veo.

No buscar hondos signos por celestes
mundos supremos.
Estrellas, a mi alcance, estos guijarros,
duros luceros.
Copia con ellos mano caprichosa
altos modelos;
fulgen, de cuarzo, las constelaciones
Cisne, Perseo.
Aquí las tengo.

Por tornasoles nunca iré al crepúsculo,
tan pasajeros.
Horizontes conozco comprimidos,
edenes ciertos.
Crepúsculos inmóviles, constantes,
sol sin descenso.
Arreboles portátiles: los llevan
las conchas dentro.
Aquí los tengo.

Que entre brumas persigan las galeras
intactos reinos,
para dar a la tierra nueva tierra,
más viento al viento.
En la playa me estoy, al horizonte,
por vago, ajeno;
mis ojos dejo que en la arena abreven
todo su anhelo.
En esos granos, que por chicos vuelan
sólo a mi aliento,
hundo la mano, y en mi palma nace
áureo imperio.
De tierras de vergel, madres de rosas,
de altos roquedos,
de campos de trigal, de parameras,
la arena, restos.
Aquí descubro yo mis continentes,
mis archipiélagos.
Glorias del Almirante, Indias levísimas,
aquí las tengo:
(Apenas; que las cojo y ya se huyen
entre los dedos.)

El futuro, distancia. No te pierda
lo venidero.
A ti te acerca tu presente. Ser
es estar siendo.
Prisa, apetito de las lejanías,
torpe atropello
de las largas dulzuras del minuto:
da tiempo al tiempo.
A la orilla del río de su calma,
quieto, contemplo.
Por la visión de lo que está delante,
dejo el proyecto.
¿A qué darle palabras al poema,
si lo estoy viendo?
Los dos amantes, dulce río abajo,
sueltan los remos;
que los lleven las ondas sosegados,
amor es lento.
El caudal de su dicha y el del agua
fluyen parejos.
Lo que ellos hablan y la espuma dice
suena de acuerdo.
Alguien que no está en ellos, y sí en ellos,
sabe su término.
Mirándose en los ojos más cercanos
se ven el puerto.

¿Es lo que veo el río, o es el río?
¿Soy yo los dos amantes, o son ellos?

Sí. Ver lo que se ve. Ya está el poema,
aquí, completo.

From *Confianza* (1955)

TO SEE WHAT I SEE

I should like, more than anything else, more than a dream, to see what I see.

Not to seek deep signs among celestial worlds on high. Stars within my reach are these pebbles, hard, shining stars. With them a capricious hand copies lofty models. The constellations Cygnus, Perseus, shine in quartz. I have them here.

Through iridescences I will never go to the sunset; they are so fleeting. I know of condensed horizons, never failing Edens. Immobile twilights, constant, sun that never sets, portable cloud-effects: seashells carry them within. I have them here.

Let galleys pursue within the mists virgin kingdoms so as to give more land to earth, more wind to wind. Indifferent to the vague horizon I will remain on the beach; the sand shall satisfy the yearning of my eyes. Into these grains of sand, so small they fly at a breath, I sink a hand and in my palm is born a golden empire of fruitful lands where roses bloom, of rocky cliffs and fields of wheat and barren wastes. The sand, the remains. Here I discover my continents, my archipelagos. Glories of Columbus, minute Indies, I have them here. (Just barely; for I clutch them and at once they flee through my fingers.)

The future is distance. Be not confounded by things to come. Your present sets you close unto yourself. To be is to stand, being.

Haste is an appetite for things remote, a clumsy trampling down of the lasting sweetnesses of the minute. Everything in its own time. On the banks of time's tranquility quietly I contemplate. I have the vision before me, I abandon planning.

Why furnish the poem with words? I am looking at it now.

The two lovers down the sweet stream abandon their oars; let the tranquil waves carry them along at peace; love is slow. The volume of their joy and the volume of the water flow equally. What they speak and what the foam says sound alike. Someone who is not in them and yet is in them, knows its terminus. Gazing into each other's eyes (these are the nearest) they see the mutual port.

Is what I see the river, or is the river what I see? Am I the two lovers, or is it they?

Yes. To see the obvious. Here's the poem, complete.

What has *sound* got to do with music?
That music must be heard is not essential.
What it sounds like may not be what it is.—Charles Ives, *About Charles Ives*

Why furnish the poem with words? I am looking at it now.—Pedro Salinas

---

The two statements just above appear to be a rejection by creative artists of the art forms with which they have worked a great deal. They are not absurd statements, but they are paradoxical if judged rationally. Ives says that it is not essential to hear how music sounds when played, and so the question arises, Not essential to what? And Salinas's statement seems to echo the romantic notion that poetry is already in the world; the poet merely transcribes it, even as Spain's great nineteenth-century romantic poet, Gustavo Adolfo Bécquer, suggested in a famous poem:

> podrá no haber poetas; pero siempre
> habrá poesía.[1]

> Perhaps poets will cease to be; but
> there will always be poetry.

But it is not essential to seek historical sources for what Ives and Salinas are saying here, because it seems evident that they are both talking not about their art as a finished product, but rather about the source of it; even Bécquer said "poetry," not "poems." After all, it is not extravagant to think of art as the by-product of a preintellectual experience, as inspiration, or Platonic possession. No reader of mystical poetry would think it strange if Saint John of the Cross had said, "What have *words* got to do with poetry?

That poetry must be written down and read is not essential. What it sounds like (to you) may not be what it is."

Saint John of the Cross could easily have said such a thing; we need only remember that he was a "professional" mystic, who also wrote poems. What he wrote was a by-product of his mystical vocation. He was first a seeker of God and secondly a poet. Had it not been so his poetry could not even have been written. So that by "essential" Ives surely means this, that in order to realize what the source of music actually is, one is not required to experience the sound of music. Indeed, if one does not already have some natural feeling for what causes art, one may never achieve it by exposing oneself to uplift.

Since we are concerned throughout these pages with the symbology of poetry and not the style, not the art, not why poems are poetic, this question of sources is central to our study, while the sound of poetry—its stylistics—is peripheral. The person who spends a lifetime working with an art form faces many times over the problem of the expressive relationship between *eros* and *logos*, between the vital source and the arranged product. It happens sometimes that a painter works for years attempting to paint *the* painting, and these many endeavors come to be known as styles, or periods. That is to say, the artist tries out ways of making manifest what spirituality actually is in the long run, trying to set effort closer to the mystery of self-transcendence. The artist may even sense at times a kind of overriding conviction that *what* one experiences is more momentous than all attempts to redeem that experience. That redemption, that salvation of the experience may seem to edge so closely onto the experience itself that the precise direction of one's vocation gets lost. One may sit back and begin to reassess the priorities of reality, for to produce poems, paintings, or symphonies may then be viewed by the artist-as-seeker as being subordinate to the seeking. If not, the artist may retreat from this lure of the oceanic consciousness and manipulate art as a feat of style, which easily leads to inflating the significance of aesthetic activity. The notion of "the Bible as literature" is an example of this.

Salinas was an excellent poet, not a giant. Because his was an integrated spirit he managed to live with a foot in either world, the world of ego-intellect and the world of Self. It may be for this reason that his interest was so often drawn to a consideration of the creative process itself as the subject of his own poems. At any rate he understood that the esthetic feat was preceded by a "pure feat" (the *hazaña pura* of "Underwood Girls"): the feat of self-transcendence, the reestablishment of contact with the roots of one's being, the renovation of one's Selfhood. And so speaking more as a layman than as a poet he can say, "Why furnish the poem with words? I am looking at it now." However the poem may turn out it is still an attempt to redeem the experience of self-transcendence. If the poem gets very close to doing that, then it gets close to being something like a carbon copy of the experience. The more faithfully it reflects that experience, the more successful it is as a poem. This observation seems to force upon us the conclusion that the most adequate poem would be the experience itself. Any attempt to transmit it aesthetically may seem like gilding the lily—a "wretched excess."

But his question here is, of course, a rhetorical one, since it occurs in a poem; when he blurts it out he is not being artistically nihilistic. He knows why you furnish the poem with words: you do it because by following your vocation you are being yourself. Salinas's vocation was to concern himself poetically with the mysterious process of self-transcendence and with the restless relationship between profane and sacred reality.

In "Ver lo que veo," a late poem, he allows himself to wax more discursive about these two worlds, and, like a debater, is inclined to the invidious comparison. To see directly the "suchness" of things, to dwell in the Eternal Now—or at least to realize with conviction that it is an abiding presence—is to experience liberation. This means liberation from suffering; not liberation from caring, not immunity to cruelty, but detachment from ego-suffering— the illusion of being vulnerable. This is salvation, becoming whole, and "Ver lo que veo" is an appropriate poem to be written by a person in the second half of life. In it Salinas bears witness to the saving grace of nonego. The thought of the poem and its diction come to grips with the eternal difference between the poetic and the nonpoetic word. Both ego-intellect and the Self use the same words with entirely different meanings, *logos* as abstraction, and *logos* as poetic symbol. The first lines of the poem initiate this wordplay: "I should like . . . to see what I see." We understand without much difficulty that the common verb *ver*, "to see," is being used in two different ways here—what we may designate as "to see$_1$" and "to see$_2$". "To see$_1$" is the primordial, preintellectual seeing, the seeing of the Seer; nonego or "magic" seeing—what the speaker of "Madrid. Calle de . . ." attributed to the mirror on vacation: "It looks today: for the first time it is eyes."

"To see$_2$" is, of course, the exploitative view of the world whereby one sets and pursues goals that can be negotiated. Since "Ver lo que veo" is concerned with liberation from the pursuit of happiness, the speaker turns from seeing$_2$ to seeing$_1$, and so we may render this as "I should like truly to see what I look at." This is not a religious goal in the strictest sense, just as Zen Buddhism is not a religion. Zen is more appropriately thought of as something akin to psychotherapy (one undertakes the task of spiritual wholeness), or as nature mysticism as opposed to theistic mysticism.[2] "Ver lo que veo" expresses the "pantheistic" acceptance of a world reality that is not the Opus No. One of Jehovah, but rather simply the obvious unity that it is. It is a sacred reality to be sure, in the sense that the exalted consciousness is an awareness of ubiquitous spirit, and falls immediately into religious expressions, as Thoreau did when he contrasted the "ingenuous worshipper" and the "ingenuous observer." It seems to be a stage that Christian theistic mystics characteristically pass through on the way to union with the God-head. Saint Teresa describes it in her autobiography: "Once when I was at prayer it was revealed to me suddenly (though I saw no actual form; but it was utterly clear to me) how all things can be seen to be in God, and how God has them all within. I do not know how to express this in writing, but it remained deeply impressed on my spirit, and it is one of the great favors that the Lord has vouchsafed me."[3] Here the experience of sudden enlighten-ment, of suddenly "catching on" to the truth of *Deus in rebus*, God in things, is expressed as suddenly seeing how all things are always quietly sitting, bathed in the "fine effluence" shed by the ground of reality. Nature mystics experience this dawning of unified consciousness, and they spontaneously attribute it to the presence of God. George Russell wrote, "I believe that most of what was said of God [by ancient seers] was in reality said of that Spirit whose body is Earth."[4]

In "Ver lo que veo" Salinas draws a big distinction between this earthly "pantheism" and theistic mysticism, because he insists throughout that he is earthbound. Russell, as a nature mystic, was not interested in how the theistic mystics may or may not have gone beyond the consciousness of *Deus in rebus;* by his statement he shows a willingness to accept the word *God* as a synonym for "Earth-Spirit." Indeed, the occidental nature mystic is typically neither a priest nor in religious orders. For such a person the initial enlight-enment of the Eternal Now is so self-fulfilling that there is no motivation (or monastic opportunity) to devote one's entire energies to professional mysti-cism. The great awakening to *Deus in rebus* brings to one a grateful accept-ance of the nature of earthly reality, and then the peace of liberation flows into the soul. One then simply rests in full trust of what may ultimately be, no matter how the sectarians may variously describe it and preach it. In "Ver lo que veo" Salinas turns from the stars in order to contemplate the sands of the shoreline, for just as Alan Watts says, "God is the most obvious thing in the world, . . . absolutely self-evident—the simplest, clearest and closest reality of life and consciousness. We are only unaware of [this] because we are too complicated, for our vision is darkened by the complexity of pride. We seek . . . beyond the horizon with our noses lifted in the air, and fail to see that [God] lies at our very feet."[5] And thus the burden of lines 3–20 of "Ver lo que veo": what I seek, that do I already have—here and now. Just as in "Crepúsculo" the speaker knows that his life must be committed to the spirit—"but not the Cross," not the self-immolating, total sacrifice of ego-consciousness to the spirit—so here he accepts that the "deep signs among celestial worlds on high" are not for him. As one of God's self-conscious creatures he contains within his spirit the whole macrocosm. Theistic mys-ticism is not his vocation, and so he accepts the fulfillment of unity, which means transcending the barrier separating the macrocosm from the micro-cosm, even as the *Zenrinkushu* recommended long ago:

> If you do not get it from yourself,
> Where will you go for it?

When the macrocosm and microcosm suddenly loom as one, then the seeker has found what was sought; hence we read in the *Zenrinkushu:*

> To have the sun and moon in one's sleeve;
> To hold the universe in the palm of one's hand.[6]

The present moment is time out of mind, a world apart from the pursuit of secular hopes and ambitions—the "dream" of the opening line: "I should like, more than anything else, more than a dream . . . ."

A characteristic of unity as the nature mystics experience it is the sense of being at the center of the universe; Sir William Ramsay's ether experiments attest to this. One is suddenly at home in the world reality; one seems to have gained everything by losing everything in egolessness. Juan Ramón Jiménez, the greatest of the modern Spanish lay mystic poets, gets at this idea by playing with the ego-meaning and meaning for the self of possessing. He exclaims, "Everything is mine now, everything! I mean, nothing is mine anymore, nothing!"[7] In similar fashion Salinas approaches the notion of possession with the recurrent "I have them here." He tells us all that is "his" in the microcosm: "Aquí descubro yo mis continentes, / mis archipiélagos," ("Here I discover my continents, my archipelagos"). But he is talking about the Eternal Now, and this is not a thing to be owned but rather an event to share in. Possession is time-bound and ego-bound; and so in lines 43–45 he backs off from the dualism that he was edging into insensibly: "Be not confounded by things to come. Your Present sets you close unto yourself." It is the same in 47–54, where the haste of karmic action—exploitative pursuit of goals—is "an appetite for things remote, a clumsy trampling down of the lasting sweetnesses of the minute . . ." and the rest of this section.

If this sounds very Buddhistic it is only because the Buddhists have made a great point of explaining that the beginning of wisdom lies in liberation from time-bound ego. All suffering comes from desire. Egolessness gives one the gift of now, wherein ego is traded off for spirit. Lines 45–46, like some Buddhist text, say:

> Your Present sets you close unto yourself. To be
> is to stand, being.

Here again Salinas is playing on the semantic differences latent in the vocabularies of Self and ego: "you_1" and "you_2," which is to say "you" as the experiencing Self (exalted consciousness) and "you" as the experiencing ego that one usually is. In the Eternal Now, *tu presente*, the Now of Self, brings "you₁" into conscious proximity; the everyday consciousness of "you₂" begins to be awash with it. (If it inundates consciousness the "worshiper" may flatly admit the "heresy," "I am God"—using the Self-meaning of "I".)

The Spanish text for lines 45–46 says, "Ser / es estar siendo," which I have translated as "To be is to stand, being." *Estar* (from L. *stare*, "to stand") has implicit an ontological meaning similar to the German *dasein*, derived from *sein*. *Sein* is "to be"; *da-sein*, "to be there," to exist by occupying space and time. Salinas's line, "Ser / es estar siendo" means "to exist is to stand existing in the world." In the Eternal Now what I am doing right now in this place is perceived as the here-and-now manifestation of the eternal Self. It is not that the"worshiper" believes that this moment will last forever (it *is* lasting forever), because to be in the Eternal Now does not mean to take leave of one's senses. One still knows that there is a tomorrow and that tomorrow may be the last day. But nevertheless, "death is impossible," and Now is Eternal in the sense that one is experiencing directly the vital principle, the *mana*, the living spirit that maintains the world reality, that has "always" maintained it and "always" will maintain it, and one sees how one is integrally a part of it forever and forever. With this experience any notion of goal-oriented activity, of "things to come" (lines 43–44) fades into insignificance. All that one ever wanted was self-fulfillment, and it suddenly dawns on one that the ego-meaning of "self-fulfillment" is irrelevant to the Self-meaning of "Self-fulfillment": realization of the Self within by raising it into awareness. The highest hope of any person is always called vaguely self-fulfillment, and that is equated with something else called happiness.

Happiness is related etymologically to the word *happen*, and to be happy is to awaken to what is actually happening here and now, before one's very eyes. It is to see truly what one is seeing. Hence the title of James Wright's poem, "Today I Was Happy, So I Made This Poem," which includes the lines,

> The moon suddenly stands up in the darkness,
> And I see that it is impossible to die.
> Each moment of time is a mountain.
> An eagle rejoices in the oak trees of heaven,
> Crying
> *This is what I wanted.*[8]

The person experiencing this may well "hastily scribble" the truth of the illumination: "To be means to be here, right now. The only way one can be is to stand here and be."

In the West this kind of enlightenment is not much respected, because it is the sort of thing about which dreamy nature mystics write poems. In the East the state of egolessness and unity appears to be more widely recognized as a human possibility, and many generations of families have sent their children to "finishing schools" where Zen Buddhists prepare them for adulthood.[9] To be here now is to attend to what is before our very eyes, and it is to overcome our deep-seated fear of the cosmos, which, we are convinced, wants to destroy us in "this great disaster of our birth." This is the great ego-ridden fear entertained by Unamuno; it is the "tragic sense of life," a thing that liberation from ego-desire and ego-suffering shows to be an illusion, more shortsighted than it is tragic.

To experience the liberation of detachment from this suffering in time means ceasing to press one's goals, for everything comes in its own due time. "On the banks of time's tranquility . . . I abandon planning." This detachment is not a monkish turning away from the world around one; on the contrary, one is fully engaged with it, truly seeing it. It is rather a liberation from the pressure of ego-oriented activity ("Haste, an appetite for things remote") whereby "happiness" is a reward in the future that is supposed to be brought about some day by one's rush through clock-time.

The fusion of macrocosm and microcosm is naturally experienced as love, and lines 57–68 express the vision in terms of two lovers in a boat downstream. They have abandoned their oars, since they are not going anywhere; they are already there, which is to say here, for there is no longer any distinction. Salinas's sense of the world reality as the ceaseless gliding of a river (the oceanic consciousness of *El Contemplado*) is the same river intuited as a serpent in "Agua en la noche," the same intuition of unity that Delmore Schwartz describes when he too awakens in the *renovatio:* his "First Morning of the Second World." Schwartz suddenly discovers that he is speaking with the voice of the Self, "a voice familiar and strange," and he looks around him to find it revealed that other people are not "other" at all:

> There they were, all of them, and I was with them,
> They were with me, and they were me, I was them, forever united
> As we all moved forward in a consonance silent and moving
>   Seated and gazing,
>   Upon the beautiful river forever.[10]

And so Salinas, contemplating the lovers who glide down the river: "Someone who is not in them and yet is in them, knows its terminus. Gazing into each other's eyes . . . they see the mutual port. . . . Am I the two lovers, or is it they?"

In line 69 Salinas again plays with the double vocabulary of ego and Self: "Is what I see the river, or is the river what I see?" The original Spanish text says, "¿Es lo que veo el río, o es el río?"—"Is what I see the river, or is [it] the river?"—which we have treated as an aposiopesis based on the repetition of *es*. It suggests the *coincidentia oppositorum* by forcing the language against itself. This is not extravagant or baroque, since we are dealing with the ahistorical problem of the language of Self. Examined logically, the question, Is what I see the river, or is it the river? does not make a great deal of sense. Formally it suggests that a choice is to be made; the English translation emphasizes this, since it must include a subject pronoun for *es*. If we exclude the subject pronoun, then the aposiopesis leaps before our eyes: "Is what I see the river, or is the river?"

With the leap out of duality and into unity the question spontaneously and naturally arises. It is a rhetorical question, of course, giving us to understand that duality has magically been transcended. Alan Watts discusses this new kind of seeing in terms of the field of vision: "The field of vision, which we take to be outside the organism, is in fact inside it because it is a translation of the external world into the form of the eye and the optical nerves. What we see is therefore a state of the organism, a state of ourselves."[11] In this way we can understand that the world reality is identical with our own mental process. We treat the phenomenon within a subject/object framework, but only a megalomaniac would maintain that the world reality is identical with ego. Yet if the world "out there" is not what ego says it is, then what is it?

The ontological question after the manner of a Bishop Berkeley is actually of no interest here, since it asks, What? What is a tree "in itself" when no one is around to see it? Answer: who wants to know? The state of unity does not reveal what anything is; rather it reveals how everything is significant—including the feat of Self-consciousness. This significance manifests itself in terms of symbolic reality, and not infrequently it appears in poems as a kind of Jungian synchronism. In "Ver lo que veo," it is a coincidence of the speaker's acutely receptive state of mind, and the flowing river with the lovers downstream. The coincidence leads to a fusion.

Synchronicity is Jung's name for "the meaningful coincidence or equivalence of a psychic and a physical state that have no causal relationship to one another."[12] This meaningful coincidence is of course related to Salinas's notion of *azar*, "chance," where an external event strikes him as matching up symbolically with his own psychic state. This is not unusual, since Salinas was a poet, and so was exceptionally receptive to the symbolic meaning of events occurring around him. To see the significance of a chance event means to be struck by the understanding that the self brings to bear on it, particularly if the event is a little more than unusual. In "Ver lo que veo," Salinas, idling by the river, sees two lovers in a boat, and this is no very amazing thing; indeed, that it is a common enough occurrence may hide from us its synchronistic significance. In order to bring out the coincidental meaning of this event, let us examine briefly two examples of synchronicity.

The first is the well-known synchronism witnessed by Jung. A patient of his was telling him of a critical dream she had had in which she was given an unusual golden beetle. At that very moment the kind of beetle described by her flew up to the windowpane and attempted to get into the room. [13] This is an unusual coincidence, but if we attribute any significance to it, it will have to be symbolic, transcending the level of meanings upon which ego-intellect operates. One would examine the symbology of the scarab and the religious significance which the Egyptians attached to it. Historically the ancient Egyptians are far removed from us, whereas symbolically, in the world of the self, they are our contemporaries.

The synchronicity of a peculiar thought and an external event such as the one just described does not seem striking to us unless the thought precedes the event, so that we exclaim, "Speak of the Devil!" When the event precedes the thought, then the connection is simple enough; we see something and it reminds us of something else. But if the event awakens us to symbolic reality, then we are struck by the presence of a remarkable sign, like that described in a poem by James Wright. He had been reading a mystical treatise by Boehme, and left the book lying open on his desk, which stood by a sunny window. Later he saw that a cricket had come in and was sunning itself on the pages of the book. This brought about a sudden enlightenment; perhaps the poet was intending to pick up the book and continue his reading, whereupon the presence of the contemplative cricket frustrated the intention, creating that blankness we have called (after Blyth) "extremity" in our discussion of "Font-Romeu." In any case the poet suddenly awakens to the symbolic significance of the event and writes his "Poems to a Brown Cricket," which include these lines:

> Here, I will stand by you, shadowless,
> At the small golden door of your body till you wake
> In a book that is shining. [14]

In ego-language the word *I* is perfectly clear; but Wright is speaking with the voice of what he calls here the "shadowless I," which is the voice of the nonmaterial spirit. His poems bear witness to the eternal presence that vitalizes the cricket, and that evolves through the millennia in order to waken into Self-consciousness as the shining vision of a mystic. For what is a mystic but a human being who has allowed the spirit to wake shining? What else is a poet?

That the cricket came in to alight on Boehme's book is not remarkable in itself. But the poet was able to experience the event as remarkable, and therefore awaken our own receptivity to such small miracles. He had been reading a book about the Self within; with the arrival of the cricket he saw that *seguro azar*, "dependable chance," was showing him the beginning and the end, the alpha and the omega of the spirit. The cricket is the very spirit of the earth, the telluric beginnings, so to speak, and there it is, in physical conjunction with the final product, the shining consciousness of the mystic. The one on the "outside," the other within.

Hence if the coincidence of a thought and an event are to be meaningful to us, we must be alive to symbolic reality, to signs, which is to say that we must do as Salinas recommends in "Ver lo que veo." We must truly see what is in front of our very eyes. It is the sort of thing that poets are characteristically aware of, and perhaps this is what makes them poets. The external event is perceived as a duplication of what is happening in their own mind, just as a position in chess is nothing more than a physical illustration of the consciousness of the players. The lay kibitzer may well see nothing significant about the chess position, even though the players may be making chess history; very well; in the same sense the possibility of synchronicity is ceaselessly taking place in the world around us, except that we are not alive to it because we have other concerns. The things around us are artifacts, useful in implementing our goals; but to switch from *negocio* to *ocio*, to see truly what is in front of us, suddenly enables us to experience the meaningful relationship between our own psychic state and the physical events before our eyes. We then see signs.

And so Salinas, in "Ver lo que veo," experiences the coincidence of a thought with an event. Gazing at the river he passes into unified consciousness and realizes that the retinal image closes the gap between the macrocosm and the microcosm. The river may or may not be "out there," but the significance of the river lies in the fact that consciousness experiences itself apperceptively as a ubiquitous flowing. Is there any difference between his psychic state and the river "out there"? They are mediated by the retinal image: does the river cause him to see it, or does his organism cause the river to be seen? It is a choice offered rhetorically, affirming the interdependence of macrocosm and microcosm, and it is not much different from the venerable question about the chicken and the egg. We may say that the Self evolved human self-consciousness to this purpose, so that it might rise up out of the river and contemplate itself doing what it does, which is to flow, in the Eternal Present. Because that is exactly what it has done, or rather what it can do, whenever one of its self-conscious creatures stumbles upon the secret of how to let the Self take over.

With this discovery of the secret of the river flooding consciousness Salinas looks downstream and a synchronic event occurs: there are two lovers in a boat, and they express precisely the significance of unified consciousness, as if they had been set there to that end. For, just as Plato has told us in the *Symposium*, it is true that each man and woman is incomplete, and that they seek completion in each other. When the right ones meet, each is a sign to the other. But if this is true, then it is also true that each ego-consciousness is incomplete, and can never find wholeness, salvation, health, except by uniting with the other half, the macrocosm. As long as ego-intellect persists in its dualism it is cut off from salvation, and erects for itself its own little grandiose "tragic sense of life." It cries out in sorrow, "*I—I* don't want to die! I want to live forever!" But unity obliterates this whole sorry tragedy at one fell swoop by decapitating the ego forthwith, whereupon one awakens as if from a nightmare.

If Salinas experiences the significance of the flowing river, he further experiences the significance of love as at-one-ment: "Am I the two lovers, or is it they?"—which we may understand as meaning, "Am I the two lovers, or are they I?" We are all in this together.

In the penultimate line of the poem we read, "Sí. Ver lo que se ve." Literally this means, "Yes. To see what is seen." But it is particularly appropriate to say that there is more to this line than meets the eye. If we look at it truly, we must sense in it a connotation at work; for *se ve* ("it is seen") is used idiomatically in Spanish to mean "it is obvious." Hence our translation, "to see the obvious," because a signal feature of unified consciousness is the open secret. We suddenly perceive that what we are now seeing has a very obvious significance, and we ask ourselves immediately, How on earth was it possible to be so blind? Then we catch on to the joke in Hsüan-chüeh's "Song of Realizing the Tao":

> The great gate is wide open to bestow alms,
> and no crowd is blocking the way.[15]

We use the word *joke* advisedly, for unified consciousness is no grave thing demanding the solemn decorum of Sunday church. Hsüan-chüeh tells us, almost as if watching us worry at some kind of Chinese puzzle, that something is obviously blocking our way to the solution, but that it is no massive physical obstacle. Once we have found out the solution, nothing could be more obvious, but until then nothing stands in the way except our own mental processes. Now, however, that crowd no longer blocks the way. Similarly, the *Zenrinkushu* tells us:

> Nothing whatever is hidden;
> From of old, all is clear as daylight.

And Soshi: "People all over the world try to know what they do not know, instead of trying to know what they already know."[16] Or, as Buber puts it, God is "the mystery of the self-evident, nearer to me than my *I*."[17] Naturally he speaks from his own experience.

In light of these observations it makes sense to read Salinas's statement "ver lo que se ve" as "to see the obvious." It comes close to the truism with which the Zen Buddhists like to play: "How can I see the Buddha-nature?" Answer: "It is obvious. Merely look at it." This may sound like Mae West's formula for living to be one hundred years old—"Don't stop breathing"—except that the advice to see the obvious, *ver lo que se ve*, is not at all tautological, since the Self, being beyond logic, is never tautological; it is real. The plane of natural mysticism can be experienced only by seeing what is most self-evident in the world, what is simplest, and one is simpler than two.

Salinas ends his poem here as he did "Cuartilla," by stating that the piece is now done: "Ya está el poema, / aquí, completo," "There's the poem, here, complete." *Ya está* conveys the notion of, "That's it; I've finished doing the job." But we have to deal with the use of the word *poema* back in line 55: "Why furnish the poem with words?" At the end of the piece he appears to be satisfied that he has closed the gap between the experience and the poem about it. "If you want to see the obvious, why then look at it. It is here, before your eyes, complete." "Here" has been a motif throughout the poem, and the last line tells us that the poem is here, complete now.

Where, then, is "here"? For the poet it is obviously the world around him that is no longer merely around him. For the reader of the poem, "here" is the text in hand. And in it the poet offers us his own "here," along with the poem. If we would do something more than enjoy his poetry we will take his advice and see what is self-evident: the here and now.

Notes

Chapter 1

1. John McHale, "The Plastic Parthenon," in *Kitsch*, ed. Gillo Dorfles (New York: Bell Publishing Co., 1969), p. 98.

2. Carl G. Jung, *The Secret of the Golden Flower: A Chinese Book of Life*, trans. Richard Wilhelm, with a commentary by Carl G. Jung (New York: Harcourt, Brace and World, 1962), p. 111.

3. Ronald G. Smith, trans., *I and Thou*, by Martin Buber (Edinburgh: T. and T. Clark, 1937), p. vii.

4. I. L. Salomon, trans., *Dino Campana: Orphic Songs* (New York: October House, 1968), p. 22.

5. *Dino Campana*, ibid., p. 27.

6. David Ignatow, *The Notebooks of David Ignatow* (Chicago: Swallow Press, 1973), pp. 219, 312.

7. The "incredible bomb" is not a nuclear device. It is much more "incredible": a supernatural bomb that destroys everything but love.

8. Pedro Salinas, *Lost Angel and Other Poems*, trans. Eleanor L. Turnbull (Baltimore: Johns Hopkins Press, 1938), p. x.

9. Pedro Salinas, *La poesía de Rubén Darío*, 3d ed. (Buenos Aires: Losada, 1968), p. 21.

10. Salinas, *Lost Angel*, p. x.

11. Ralph Adam Fine, *Mary Jane versus Pennsylvania* (New York: McCall Publishing Co., 1970), p. 116.

12. Ibid.

13. Jack S. Margolis and Richard Clorfene, *A Child's Garden of Grass* (New York: Pocket Book Editions, 1970), p. 27.

14. William James, *The Varieties of Religious Experience* (New York: New American Library, 1958), p. 298.

15. Maurice Nicoll, *Living Time* (New York: Hermitage House, 1953), p. 143.

16. Jorge Guillén, a major poet of Salinas's generation and a close friend of Salinas, wrote about a piece of furniture in this fashion. The title of the poem is "Beato sillón," i.e., "Holy Armchair," or "Beatified Armchair." (See his *Cántico* [Buenos Aires: Editorial Sudamericana, 1950], p. 235.)

17. Hsüan-chüeh, *Song of Realizing the Tao*, quoted in Alan Watts, *The Way of Zen* (New York: Pantheon Books, 1957), p. 145.

18. Henry David Thoreau, *Journal*, May 12, 1851, in *The Writings of Henry David Thoreau* (New York: Houghton, Mifflin and Co., 1906), 8:194.

19. James, *Varieties of Religious Experience*, p. 298.

20. Suso, quoted in Claudio Naranjo and Robert Ornstein, *On the Psychology of Meditation* (New York: Viking Press, 1971), p. 22.

21. Note here that this is not solipsism (the theory that the self can be aware of nothing but its own experience), because in the state of unity there is no difference between the "self" and what it experiences; but language, the tool of ego-intellect, will always suggest duality.

22. Nicoll, *Living Time*, pp. 149, 146.
23. Thoreau, *Journal*, March 17, 1852, 9:354.
24. David Ignatow, *Poems: 1934–1969* (Middletown, Conn.: Wesleyan University Press, 1970), pp. 125–26.
25. Charles A. Bennett, *A Philosophical Study of Mysticism* (New Haven: Yale University Press, 1923), p. 15.
26. This attitude can be carried over into the drug-induced *coincidentia oppositorum*, where it produces the "bad trip."
27. Helton G. Baynes, *Mythology of the Soul* (New York: Humanities Press, 1955), p. 367.

Chapter 2

1. Case (not drug-induced) cited in Walter H. Clark, *Chemical Ecstasy: Psychedelic Drugs and Religion* (New York: Sheed and Ward, 1969), p. 20.
2. Quoted in Charles A. Bennett, *A Philosophical Study of Mysticism* (New Haven: Yale University Press, 1923), pp. 73–74.
3. Reginald H. Blyth, *Haiku*, 4 vols. (Tokyo: Hokuseido Press, 1949–1952), 1:63.
4. See Alan Watts, *The Way of Zen* (New York: Pantheon Books, 1957), p. 75.
5. "El desnudo impecable," in *El desnudo impecable y otras narraciones* (Mexico: Tezontle, 1951), p. 123 (my translation). Jorge Guillén uses the singular *vacación* in the same way; see his poem "Vacación," in *Cántico* (Buenos Aires: Editorial Sudamericana, 1950), pp. 138–39; also the *vacante* ("the vacant person") of his "El distraído," in ibid, p. 191.
6. The title of the poem in Spanish has the force of "Madrid: Street *X*," or "Madrid: Street Such-and-such." I translate by analogy with Stanley J. Kunitz's poem, "Promenade on Any Street," in *Intellectual Things* (New York: Doubleday, Doran and Co., 1930), p. 56.
7. Shunryu Suzuki Roshi, in Jacob Needleman, *The New Religions* (New York: Doubleday and Co., 1970), p. 56.
8. "Dedicarse . . . enteramente a un ejercicio determinado."
9. Fr. Luis de Granada, *Obras de Fr. Luis de Granada*, Biblioteca de autores españoles, vol. 11 (Madrid: Rivadeneyra, 1915), p. 285; Juan de los Angeles, *Conquista del reino de Dios* (Madrid: Rialp, 1958), p. 423 (Fr. Juan here contrasts *ocio* and *negocio*); Miguel de Molinos, *Guía espiritual* (Madrid: Aguilar, 1935?), pp. 225–26.
10. Te-shan, quoted in Robert Powell, *Zen and Reality* (London: Allen and Unwin, 1961), p. 44.
11. Johan Huizinga, *Homo Ludens* (Boston: Beacon Press, 1955), p. 161; Lao Tzu, *Tao Te Ching*, XI ("Thirty spokes"), in *Zen in English Literature and Oriental Classics*, trans. Reginald H. Blyth (Tokyo: Hokuseido Press, 1942), p. 248.
12. Charles Reznikoff, "Autobiography," in *Going To and Fro and Walking Up and Down* (New York: Futuro Press, 1941), p. 28.
13. Cf. the traditional motifs of storks nesting on rooftops and bringing babies; Keigo Seki, *Folktales of Japan* (Chicago: University of Chicago Press, 1963), p. 78n;

Helton G. Baynes, *Mythology of the Soul* (New York: Humanities Press, 1955), p. 698; Robert Graves, *Difficult Questions, Easy Answers* (London: Cassell, 1972), p. 3.

14. Carl G. Jung, *The Secret of the Golden Flower*, trans. Richard Wilhelm (New York: Harcourt, Brace and World, 1962), p. 132.

15. Robert Graves, *Goodbye to All That* (London: Cassell, 1957), p. 264.

16. Heinrich Zimmer, *Philosophies of India* (New York: Pantheon Books, 1951), p. 285.

17. See John Crispin, *Pedro Salinas* (New York: Twayne Publishers, 1974), p. 26.

18. Carlos Feal Deibe rightly sees this poem as concerned with the escape from a prose reality (*La poesía de Pedro Salinas* [Madrid: Editorial Gredos, 1965], p. 49), but because he casts only a cursory glance at the text, he reads it animistically as the description of a street that has magically come to life (in the fashion of the animated artifacts of Hans Christian Andersen) and that is now discovering its true being (*su ser íntimo*) (ibid., pp. 46–47). Various critics of Salinas use the animistic approach, since Salinas wrote so frequently about reality in terms of artifacts, but this will not stand much scrutiny, since it is alien to the sophistication of Salinas's symbolism.

Chapter 3

1. Okakura Kakuzo, *The Book of Tea* (Rutland, Vt.: Charles E. Tuttle, 1956), p. 91.

2. Alan Watts, *The Way of Zen* (New York: Pantheon Books, 1957), p. 146.

3. Wallace Stevens, "Someone Puts a Pineapple Together," in *The Palm at the End of the Mind* (New York: Random House, 1972), p. 295.

4. Jacob Grimm, *Teutonic Mythology*, 4 vols. (New York: Dover, 1966), 2:585.

5. See Richard Burton, *The Book of the Thousand Nights and a Night*, 10 vols., privately printed by the Burton Club, n.d. 5:302n.

6. Alfred Métraux, *Voodoo in Haiti* (New York: Oxford University Press, 1959), p. 361.

7. Mircea Eliade, *Australian Religions: An Introduction* (Ithaca, N.Y.: Cornell University Press, 1973), p. 109. He is quoting Adolphus Elkin.

8. Edgar Thurston, *Omens and Superstitions of Southern India* (New York: McBride, Nast, 1912), p. 90.

9. Ibid., p. 91.

10. Edgar Herzog, *Psyche and Death* (London: Hodder and Stoughton, 1966), p. 58.

11. Henry David Thoreau, *Journal*, Aug. 17, 1851, in *The Writings of Henry David Thoreau* (New York: Houghton, Mifflin and Co., 1906), 8:392–93.

12. Ernest Jones, *Nightmare, Witches, and Devils* (New York: W. W. Norton, 1931), p. 94.

13. Delmore Schwartz, "O Child, Do Not Fear the Dark and Sleep's Dark Possession," in *Summer Knowledge: New and Selected Poems, 1938–1958* (Garden City, N.Y.: Doubleday and Co., 1959), p. 162.

14. Saint Teresa, *Vida y obras*, 3 vols. (Madrid: Felipe G. Rojas, 1902), 1:405; Saint John of the Cross, *Vida y obras* (Madrid: Biblioteca de Autores Cristianos, 1950), p. 1039; Miguel de Molinos, *Guía espiritual* (Madrid: Aguilar, 1935?), p. 196.

15. William Butler Yeats, *Ideas of Good and Evil* (London: A. H. Bullen, 1908), p. 124.

16. Aelian, *On the Characteristics of Animals* (Cambridge: Harvard University Press, 1958–1959), 11.16.

17. Herodotus (New York: C. Scribner's Sons, 1897), 8.41.

18. Heinrich Zimmer, *The Art of Indian Asia*, 2 vols. (New York: Pantheon Books, 1955), 1:59.

Chapter 4

1. The list of yin and yang characteristics, so convenient for present purposes, appears in the *Time-Life* book, *The World's Great Religions* (New York: Time, Inc., 1957), p. 77.

2. Charles Reznikoff, "Autobiography," in *Going To and Fro and Walking Up and Down* (New York: Futuro Press, 1941), p. 35.

3. Edmund Carpenter, "Interval," in *They Became What They Beheld* (New York: Outerbridge and Dienstfrey, 1970), unpaginated.

4. Idem, "Hardedge," in ibid.

5. Reginald H. Blyth, *Haiku*. 4 vols. (Tokyo: Hokuseido Press, 1949–1952), 3: 370, 371.

6. Ibid., 2:83.

7. Ibid., 2:88.

8. Theodore Roethke, *Words For the Wind* (New York: Doubleday and Co., 1958), p. 102

9. Frances G. Wickes, *The Inner World of Man* (New York: H. Holt, 1948), p. 23.

10. William Desmonde, *Magic, Myth, and Money* (New York: Free Press of Glencoe, 1962) pp. 124–26; Helton G. Baynes, *Mythology of the Soul* (New York: Humanities Press, 1955), p. 225.

11. Desmonde, *Magic, Myth, and Money*, p. 126.

12. Ibid.

13. Ibid., p. 125

Chapter 5

1. Carl G. Jung, *Psychological Types* (New York: Harcourt, Brace and Co., 1926), pp. 588–99.

2. Helton G. Baynes, *Mythology of the Soul* (New York: Humanities Press, 1955), p. 162.

3. Frances G. Wickes, *The Inner World of Man* (New York: H. Holt, 1948), p. 94.

4. François Duyckaerts, *The Sexual Bond* (New York: Delacorte Press, 1970), p. 168.

5. Cited in W. H. Auden, *A Certain World: A Commonplace Book* (New York: The Viking Press, 1970), p. 243.

6. Baynes, *Mythology of the Soul*, pp. 333, 649.

7. Robert Charles Hope, *The Legendary Lore of the Holy Wells of England* (London: Elliot Stock, 1893), p. 45.

8. See also Rupert Allen, *Psyche and Symbol in the Theater of Federico García Lorca* (Austin: University of Texas Press, 1974), pp. 199–211.

9. Andrew Lang, ed., *Yellow Fairy Book* (New York: Longmans, Green and Co., 1948), p. 62.

10. Ira Progoff, *Depth Psychology and Modern Man* (New York: Julian Press, 1959), pp. 84–106.

11. Théophile Gautier, *The Complete Works*, trans. Frédéric C. de Sumichrast, 12 vols. (New York: Bigelow, Smith, 1900), 7: 365, 368.

12. Semper Idem [pseud.], *The "Blue Book": A Bibliographical Attempt to Describe the Guide Books to the Houses of Ill Fame in New Orleans as They Were Published There* (New Orleans, 1936), p. 61.

13. Curt Gentry, *The Madams of San Francisco* (New York: Doubleday and Co., 1964), p. 111.

14. John Gosling and Douglas Warner, *The Shame of a City: An Inquiry into the Vice of London* (London: W. H. Allen, 1960), pp. 193–94.

15. Gentry, *Madams*, p. 110.

16. George J. Kneeland, *Commercial Prostitution in New York City* (New York: Century Co., 1913), p. 30.

17. Ibid., p. 52.

18. Ibid., p. 68.

19. Robert A. Wilson, ed., *Playboy's Book of Forbidden Words* (Chicago: Playboy Press, 1972), pp. 57–58. In Mexico the taxi dancers are also called *ficheras*, because they receive a negotiable chit (*ficha*) for each drink they persuade a customer to buy them. The availability of the *fichera* as prostitute is generally recognized.

20. Wilhelm Stekel, in his *The Interpretation of Dreams* (New York: Washington Square Press, 1967), discusses the taxicab metaphor in terms of a promiscuous female patient who dreamed about getting into a taxicab. See pp. 105–6. The Spanish text of "Font-Romeu" says of the woman, "Es *un* taxi," employing the masculine gender, and not "es *una* taxi." Simply to describe the woman's occupation, using the idiomatic language of the milieu, one would say, "Es una taxi" ("she is a taxi dancer"); to bring out the satirical force of the expression Salinas says, "Es un taxi" ("she is [like] a taxicab"), meaning what the expression originally implied.

21. John Canady, *Metropolitan Seminars in Art*, Portfolio 11, "The Artist as a Social Critic" (New York: The Metropolitan Museum of Art, 1959), p. 25.

22. C. H. Rolph [pseud.], *Women of the Streets* (London: Secker & Warburg, 1955), p. 92. The other group are clients seeking "kinky" sex.

23. Ibid., p. 116.

24. Polly Adler, *A House Is Not a Home* (New York: Rinehart and Co., 1953), p. 125.

25. Rolph, *Women of the Streets*, pp. 118, 87, 91.

26. Adler, *A House Is Not a Home*, p. 130.

27. Rolph, *Women of the Streets*, p. 119.

28. I have adapted Kohyo's haiku as given by Blyth: "The dragon-fly / Perches on the stick / That strikes at him," *Haiku* (Tokyo: Hokuseido Press, 1949–1952), 4:77.

29. Ibid., 3:42, 4:259.

30. Rolph, *Women of the Streets*, p. 90.

31. Ibid., p. 107.

32. Blyth, *Haiku*, 4:222.

33. Rolph, *Women of the Streets*, p. 107.

34. Kneeland, *Commercial Prostitution*, p. 108.

35. Erich Neumann, *The Origins and History of Consciousness* (Princeton: Princeton University Press, 1970), pp. 92, 141–43, 158–59, 203, 253–54, 310–11, 319.

36. Ibid., p. 318. See also Frances G. Wickes, *The Inner World of Man* (New York: H. Holt, 1948), p. 91.

37. Martin Buber, *I and Thou* (Edinburgh: T. and T. Clark, 1937), p. 64.

38. Quoted in Blyth, *Haiku*, 1:335.

39. New York: Putnam, 1964. By *myth* Hays means "popular misconception."

40. William Henry Hudson, *A Traveller in Little Things* (London: J. M. Dent, 1932), p. 81.

41. *The Complete Grimm's Fairy Tales* (New York: Pantheon Books, 1972), p. 676.

42. Adler, *A House Is Not a Home*, p. 58.

43. Helton G. Baynes, *Mythology of the Soul* (New York: Humanities Press, 1955), p. 811.

Chapter 6

1. The various meanings for the Sp. *fábula* given by the Royal Academy are in the same spirit, e.g., "relación falsa, mentirosa, de pura invención, destituída de todo fundamento"; "composición . . . en que . . . se da una enseñanza útil o moral"; "cualquiera de las ficciones de la mitología."

2. Henry David Thoreau, *Journal*, Feb. 5, 1854, in *The Writings of Henry David Thoreau* (New York: Houghton, Mifflin and Co., 1906), 12:99.

3. Ibid., May 10, 1853, 11:135.

4. As Thoreau puts it: "I perceived distinctly that man melts at the sound of music, just like a rock exposed to a furnace heat. They need not have fabled that Orpheus moved the rocks and trees, for there is nothing more insensible than man; he sets the fashion to the rocks, and it is as surprising to see him melted, as when children see the lead begin to flow in a crucible." Ibid., April 12, 1854, 12:193.

5. Jorge Guillén, "Los jardines," in *Cántico* (Buenos Aires: Editorial Sudamericana, 1950), p. 315.

6. Gerardo Diego, "Salmo de la Transfiguración," in *Segunda antología de sus versos (1941–1967)* (Madrid: Espasa-Calpe, 1967), p. 103.

7. S. Tolkowsky's massively documented symbological study, *Hesperides: A History of the Culture and Use of Citrus Fruits* (London: J. Bale, Sons and Curnow, 1938), sets the matter beyond all dispute (see, for example, pp. 47, 69, 75, 115, 260); see also Alexander Porteous, *Forest Folklore, Mythology, and Romance* (London: Allen and Unwin, 1928), p. 389; and Ernst Lehner and Johanna Lehner, *Folklore and Symbolism of Flowers, Plants and Trees* (New York: Tudor Publishing Co., 1960), p. 75.

8. Heinrich Zimmer, *The King and the Corpse: Tales of the Soul's Conquest of Evil* (New York: Pantheon Books, 1948), pp. 46–47.

9. Francis Hindes Groome, *Gypsy Folk-Tales* (London: Hurst and Blackett, 1899), p. 36.

10. Hans Licht [pseud.], *Sexual Life in Ancient Greece* (London: Routledge and K. Paul, 1932), p. 207.

11. T. F. Thiselton-Dyer, *The Folk-Lore of Plants* (New York: D. Appleton, 1889), p. 99. Thiselton's source is Robert Burns.

12. H. R. Ellis Davidson, *Scandinavian Mythology* (New York: Hamlyn, 1969), p. 90.

13. Ralph Waldo Emerson, "Love" in *Essays* (New York: Thomas Y. Crowell, 1926), p. 124.

Chapter 7

1. Jorge Guillén, *Cántico* (Buenos Aires: Editorial Sudamericana, 1950), p. 76. Guillén uses the word *persianas* for "matchstick blinds."

2. Shirley Goulden, *Chinese Fairy Tales* (Milan: Duell, Sloan and Pearce, 1958), pp. 15–24.

3. See my *Symbolic World of Federico García Lorca* (Albuquerque: University of New Mexico Press, 1972), pp. 61–64, where this aspect of the fairy tale is discussed in some detail.

4. In this connection it is to be noted in passing that Thoreau, the transcendental naturalist who spent his life immersed in the world of eros, was a surveyor by profession.

5. Mircea Eliade, *Shamanism: Archaic Techniques of Ecstasy* (New York: Pantheon Books, 1964), p. 137.

6. Idem, *The Forge and the Crucible* (New York: Harper and Bros., 1956), p. 19.

7. See below, where the greater implications of the *déjà vu* are discussed.

Chapter 8

1. Bruce Bliven, Jr., *The Wonderful Writing Machine* (New York: Random House, 1954), pp. 132, 131.

2. See ibid., chap. 8, "Race against Time," especially pp. 114–19.

3. The Corona XC-D. See *The Typewriter: History and Encyclopedia* (New York: Business Equipment Publishing Co., 1923?), p. 26.

4. Diana Ramírez de Arellano, *Caminos de la creación poética en Pedro Salinas* (Madrid: J. Romo Arregui, 1956), reproduces several facsimiles of typewritten drafts of poems by Salinas. See pp. 52, 103–4, 148–49, 152–53.

5. *The Cloud of Unknowing* (London: Oxford University Press, 1944), pp. 125, 62.

6. See Federico García Lorca, "La imagen poética de don Luis de Góngora," in *Obras completas* (Madrid: Aguilar, 1967), p. 74.

7. Alan Gauld, "Automatic Art," in *Man, Myth and Magic: An Illustrated Encyclopedia of the Supernatural* (New York: Marshall Cavendish Corp., 1970).

8. Rosalind Heywood, "Ouija Boards," in *Man, Myth and Magic*.

Chapter 9

1. Jakob and Wilhelm Grimm, eds., "Der gläserne Sarg," in *Grimm Kinder- und Hausmärchen*. 2 vols. (Berlin: Deutsches Verlagshaus Bon & Co., n.d.), 2:207–12.

The term *signos misteriosos* appears in the Spanish-language edition, *cuentos de Grimm*, prepared by María Edmée Alvarez (Mexico: Porrúa, 1974), p. 139. For the English version of the tale see *The Complete Grimm's Fairy Tales* (New York: Pantheon Books, 1972), pp. 672–78.

2. So runs the opening line of "The Iron Stove" (ibid., p. 571).

3. John Collier, "Sleeping Beauty," in *The Best of John Collier* (New York: Pocket Books, 1975), p. 308.

4. Pedro Salinas, "Defensa de la lectura," in *El defensor* (Madrid: Alianza Editorial, 1967), pp. 195, 196.

5. See Howard C. Warren, ed., *Dictionary of Psychology* (New York: Houghton Mifflin Co., 1934). Freud himself used the word *Besetzung*, meaning "the casting of characters in a drama" (dramatis personae), since the subject sees objects and people as characters in the inner *Seelendrama*.

6. George Russell [Æ], *The Candle of Vision* (London: Macmillan and Co., 1918), p. 46.

Chapter 10

1. One thinks of the primitivism in early twentieth-century painting, and of the Fauves in particular.

2. Eric Maple, *Superstition and the Superstitious* (London: W. H. Allen, 1971), p. 53.

3. Gustav Jahoda, *The Psychology of Superstition* (London: The Penguin Press, 1969), pp. 15–16. Jahoda says "the thought obtruded itself," that is, it was spontaneous. The divinatory activity, once it has been raised to consciousness, may of course become degraded as a silly piece of busywork on the part of ego-intellect; cf. the judge (!) in Tolstoi's *Resurrection:* "He had a meditative air, resulting from a habit he had of deciding, by different curious means, all sorts of self-put questions. Just now he had asked himself whether [his doctor's] new treatment would be beneficial, and had decided that it would cure his catarrh if the number of steps from the door to his chair would divide by three. He made 26 steps, but managed to get in a 27th just by his chair."

4. Readers familiar with the Eleanor Turnbull translation of selected poems by Salinas (*Lost Angel and Other Poems* [Baltimore: Johns Hopkins Press, 1938]) may note that I disagree with her rendering of lines 13–14 of "Cuartilla"; she writes that the doves "withhold / the whiteness of their wings," whereas I take *aplazan* to mean "invoke." I believe the Turnbull translation to be in error in spite of the fact that she says in her foreword that Salinas himself "has kindly gone over each poem, and wishes it said that the slight changes that may be found in the English translations have been made with his entire appproval." I do not know what is meant by "going over" the poems, but in any case the Turnbull translations cannot be considered authoritative, since they contain a number of errors, whether Salinas sanctioned them or not. Examples may be found on p. 11, last line, "yours" for *suyo*, which is an undergraduate boner; p. 17, line 4, "Who was going to tell me?" missing the idiomatic force of the Spanish *¿Quién me iba a decir?* expressing amazement (i.e., "Who would ever have thought it!"); p. 33, first line, the meaningless "With what am

I going to deck you?" missing the idiomatic meaning of *¿Qué voy a ponerte a ti?* ("What name shall I give you?").

5. This kind of losing is an aspect of the "bad trip."

Chapter 11

1. Henry David Thoreau, *Journal*, March 7, 1859, in *The Writings of Henry David Thoreau* (New York: Houghton, Mifflin and Co., 1906), 18:23.

2. Mircea Eliade, *Mephistopheles and the Androgyne* (New York: Sheed and Ward, 1965), p. 158.

3. Or: "the window opens a steady eye."

4. Cicero, *De senectute, de amicitia, de divinatione* (London: William Heinemann, 1927), pp. 301, 315, 342, 353, 361–63.

5. In Salinas's poem "La otra" (No. 3 of *Fábula y signo*), an adolescent girl matures into an arid materialist, and Salinas uses the telephone to symbolize her remoteness from the self: she puts in a long-distance call in order to tell it to be silent.

6. See Theodore Besterman, *Crystal-Gazing* (New York: University Books, 1965), p. 160.

7. Désirée Hirst, *Hidden Riches: Traditional Symbolism from the Renaissance to Blake* (London: Eyre and Spottiswoode, 1964), p. 85.

8. Cited by Besterman, *Crystal-Gazing*, p. 51.

9. See Marcel Mauss, *A General Theory of Magic* (London: Routledge & Kegan Paul, 1972), p. 45. Lang is cited in Besterman, *Crystal-Gazing*, p. 104.

10. Cited in Reginald. H. Blyth, *Haiku* (Tokyo: Hokuseido Press, 1949–1952), 1:72.

11. Besterman, *Crystal-Gazing*, p. 90.

12. E. A. Wallis Budge, *Amulets and Talismans* (New York: University Books, 1961) p. 312.

13. Edward Gibbon, *The Decline and Fall of the Roman Empire*, 3 vols. (New York: Random House, 1932), 1:764.

14. Ibid., p. 768.

15. Albert Giraud, "Les Croix," in *Pierrot Lunaire* (Paris: Alphonse Lemerre, 1884), p. 59. My translation.

16. Quoted in Samuel French Morse, *Wallace Stevens: Life as Poetry* (New York: Pegasus, 1970), p. 21.

17. Quoted in Joachim Seyppel, *T. S. Eliot* (New York: Frederick Ungar Publishing Co., 1972), p. 44.

18. Quoted in Dom Cuthbert Butler, *Western Mysticism* (New York: Barnes and Noble, 1968), pp. 166–67.

19. Robert C. Zaehner, *Mysticism Sacred and Profane* (Oxford: Clarendon Press, 1957), p. 149.

20. Michel Foucault, *Madness and Civilization: A History of Insanity in the Age of Reason* (New York: Pantheon Books, 1965), p. 79.

21. Miguel de Molinos, *Guía espiritual* (Madrid: Aguilar, 1935?), p. 91. My translation.

Chapter 12

1. See Sheila Ostrander and Lynn Schroeder, "Kirlian Photography," in *Handbook of Psychic Discoveries* (New York: Berkeley Publishing Corp., 1974), pp. 59–79.

2. Henry David Thoreau, *Journal*, Feb. 20, 1857, in *The Writings of Henry David Thoreau* (New York: Houghton, Mifflin and Co., 1906), 15:274–75.

3. George Russell [Æ], *The Candle of Vision* (London: Macmillan and Co., 1918), p. 114. It is this experience of signs in nature that no doubt gave rise to the so-called doctrine of signatures which was practiced superstitiously as folk-medicine. See, for example, Thiselton-Dyer, "Doctrine of Signatures," in *The Folk-Lore of Plants* (New York: D. Appleton, 1889), pp. 201–15. The connection between the doctrine of signatures and the higher spirituality of natural signs is apparent in what we read about the mystic Jacob Boehme, who, "going abroad into the fields to a green, . . . he there sat down, and viewing the herbs and grass of the field, in his inward light he saw into their essences, use, and properties, which was discovered to him by their lineaments, figures, and signatures." Edward Taylor, quoted in William James, *The Varieties of Religious Experience* (New York: New American Library, 1958), p. 315n.

4. Rainer Maria Rilke, *Duino Elegies*, trans. J. B. Leishman and Stephen Spender (New York: W. W. Norton, 1939), p. 73, lines 7–9.

5. Thoreau, *Journal*, Feb. 18, 1852, 9:311.

6. Fitz Hugh Ludlow, *The Hasheesh Eater* (New York: Harper and Bros., 1857), p. 178.

7. Russell, *Candle of Vision*, pp. 5–6.

8. Denise Levertov, "The Open Secret," in *Relearning the Alphabet* (New York: New Directions, 1966), p. 73.

9. Gustavo Adolfo Bécquer, *Rimas* (Madrid: Espasa-Calpe, 1968), pp. 47–48. My translation.

10. Ludlow, *Hasheesh Eater*, p. 151.

11. Reginald H. Blyth, *Haiku* (Tokyo: Hokuseido Press, 1949–1952), 4:31.

Chapter 13

1. Robert C. Zaehner, *Mysticism Sacred and Profane* (Oxford: Clarendon Press, 1957), p. 162.

2. E. Robert Sinnet, "Experience and Reflections," in *Psychedelics: The Uses and Implications of Hallucinogenic Drugs*, ed. Bernard Aaronson and Humphry Osmond (New York: Anchor Books, 1970), p. 34.

3. Georg Christoph Lichtenberg, quoted in W. H. Auden, *A Certain World: A Commonplace Book* (New York: Viking Press, 1970), pp. 136–37.

4. Alan Watts, *The Joyous Cosmology* (New York: Random House, 1962), p. 61.

5. Lao Tzu, *Tao Te Ching*, trans. Raymond B. Blakney (New York: New American Library, 1955), p. 53.

6. Ibid., p. 77.

Chapter 14

1. George Henry Lewes, *History of Philosophy* (London: Longmans, Green and Co., 1871), 1: 245, 246, 252, 259, 260, 261.

2. I have translated *tierra y cielo* as "earth and sky" in preference to "earth and heaven," since the latter allows for confusion with Plato's notion of celestial Ideas and mundane phenomena.

3. J. B. Priestley, *Man and Time* (New York: Doubleday and Co., 1964), pp. 306–7.

4. Theodore Roethke, *Words for the Wind* (New York: Doubleday and Co., 1958), p. 196.

5. *The Notebooks of David Ignatow* (Chicago: Swallow Press, 1973), p. 13.

6. Aldous Huxley, *The Doors of Perception* (New York: Harper and Row, 1970), pp. 17–18.

7. Lewes, *History of Philosophy*, p. 253.

8. William A. Lessa, *Chinese Body Divination* (Los Angeles: United World, 1968), p. 138.

9. Mircea Eliade, *Shamanism: Archaic Techniques of Ecstasy* (New York: Pantheon Books, 1964), pp. 98, 481.

10. Jack Lindsay, *The Clashing Rocks: A Study of Early Greek Religion and Culture and the Origins of Drama* (London: Chapman and Hall, 1965), p. 252.

11. Meister Eckhart, *Sermons and Collations, Tractates, Sayings* (London: John M. Watkins, 1956), p. 79.

12. Sir John Mandeville, *Travels* (London: The Hakluyt Society, 1953), p. 137.

13. Delmore Schwartz, *Summer Knowledge: New and Selected Poems, 1938–1958* (Garden City, N.Y.: Doubleday and Co., 1959), p. 189; Roethke, *Words for the Wind*, p. 110; David Ignatow, "All Comes," in *Earth Hard* (London: Rapp and Whiting, 1968), p. 48.

14. *Notebooks of David Ignatow*, p. 33.

15. Sandburg is cited in Juan Ramón Jiménez, *Libros de poesía* (Madrid: Aguilar, 1957), p. lix; Rubén Darío, *Cantos de vida y esperanza* (Madrid: Afrodisio Aguado, 1949), pp. 137–40.

16. Reginald H. Blyth, *Zen in English Literature and Oriental Classics* (Tokyo: Hokuseido Press, 1942), p. 26; Hauptmann is quoted in Joseph Campbell, *The Masks of God: Creative Mythology* (New York: The Viking Press, 1970), p. 93. For "Word" Hauptmann uses *Urwort*, "primordial word": "Dichten heisst, hinter Worten das Urwort erklingen lassen."

Chapter 15

1. Aldous Huxley, *The Perennial Philosophy* (New York: Harper and Row, 1970), p. 2.

2. Percy Bysshe Shelley, *Defence of Poetry* (Oxford: Basil Blackwell, 1947), p. 54.

3. Ibid., pp. 54–55, 53.

4. Robert Graves, *Goodbye to All That* (London: Cassell, 1957), p. 264.

5. Shelley, *Defence of Poetry*, p. 57.

6. Quoted in Walter A. Strauss, *Descent and Return: The Orphic Theme in Modern Literature* (Cambridge: Harvard University Press, 1971), p. 64.

7. Quoted in Reginald H. Blyth, *Haiku* (Tokyo: Hokuseido Press, 1949–1952), 1:241.

8. Shelley, *Defence of Poetry*, p. 56.

9. Blyth, *Haiku*, 3:14–15.

10. Charles A. Bennett, *A Philosophical Study of Mysticism* (New Haven: Yale University Press, 1923), p. 19.

11. Pedro Salinas, "Defensa del lenguaje," in *El defensor* (Madrid: Alianza Editorial, 1967), pp. 288, 289.

12. Huxley, *Perennial Philosophy*, pp. 1–2.

13. Lao Tzu, *Tao Te Ching* trans. Dim Cheuk Lau (London: Penguin Books, 1975), p. 82; ibid., trans. Raymond B. Blakney (New York: New American Library, 1955), p. 77.

14. Gustavo Correa, "El simbolismo del mar en la poesía española," *Revista Hispánica Moderna* 22 (1966):71.

15. Raymond B. Blakney, trans., *Tao Te Ching*, p. 53.

16. Blyth, *Haiku*, 4:348–49.

17. Quoted in Frances A. Yates, *Giordano Bruno and the Hermetic Tradition* (Chicago: University of Chicago Press, 1964), pp. 212–13.

18. Quoted in William James, *The Varieties of Religious Experience* (New York: New American Library, 1958), p. 299n.

19. Judith Feldbaum, "El trasmundo de la obra poética de Pedro Salinas," *Revista Hispánica Moderna* 22 (1956):29; Correa, "El simbolismo," p. 71; Elsa Dehennin, *Passion d'Absolu et tension expressive dans l'oeuvre poétique de Pedro Salinas* (Ghent: Romanica Gandensia, 1957), p. 78; Francisco Matos Paoli, "Visión de nuestro mar en Pedro Salinas," *Asomante* 2, no. 3 (1946):76 (Matos Paoli misquotes the passage in question, inserting a comma: "Si te nombro, soy tu amo, de un segundo"; Adriana Lewis de Galanes, " 'El Contemplado': El infinito poseído por Pedro Salinas," *Revista Hispánica Moderna* 33 (1967):39 (Lewis de Galanes never explains how the meaning of the title could be possible); Margot Arce de Vásquez, cited approvingly in Alma de Zubizarreta, *Pedro Salinas: El diálogo creador* (Madrid: Gredos, 1969), p. 72n.

20. Alan Watts, *The Book: On the Taboo against Knowing Who You Are* (New York: Pantheon Books, 1966), pp. 14, 17.

21. Theodore Roethke, "Fourth Meditation," from "Meditations of an Old Woman," in *Words for the Wind* (New York: Doubleday and Co., 1958), p. 205.

22. Walter Houston Clark, *Chemical Ecstasy: Psychedelic Drugs and Religion* (New York: Sheed and Ward, 1969), p. 71; Tennyson is quoted in William James, *Varieties of Religious Experience*, p. 295n.

23. Delmore Schwartz, "The First Morning of the Second World," in *Summer Knowledge: New and Selected Poems, 1938–1958* (Garden City, N.Y.: Doubleday and Co., 1959), p. 152.

24. Blyth, *Haiku*, 3:72.

25. Ibid., 1:18.

26. Daisetz Teitaro Suzuki, *Mysticism: Christian and Buddhist* (New York: Harper, 1957), p. 9.

27. Heinrich Zimmer, *The Art of Indian Asia*, 2 vols. (New York: Pantheon Books, 1955), 1:80.

28. See Julian Palley, *La luz no usada: La poesía de Pedro Salinas* (Mexico: Ediciones De Andrea, 1966), p. 91.

29. Henry David Thoreau, *Journal*, Dec. 1838, in *The Writings of Henry David Thoreau* (New York: Houghton, Mifflin and Co., 1906), 7:64.

30. Juan Ramón Jiménez, "Todo," in *Libros de poesía* (Madrid: Aguilar, 1957), p. 489.

31. Quoted in Alan Watts, *Behold the Spirit: A Study in the Necessity of Mystical Religion* (New York: Pantheon Books, 1971), p. 176. Readers should also note the passage from Traherne's *Centuries of Meditation* cited in Bartlett's *Familiar Quotations*.

Chapter 16

1. Quoted in Claudio Naranjo and Robert Ornstein, *On the Psychology of Meditation* (New York: Viking Press, 1971), p. 30.

2. Aldous Huxley, *The Doors of Perception* (New York: Harper and Bros., 1954), p. 35.

3. Federico García Lorca, "Romance sonámbulo," in *Obras completas* (Madrid: Aguilar, 1967), p. 431.

4. "La luz, que nunca sufre, / Me guía bien." From the last strophe of Guillén's "Muchas gracias, adiós," in *Cántico* (Buenos Aires: Editorial Sudamericana, 1950), p. 73.

5. Richard Alpert, *Remember: Be Here Now* (San Cristobal, N.M.: Lama Foundation, 1971), unpaginated, p. 19.

6. George Santayana, Sonnet XXV, in *Poems* (New York: Charles Scribner's Sons, 1946), p. 29.

7. Martin Buber, *I and Thou* (Edinburgh: T. and T. Clark, 1937), p. 46.

8. *The Complete Grimm's Fairy Tales* (New York: Pantheon Books, 1972), p. 652.

9. Chan Sei Ghow, *Short Footsteps on a Long Journey* (St. Louis, Mo.: Folkestone Press, 1967), p. 44.

10. Walter H. Clark, *Chemical Ecstasy: Psychedelic Drugs and Religion* (New York: Sheed and Ward, 1969), p. 110.

11. Maurice Nicoll, *Living Time* (New York: Hermitage House, 1953), p. 144.

12. Other explanations tend to be elaborate, and therefore unconvincing: "The person in question experiences the recollection of a certain *emotion* of his past. He fails, however, to recognize it as identical with the previous one; he then displaces his feelings and believes it is the environment that is identical to one of the past." Emil A. Gutheil, *The Language of the Dream* (New York: Macmillan, 1939), p. 48. Again, John W. Dunne says that the *déjà vu* is really the sudden recollection of "an apparently forgotten dream because . . . something occurs which reminds [one] of . . . the dream." *An Experiment with Time* (New York: Macmillan, 1937), p. 75. Dunne maintains that what happens to one has already been dreamt about.

13. George Russell [Æ] "A New World," in *Collected Poems* (London: Macmillan and Co., 1917), pp. 52–53.

14. Alan Watts, *The Joyous Cosmology* (New York: Random House, 1962), pp. 44–45.

15. Robert Powell, *Zen and Reality* (London: Allen and Unwin, 1961), p. 66.

16. Delmore Schwartz, "The First Morning of the Second World," in *Summer Knowledge: New and Selected Poems, 1938–1958* (Garden City, N.Y.: Doubleday and Co., 1959), p. 156.

Chapter 17

1. Gustavo Aldolfo Bécquer, *Rimas* (Madrid: Espasa-Calpe, 1968), p. 18.

2. See, for example, Alan Watts, *Psychotherapy East and West* (New York: Ballantine Books, 1961); and Robert C. Zaehner, *Mysticism Sacred and Profane* (Oxford: Clarendon Press, 1957). The titles speak for themselves.

3. Saint Teresa, *Vida y obras* (Madrid: Felipe G. Rojas, 1902), 1:424. My translation.

4. George Russell [Æ], *The Candle of Vision* (London: Macmillan and Co., 1918), p. 31.

5. Alan Watts, *Behold the Spirit* (New York: Pantheon Books, 1971), p. 91.

6. Cited in Reginald H. Blyth, *Haiku* (Tokyo: Hokuscido Press, 1949–1952), 1:17.

7. Juan Ramón Jiménez, "Todo," in *Libros de poesía* (Madrid: Aguilar, 1957), p. 489.

8. James Wright, "Today I was Happy, So I Made This Poem," in *Collected Poems* (Middletown, Conn.: Wesleyan University Press, 1971), p. 133. I have corrected the misprint that appears in the title.

9. See Alan Watts, *The Way of Zen* (New York: Pantheon Books, 1957), p. 104.

10. Delmore Schwartz, "The First Morning of the Second World," in *Summer Knowledge: New and Selected Poems, 1938–1958* (Garden City, N.Y.: Doubleday and Co., 1959), p. 153.

11. Watts, *Psychotherapy East and West*, pp. 96–97.

12. Carl G. Jung, "Synchronicity: An Acausal Connecting Principle," in *The Interpretation of Nature and the Psyche* (New York: Pantheon Books, 1955), p. 138.

13. Ibid., p. 31.

14. James Wright, "Poems to a Brown Cricket," in *Collected Poems*, p. 167.

15. Cited in Alan Watts, *The Way of Zen* (New York: Pantheon Books, 1957), p. 145.

16. The *Zenrinkushu* and Soshi are cited in Blyth, *Haiku*, 1: 18, 241.

17. Martin Buber, *I and Thou* (Edinburgh: T. and T. Clark, 1937), p. 79.

Bibliography

Aaronson, Bernard, and Humphry Osmond. *Psychedelics: The Uses and Implications of Hallucinogenic Drugs*. New York: Anchor Books, 1970.

About Charles Ives. PBS Television Special. September 15, 1975.

Adler, Polly. *A House Is Not a Home*. New York: Rinehart and Co., 1953.

Aelian. *On the Characteristics of Animals*. 3 vols. Cambridge: Harvard University Press, 1958–1959.

Allen, Rupert C. *Psyche and Symbol in the Theater of Federico García Lorca*. Austin: University of Texas Press, 1974.

———. *The Symbolic World of Federico García Lorca*. Albuquerque: University of New Mexico Press, 1972.

Alpert, Richard. *Remember: Be Here Now*. San Cristobal, N.M.: Lama Foundation, 1971.

Alvarez, María Edmée, ed. *Cuentos de Grimm*. Mexico: Porrúa, 1974.

Auden, W. H. *A Certain World: A Commonplace Book*. New York: The Viking Press, 1970.

Baum, L. Frank. *The Scarecrow of Oz*. New York: Rand McNally, 1915.

Baynes, H. G. *Mythology of the Soul*. New York: Humanities Press, 1955.

Beagle, Peter S. *A Fine and Private Place*. New York: Dell, 1960.

Bécquer, Gustavo Adolfo. *Rimas*. Madrid: Espasa-Calpe, 1968.

Bennett, Charles A. *A Philosophical Study of Mysticism*. New Haven: Yale University Press, 1923.

Besterman, Theodore. *Crystal-Gazing*. New York: University Books, 1965.

Bliven, Bruce, Jr. *The Wonderful Writing Machine*. New York: Random House, 1954.

Blyth, R. H. *Haiku*. 4 vols. Tokyo: Hokuseido Press, 1949–1952.

———. *Zen in English Literature and Oriental Classics*. Tokyo: Hokuseido Press, 1942.

Buber, Martin. *I and Thou*. Translated by R. G. Smith. Edinburgh: T. and T. Clark, 1937.

Budge, E. A. Wallis. *Amulets and Talismans*. New York: University Books, 1961.

Burton, Richard. *The Book of the Thousand Nights and a Night*. 10 vols. Privately printed by the Burton Club, n.d.

Butler, Dom Cuthbert. *Western Mysticism*. 3d ed. New York: Barnes and Noble, 1968.

Campbell, Joseph. *The Masks of God: Creative Mythology*. New York: The Viking Press, 1970.

Canady, John. *Metropolitan Seminars in Art*. 24 portfolios. New York: The Metropolitan Museum of Art, 1959.

Carpenter, Edmund. *They Became What They Beheld*. New York: Outerbridge and Dienstfrey, 1970.

Cicero. *De senectute, de amicitia, de divinatione*. Translated by William Armistead Falconer. London: William Heinemann, 1927.

Clark, Walter Houston. *Chemical Ecstasy: Psychedelic Drugs and Religion*. New York: Sheed and Ward, 1969.

The Cloud of Unknowing. London: Oxford University Press, 1944.

Collier, John. *The Best of John Collier*. New York: Pocket Books, 1975.

The Complete Grimm's Fairy Tales. New York: Pantheon Books, 1972.

Correa, Gustavo. "El simbolismo del mar en la poesía española." *Revista Hispánica Moderna* 32 (1966): 62–86.

Crispin, John. *Pedro Salinas*. New York: Twayne Publishers, 1974.

Darío, Rubén. *Cantos de vida y esperanza*. Madrid: Afrodisio Aguado, 1949.

Davidson, H. R. Ellis. *Scandinavian Mythology*. New York: Hamlyn, 1969.

Dehennin, Elsa. *Passion d'Absolu et tension expressive dans l'oeuvre poétique de Pedro Salinas*. Ghent: Romanica Gandensia, 1957.

Desmonde, William H. *Magic, Myth, and Money*. New York: Free Press of Glencoe, 1962.

Diego, Gerardo. *Segunda antología de sus versos (1941–1967)*. Madrid: Espasa Calpe, 1967.

Dorfles, Gillo, ed. *Kitsch: The World of Bad Taste*. New York: Bell Publishing Co., 1969.

Dunne, J. W. *An Experiment with Time*. New York: Macmillan, 1937.

Duyckaerts, François. *The Sexual Bond*. New York: Delacorte Press, 1970.

Eckhart, Meister. *Sermons and Collations, Tractates, Sayings*. London: John M. Watkins, 1956.

Eliade, Mircea. *Australian Religions: An Introduction*. Ithaca, New York: Cornell University Press, 1973.

———. *The Forge and the Crucible*. New York: Harper and Bros., 1956.

———. *Mephistopheles and the Androgyne*. New York: Sheed and Ward, 1965.

———. *Shamanism: Archaic Techniques of Ecstasy*. New York: Pantheon Books, 1964.

Emerson, Ralph Waldo. *Essays*. New York: Thomas Y. Crowell, 1926.

Feal Deibe, Carlos. *La poesía de Pedro Salinas*. Madrid: Editorial Gredos, 1965.

Feldbaum, Judith. "El trasmundo de la obra poética de Pedro Salinas." *Revista Hispánica Moderna* 22 (1956): 12–34.

Fine, Ralph Adam. *Mary Jane versus Pennsylvania*. New York: McCall Publishing Co., 1970.

Foucault, Michel. *Madness and Civilization: A History of Insanity in the Age of Reason*. New York: Pantheon Books, 1965.

García Lorca, Federico. *Obras completas*. 13th ed. Madrid: Aguilar, 1967.

Gautier, Théophile. *The Complete Works*. Translated by F. C. de Sumichrast. 12 vols. New York: Bigelow, Smith, n.d.

Gentry, Curt. *The Madams of San Francisco*. New York: Doubleday and Co., 1964.

Ghow, Chan Sei. *Short Footsteps on a Long Journey*. Translated by W. Robert Miller. St. Louis, Missouri: The Folkestone Press, 1967.

Gibbon, Edward. *The Decline and Fall of the Roman Empire*. 3 vols. New York: Random House, 1932.

Giraud, Albert. *Pierrot Lunaire*. Paris: Alphonse Lemerre, 1884.

Gosling, John, and Douglas Warner. *The Shame of a City: An Inquiry into the Vice of London*. London: W. H. Allen, 1960.

Goulden, Shirley. *Chinese Fairy Tales*. Milan: Duell, Sloan and Pearce, 1958.

Granada, Fr. Luis de. *Obras de Fr. Luis de Granada*. Biblioteca de autores españoles, vol. 11. Madrid: Rivadeneyra, 1915.

Graves, Robert. *Difficult Questions, Easy Answers*. London: Cassell, 1972.
————. *Goodbye to All That*. London: Cassell, 1957.
Grimm, Jacob. *Teutonic Mythology*. 4 vols. New York: Dover, 1966.
Grimm Kinder- und Hausmärchen. 2 vols. Berlin: Deutsches Verlagshaus Bon &
    Co., n.d.
Groome, Francis Hindes. *Gypsy Folk-Tales*. London: Hurst and Blackett, 1899.
Guillén, Jorge. *Cántico*. Buenos Aires: Editorial Sudamericana, 1950.
Gulik, Robert Hans van. *Sexual Life in Ancient China*. Leiden: E. J. Brill, 1961.
Gutheil, Emil A. *The Language of the Dream*. New York: Macmillan, 1939.
Hays, H. R. *The Dangerous Sex: The Myth of the Feminine Evil*. New York: Putnam,
    1964.
Herodotus. Translated by Canon Rawlinson. 2 vols. New York: C. Scribner's Sons,
    1897.
Herzog, Edgar. *Psyche and Death*. London: Hodder and Stoughton, 1966.
Hirst, Désirée. *Hidden Riches: Traditional Symbolism from the Renaissance to
    Blake*. London: Eyre and Spottiswoode, 1964.
Hope, Robert Charles. *The Legendary Lore of the Holy Wells of England*. London:
    Elliot Stock, 1893.
Hudson, William Henry. *A Traveller in Little Things*. London: J. M. Dent, 1932.
Huizinga, J. *Homo Ludens*. Boston: The Beacon Press, 1955.
Huxley, Aldous. *The Doors of Perception*. New York: Harper and Bros., 1954.
————. *The Perennial Philosophy*. New York: Harper and Row, 1970.
Ignatow, David. *Earth Hard*. London: Rapp and Whiting, 1968.
————. *The Notebooks of David Ignatow*. Chicago: Swallow Press, 1973.
————. *Poems: 1934–1969*. Middletown, Conn.: Wesleyan University Press, 1970.
Jahoda, Gustav. *The Psychology of Superstition*. London: The Penguin Press, 1969.
James, William. *The Varieties of Religious Experience*. New York: New American
    Library, 1958.
Jiménez, Juan Ramón. *Libros de poesía*. Madrid: Aguilar, 1957.
Joannes Climacus, Saint. *Escala espiritual*. Translated by Fr. Luis de Granada.
    Biblioteca de autores españoles, vol. 11. Madrid: M. Rivadeneyra, 1915.
Jones, Ernest. *Nightmare, Witches, and Devils*. New York: W. W. Norton, 1931.
Juan de la Cruz. *Vida y obras*. Madrid: Biblioteca de Autores Cristianos, 1950.
Juan de los Angeles. *Conquista del reino de Dios*. Madrid: Rialp, 1958.
Jung, Carl G. *The Interpretation of Nature and the Psyche*. New York: Pantheon
    Books, 1955.
————. *Psychological Types*. New York: Harcourt, Brace and Co., 1926.
Kneeland, George J. *Commercial Prostitution in New York City*. New York: The
    Century Co., 1913.
Kunitz, Stanley J. *Intellectual Things*. New York: Doubleday, Doran and Co., 1930.
Lang, Andrew, ed. *Yellow Fairy Book*. New York: Longmans, Green and Co., 1948.
Lao Tzu. *Tao Te Ching*. Translated by D. C. Lau. London: Penguin Books, 1975.
————. *The Way of Life (Tao Te Ching)*. Translated by R. B. Blakney. New York:
    New American Library, 1955.
Lehner, Ernst and Johanna. *Folklore and Symbolism of Flowers, Plants and Trees*.
    New York: Tudor Publishing Co., 1960.
Lessa, William A. *Chinese Body Divination*. Los Angeles: United World, 1968.

Levertov, Denise. *Relearning the Alphabet*. New York: New Directions, 1966.

Lewes, George Henry. *The History of Philosophy*. 2 vols. London: Longmans, Green and Co., 1871.

Lewis de Galanes, Adriana. " 'El Contemplado': El infinito poseído por Pedro Salinas." *Revista Hispánica Moderna* 33 (1967): 38–54.

Licht, Hans [pseud.]. *Sexual Life in Ancient Greece*. London: Routledge and K. Paul, 1932.

Lindsay, Jack. *The Clashing Rocks: A Study of Early Greek Religion and Culture and the Origins of Drama*. London: Chapman and Hall, 1965.

Ludlow, Fitz Hugh. *The Hasheesh Eater*. New York: Harper and Bros., 1857.

Man, Myth and Magic: An Illustrated Encyclopedia of the Supernatural. 24 vols. New York: Marshall Cavendish Corp., 1970.

Mandeville, Sir John. *Travels*. London: The Hakluyt Society, 1953.

Maple, Eric. *Superstition and the Superstitious*. London: W. H. Allen, 1971.

Margolis, Jack S., and Richard Clorfene. *A Child's Garden of Grass*. New York: Pocket Book Editions, 1970.

Matos Paoli, Francisco. "Visión de nuestro mar en Pedro Salinas." *Asomante* 2, no. 3 (1946): 75–80.

Mauss, Marcel. *A General Theory of Magic*. London: Routledge & Kegan Paul, 1972.

Métraux, Alfred. *Voodoo in Haiti*. New York: Oxford University Press, 1959.

Mills, Ralph J., ed., *The Notebooks of David Ignatow*. Chicago: The Swallow Press, 1973.

Molinos, Miguel de. *Guía espiritual*. Madrid: Aguilar, 1935?

Morse, Samuel French. *Wallace Stevens: Life as Poetry*. New York: Pegasus, 1970.

Naranjo, Claudio, and Robert Ornstein. *On the Psychology of Meditation*. New York: The Viking Press, 1971.

Needleman, Jacob. *The New Religions*. New York: Doubleday and Co., 1970.

Neumann, Erich. *The Origins and History of Consciousness*. Princeton: Princeton University Press, 1970.

Nicoll, Maurice. *Living Time*. New York: Hermitage House, 1953.

Okakura Kakuzo. *The Book of Tea*. Rutland, Vermont: Charles E. Tuttle, 1956.

Ostrander, Sheila, and Lynn Schroeder. *Handbook of Psychic Discoveries*. New York: Berkeley Publishing Corp., 1974.

Palley, Julian. *La luz no usada: La poesía de Pedro Salinas*. Mexico: Ediciones De Andrea, 1966.

Porteous, Alexander. *Forest Folklore, Mythology, and Romance*. London: Allen and Unwin, 1928.

Powell, Robert. *Zen and Reality*. London: Allen and Unwin, 1961.

Priestley, J. B. *Man and Time*. New York: Doubleday and Co., 1964.

Progoff, Ira. *Depth Psychology and Modern Man*. New York: Julian Press, 1959.

Ramírez de Arellano, Diana. *Caminos de la creación poética en Pedro Salinas*. Madrid: J. Romo Arregui, 1956.

Reznikoff, Charles. *Going To and Fro and Walking Up and Down*. New York: Futuro Press, 1941.

Rilke, Rainer Maria. *Duino Elegies*. Translated by J. B. Leishman and Stephen Spender. New York: W. W. Norton, 1939.

Roethke, Theodore. *Words for the Wind.* New York: Doubleday and Co., 1958.

Rolph, C. H. [pseud.], ed. *Women of the Streets: A Sociological Study of the Common Prostitute.* London: Secker and Warburg, 1955.

Russell, George [Æ]. *The Candle of Vision.* London: Macmillan and Co., 1918.

———. *Collected Poems.* London: Macmillan and Co., 1917.

Salinas, Pedro. *El defensor.* Madrid: Alianza Editorial, 1967.

———. *El desnudo impecable y otras narraciones.* Mexico: Tezontle, 1951.

———. *Lost Angel and Other Poems.* Translated by Eleanor L. Turnbull. Baltimore: The Johns Hopkins Press, 1938.

———. *La poesía de Rubén Darío.* 3d ed. Buenos Aires: Losada, 1968.

———. *Poesías completas.* Barcelona: Barral Editores, 1971.

Salomon, I. L., trans. *Dino Campana: Orphic Songs.* New York: October House, 1968.

Santayana, George. *Poems.* New York: Charles Scribner's Sons, 1946.

Schwartz, Delmore. *Summer Knowledge: New and Selected Poems, 1938–1958.* Garden City, N.Y.: Doubleday and Co., 1959.

Seki, Keigo. *Folktales of Japan.* Chicago: University of Chicago Press, 1963.

Semper Idem [pseud.]. *The "Blue Book": A Bibliographical Attempt to Describe the Guide Books to the Houses of Ill Fame in New Orleans as They Were Published There.* New Orleans: privately printed, 1936.

Seyppel, Joachim. *T. S. Eliot.* New York: Frederick Ungar Publishing Co., 1972.

Shelley, Percy Bysshe. *Defence of Poetry.* Oxford: Basil Blackwell, 1947.

Stekel, Wilhelm. *The Interpretation of Dreams.* New York: Washington Square Press, 1967.

Stevens, Wallace. *The Palm at the End of the Mind.* New York: Random House, 1972.

Strauss, Walter A. *Descent and Return: The Orphic Theme in Modern Literature.* Cambridge: Harvard University Press, 1971.

Suzuki, Daisetz Teitaro. *Mysticism: Christian and Buddhist.* New York: Harper, 1957.

Teresa de Jesús, Saint. *Vida y obras.* 3 vols. Madrid: Felipe G. Rojas, 1902.

Thiselton-Dyer, T. F. *The Folk-Lore of Plants.* New York: D. Appleton, 1889.

Thoreau, Henry David. *Journal.* Vols. 7–20 of *The Writings of Henry David Thoreau.* New York: Houghton, Mifflin and Co., 1906.

Thurston, Edgar. *Omens and Superstitions of Southern India.* New York: McBride, Nast, 1912.

Tolkowsky, S. *Hesperides: A History of the Culture and Use of Citrus Fruits.* London: J. Bale, Sons and Curnow. 1938.

Tolstoi, Lev N. *Resurrection.* Translated by Louise Maude. 2 vols. London: Oxford University Press, 1952.

The Typewriter: History and Encyclopedia. New York: Business Equipment Publishing Co., 1923?

Warren, Howard C., ed. *Dictionary of Psychology.* New York: Houghton Mifflin, 1934.

Watts, Alan W. *Behold the Spirit: A Study in the Necessity of Mystical Religion.* New York: Pantheon Books, 1971.

———. *The Book: On the Taboo against Knowing Who You Are.* New York: Pantheon Books, 1966.

———. *The Joyous Cosmology*. New York: Random House, 1962.

———. *Psychotherapy East and West*. New York: Ballantine Books, 1961.

———. *The Way of Zen*. New York: Pantheon Books, 1957.

Wickes, Frances G. *The Inner World of Man*. New York: H. Holt, 1948.

Wilhelm, Richard, trans. *The Secret of the Golden Flower: A Chinese Book of Life*. With a commentary by C. C. Jung. New York: Harcourt, Brace and World, 1962.

Wilson, Robert A., ed. *Playboy's Book of Forbidden Words*. Chicago: Playboy Press, 1972.

The World's Great Religions. New York: Time, Inc., 1957.

Wright, James. *Collected Poems*. Middletown, Conn.: Wesleyan University Press, 1971.

Yates, Frances A. *Giordano Bruno and the Hermetic Tradition*. Chicago: University of Chicago Press, 1964.

Yeats, William Butler. *Ideas of Good and Evil*. London: A. H. Bullen, 1908.

Zaehner, R. C. *Mysticism Sacred and Profane*. Oxford: Clarendon Press, 1957.

Zimmer, Heinrich. *The Art of Indian Asia*. 2 vols. New York: Pantheon Books, 1955.

———. *The King and the Corpse: Tales of the Soul's Conquest of Evil*. New York: Pantheon Books, 1948.

———. *Philosophies of India*. New York: Pantheon Books, 1951.

Zubizarreta, Alma de. *Pedro Salinas: El diálogo creador*. Madrid: Gredos, 1969.

Index